Flavors of India

Vegetarian Indian Cuisine

by

Shanta Nimbark Sacharoff

Book Publishing Company
Summertown, Tennessee

Cover design by Sheryl Karas
Illustrations by Linda Robertson Hogan
                    Kim Trainor
                    Otis Maly
                    Jerry Lee Hutchens

© 1996 Shanta Nimbark Sacharoff

Published in the United States by
Book Publishing Company
P.O. Box 99
Summertown, TN 38483

ISBN 1-57067-023-4

Sacharoff, Shanta Nimbark.
     Flavors of India : vegetarian Indian cuisine / by
Shanta Nimbark Sacharoff.
          p. cm.
     Includes index.
     ISBN 1-57067-023-4
     1. Vegetarian cookery. 2. Cookery, Indic. I.
Title.
     TX837.S2123 1996
     641.5'636'0954--dc20   96-31917
                              CIP

Contents

INTRODUCTION 4

1 - VEGETARIAN NUTRITION 7

2 - THE HEALTHFUL INDIAN PANTRY 13

3 - BASIC RECIPES 29

4 - APPETIZERS, SNACKS & CHUTNEYS 45

5 - VEGETABLES AND SALADS 76

6 - DALS AND BEAN-BASED DISHES 110

7 - RICE AND RICE DISHES 131

8 - BREADS 141

9 - SWEETS 157

10 - BEVERAGES 173

11 - SIMPLE MEALS, PICNICS & FEASTS 181

MAIL ORDER SOURCES 187
GLOSSARY 188
INDEX 189

INTRODUCTION

There are hundreds of millions of vegetarians in this world. Among those are religious Hindus, Buddhists, and Jains, as well as many other individuals who respect and honor animal life. There are also many people who cannot afford to eat meat or do not have the means to preserve it. In addition, many conscientious people avoid meat because of the many health hazards associated with it or because it is ecologically infeasible for our planet.

Historically, India has had a large vegetarian population. The Indian vegetarian diet evolved from the basic Hindu belief that all beings are sacred and that the human being is just one of them. It is not known exactly when Hindus began to restrict meat from their diet, but the vegetarian way of life in India goes beyond religious conviction.

The mostly rural economy of India depends on animals for agricultural support rather than as dietary staples. Thus, the cow has become a symbol of mother earth in Hinduism for her ability to produce milk and give birth to the bullocks that are still used to plow Indian farms today. For all these reasons, a large portion of India's population still remains vegetarian.

Indian cuisine has also been influenced by cultures from outside and has adopted many interesting traits. For instance, the British and Moguls (Muslims of Mongol, Turkish, and Persian descent) influenced Indian cookery by combining meat with various spiced sauces, which later became "curries." It was fashionable among certain Westernized Indians to include meat in their diet during and after the "raj" era of British rule. Currently, the trend is reversing as educated Indians rediscover the virtues of their vegetarian heritage. Although Indian restaurants catering to an omnivorous clientele may offer more meat entrees than vegetarian dishes, Indian home cooking remains mostly vegetarian.

In India, where food is not always abundant, seasonal and dried foods are utilized carefully to create the daily menu. Here in the United States, the proverbial land of melting pots where a bounteous variety of food is always around, a meatless menu is rather easy to put together. Why then do many Americans find it difficult to sustain a meatless diet? A lack of satisfying taste and a concern over nutrition are the two most common reasons given by people who struggle to maintain a vegetarian diet in the West. There is another important factor which makes it difficult for vegetarians to maintain their life style. There is a noticeable lack of cultural support for vegetarians in our Western, meat-centered society. Even after widely publicized research exposing the connections between heart disease and meat consumption, many restaurants in the United States do not even have vegetarian entrees!

This book is a gift to you—the vegetarians who want to add new flavor to your daily menu, who want to be more confident about its nutritional value, and who want to find support in sustaining a vegetarian path. The book is also for those adventurous and professional chefs who simply want to expand their culinary repertoire by adding ethnic vegetarian entrees.

The first two chapters provide basic information regarding vegetarian nutrition. Some of the traditional recipes which follow have been altered by me to make them more nutritious. Some of the changes I offer will delightfully surprise you by showing you how simple, yet nutritious, Indian food can be when incorporated with local, seasonal foods.

It is easy to maintain a meatless diet using Indian vegetarian recipes in general and this book in particular for these reasons:

1) The food is colorful and appetizing.
2) Regional variations make Indian menus quite diverse.
3) The menus can be nutritionally balanced easily.

In India, my family was always attentive to the subtle flavors of food. Later, in America, I learned about the nutritional quality of food. I offer you the results! Here is a book that combines traditional Indian dishes with an eye for their nutritional value and a touch of my own imagination, which is what cooking is all about. Food made with recipes from this book are nutritious, inexpensive, and delicious!

CHAPTER ONE
VEGETARIAN NUTRITION

Nutrition is the sacred tie between the foods we eat and how our bodies utilize them; good nutrition ensures good health. In addition, nutrition can explain how people are connected socially, economically, and spiritually through the food they eat and share. A complete understanding of nutrition requires not only a knowledge of how the body uses food, but an awareness of the role society plays in shaping how people of different cultures treat the food they eat.

In this chapter and the next, you will get a brief introduction to the immensely complex subject of nutrition. It will include information on maintaining a well-balanced diet in general and a vegetarian diet in particular, with a focus on the traditional menus of India. Social factors have had an adverse effect on diet in modern societies, so a list of recommendations to remedy poor eating habits is also included.

Proper nutrition provides the body with the elements necessary for optimal growth and health, better known as *nutrients*. Most books on nutrition provide information on a simplified "balanced diet," which divides food into four major food groups—proteins, carbohydrates, fats, and micronutrients (vitamins and minerals). Proteins (meat, dairy, beans, nuts, etc.) are usually placed on top of the nutrition chart as body-building nutrients (recommending generous servings); followed by carbohydrates (grains, starches, and cereals) as the ideal fuel foods; fats (oil, butter) as the energy store house; and vitamins and minerals (fruits and vegetables) as the regulators of all these functions. This simplistic analysis is adequate, but limited, in light of new research in the areas of food and nutrition.

Based on this research, there are recently published books on vegetarian nutrition which challenge the now outdated, but still popular, notions of the four separate food groups. The complex machinery of our bodies utilizes all of the nutrients listed in the four food groups simultaneously and interdependently. Therefore, no one food is more important than the other, although the body's need for each nutrient may vary in quantity depending on many factors, such as life-style, gender, age, climate, activity, and general state of health.

The Recommended Daily Dietary Allowances (RDAs) recommended by the Food and Nutrition Board of the National Research Council are only estimated values for the various major nutrients we need for growth and good health and represent only a generalized picture of the body's daily need for these nutrients. Specific needs for a particular group (or individual) should be taken into account. People engaging in heavy physical labor need more carbohydrates than office workers. A pregnant woman may need more protein than her husband. A cold climate may require consumption of more fats than a hot climate. Some research points out that the body can even adapt to a limited amount of nutrients if not all the nutrients are sufficiently available. Such is the case among some poor farmers in India who work all day long with a meager diet of few rotis (bread) and little bit of *dal* (beans) and vegetables, and still remain quite healthy.

Most foods also contain more than one nutrient. Beans are rich in proteins but also are a good source of carbohydrates and minerals. Similarly, grains are an excellent source of carbohydrates, but also contribute a good deal of protein. So our Indian ancestors combined beans with rice to get protein and carbohydrates from both sources. Today, we need to re-learn this wisdom and step beyond the separate "food groups." Here the food groups are discussed in terms of how they work together; in later chapters their team work will be demonstrated in planned menus.

Often the students in my cooking class ask me: What do vegetarians eat, besides vegetables? The answer should be quite obvious in most parts of the United States, where a variety of grains, nuts, seeds, and beans are available year-around, in addition to frozen, canned, dried, and seasonal fresh produce. In India, as in many other countries, people eat only what is in season, plus beans and grains, and still get enough nutrients to stay healthy. It is how you prepare seasonal, fresh foods with other ingredients that makes a vegetarian diet nutritionally sound. Learning to present this diet in a palatable fashion will make you a good cook. After all, when we sit down with the anticipation of enjoying a good dinner, we don't think about nutrients; we fancy an elegant, good-tasting meal.

PROTEIN FOR VEGETARIANS
USING INDIAN FOODS

Another frequently asked question is how vegetarians get enough protein without eating animal products. Most nutritionists consider protein to be of "prime importance" (its literal meaning in Greek) because of its primary role in maintaining the body's growth and repairing tissue. Foods containing a good deal of protein need to be in our diet regularly since, unlike fat, protein cannot be stored in our bodies for very long. Therefore, some concern regarding your protein intake is understandable. However, most people in the Western world (vegetarians included) get more than enough of this essential nutrient.

What is "good quality protein?" Previous research on protein (up until the '50s) focused on complete vs. incomplete proteins. According to these findings "complete" proteins were defined as those foods which contain all of the essential amino acids required for tissue growth. Some examples of these complete protein foods were milk, meat, and eggs. Likewise, "incomplete" protein foods were defined as those having some, but not all, of these essential amino acids in sufficient amounts. This theory listed most beans, whole grains, nuts, and seeds as "incomplete" proteins. Based on this research, many vegetarians were worried about the kind of protein they would get from a meatless diet. A few pioneering books on vegetarian diet—such as

Diet for a Small Planet—tried to rid us of this anxiety by offering a solution: If you ate grains and legumes at the same meal, you could eliminate meat without sacrificing the benefits of complete protein. However, the most recent research on human needs for protein has shown that it is easier to get good quality protein from a vegetarian diet than we were led to believe. First of all, we do not need to worry about complete vs. incomplete protein, since plant proteins are not incomplete; all of the essential amino acids are actually present in various amounts. Secondly, amino acids from foods eaten throughout the day form an amino acid pool in the body from which protein needs can be met throughout the day.

However, it is important to note that including a variety of food in your diet is very important, since foods high in protein have their strengths and weakness in terms of the amino acids they contain. Also, unlike proteins obtained from a single source such as meat, protein from combined vegetarian sources, such as grains and beans, also contain a large amount of another nutrient—carbohydrate. It is interesting to note that many traditional Indian dishes combine grains and beans (the amount of certain amino acids in grains complements the amounts of other amino acids in beans). Some examples are *khichadi* on page 136 and *dosa* on page 59. It seems that the diet of our ancestors years ago is being proven by science to be the best choice for us today.

CARBOHYDRATES

One important concern for those seeking to maintain a healthful diet is getting enough calories from complex carbohydrates. Whole grains provide the body with other vital nutrients besides energy, as opposed to the "empty calories" of processed and/or fatty foods, such as white flour, refined sweeteners, and many snack foods. An Indian menu which includes a lot of whole grains, beans, nuts, and seeds will provide plenty of complex carbohydrates. Many of these whole foods also provide the body with another type of carbohydrate called fiber, which does not contain a large amount of nutrients, but is very important to the digestive system. Simple carbohydrates, such as some sweeteners and refined starches, provide the body with quick energy. However, since they are devoid of other nutrients, they are less nutritious. Chapter Two will provide information on how to stock up your panty with many healthful carbohydrates for your Indian cooking.

FATS

Fats are the most concentrated sources of energy in the foods we eat. They can supply our bodies with twice as much energy as an equal weight of protein. Fats also store and transport fat-soluble nutrients, such as vitamin A and E. Fat insulates and pads many delicate, vital organs, so some fat is important in our daily diet. Also, it helps transport flavors to our taste buds, thus enhancing our enjoyment of the foods we eat. However, only a small amount of fat is necessary to meet your body's daily requirement. All of the fat that your body needs can be supplied naturally from many whole foods, such as grains and some vegetables. Added fat is hardly needed for optimum health. Most people, vegetarians and meat eaters alike, consume too much fat, which is a health hazard in our modern society. Ideally, most of our caloric needs should be met through complex carbohydrates and not from added fats. However, since fats are an attractive and tasty medium for cooking and a moderate amount is not harmful to most people, let's discuss which fats are good for you, nutritionally.

There are two types of dietary fats, saturated and unsaturated. Saturated fats are considered unhealthful because they contribute to arteriosclerosis or hardening of the arteries. Moderate use of unsaturated fats is advisable because they contain linoleic and linolenic acids, both essential for many functions in the body.

All saturated fats appear solid at room temperature and almost always come from animal sources. One major exception is coconut oil, which is plant-derived, yet highly saturated. Other examples of saturated fats are animal fats, such as lard and butter or *ghee* (clarified butter). Unsaturated fats are usually liquid at room temperature and are derived from vegetable sources. Examples of unsaturated fats are corn oil, canola oil, safflower oil, sunflower seed oil, and peanut oil. Vegetable shortenings such as margarine are processed from unsaturated fats. However, they undergo a chemical transformation called *hydrogenation* which enables the liquid oil to become solid, like butter. It also chemically alters the fat so that it acts more like a saturated fat in the body and therefore is not a wise choice as a cooking medium. It would be better to use a bit of butter now and then.

Another fatty substance which merits mention here is cholesterol. Cholesterol is a substance manufactured by the body to metabolize proteins and other nutrients. It is neither necessary nor healthful to add cholesterol to our diet; the body usually manufactures all it needs. Cholesterol is a culprit in many heart-related diseases. All fast foods, as well as meat, creamy sauces, butter, and eggs, contain too much cholesterol. Reduced intake of both cholesterol and saturated fat would greatly benefit a healthy heart. And a marked reduction of all fats (even the good types) increases your potential for good health. The next chapter will provide information regarding the type of cooking fats suitable for nutritious Indian cooking.

MICRONUTRIENTS— VITAMINS AND MINERALS

The body needs vitamins and minerals in very small amounts. Since many of these nutrients cannot be stored in the body for a long time, they must be consumed on a regular basis, due to the vital role that they play in controlling other major nutrients. A nation-wide nutrition survey conducted in the United States in 1978 showed that many well-fed people who consume plenty of protein showed a deficiency of some micronutrient.

Vegetarians usually consume a lot of whole grains and fresh produce and so they get most of their vitamins and minerals from their diet. However, there is a certain micronutrient which is difficult to find in the vegan diet: vitamin B_{12}. This vitamin is found in animal products and, therefore, is easy to get from Indian foods which contain dairy products. Vegans are advised to take B_{12} supplements—about 2 micrograms a day for adults. A good dietary supplement is nutritional yeast which has had B_{12} added to it.

Two other micronutrients that are important to get good quantities of in a vegan diet are iron and calcium. Good food sources of iron are green leafy vegetables, dried fruits, and beans. Tofu and other bean products, seeds, and corn provide a good amount of calcium.

WATER

Water is an important element in our diet; about 60% of our body weight is water, and we need water for carrying other nutrients throughout the body. These days, people forget to drink water and often substitute other beverages. An Indian meal is always served with water. Filter your drinking water to remove chlorine and other impurities; your water will be tastier and more appealing to drink.

CHAPTER TWO
THE HEALTHFUL INDIAN PANTRY

Not too long ago, food was grown simply, without the use of machines or chemicals. Cultivation was done with the aid of domestic animals, using natural waste products as fertilizers. Even today, in many parts of India where technology is minimal, food is produced mostly by hand with generous help from bullocks, the common draft animals of India.

The introduction of modern technology to agriculture made food production and its distribution easier. This helped reduce the problem of hunger throughout the world, especially in the highly populated subcontinent of India. Machines made many agricultural tasks simpler and faster. Anyone who has hulled peanuts for farm seeds, as I have in my youth, knows the sweet benefits of simple machines.

However, as the food industry became a business which turned food production and its distribution into a commodity, food technology began to be misused by food growers, distributors, and even consumers. The same machines which were introduced to free us from difficult farm labor made it easier to deteriorate the quality of our food supply. For example, the milling of grains scraped away the outer nutrients from the hull so that the grain could be transported great distances and stored for long periods without spoiling. Manufacturers began to popularize such grains in the name of convenience and economy. Presently, using modern farming methods, much of the modernized world may be overfed but undernourished, according to current nutritional surveys.

As food technology advances, more and more Indians have begun to use processed foods for convenience or as a status symbol. A good example of how technology has affected the food habits of Indian people is shown in their almost exclusive preference for milled white rice. Traditionally, rice was hand-pounded to remove the outermost layer—the husk—which is indigestible. Underneath the husk is nutritious brown rice. The modern milling of rice made husking easier, but it went a step further by scraping the kernel until it was completely polished—devoid of most of the micronutrients and fiber which the original grain contained. In modern India, only villagers and poor people use the more nutritious brown rice as a staple because they cannot afford milled rice.

Modern food technology also overuses chemicals such as synthetic fertilizers, pesticides, and additives to increase food production and to make its transportation easier. The possible health hazards of some of these chemicals are currently well-publicized. In India, much of the food supply is still relatively free of chemicals by default because of their high cost. However, even in that country, the indiscriminate use of harmful chemicals in farming is a growing concern among many health-conscious groups. The excessive use of chemicals threatens our health, the environment at large, and erodes nutrients away from soil which was once organically nourished with animal waste products and humus.

How can we, as concerned consumers, reconcile our dependence on food technology with its many drawbacks? Some aspects of modern technology may be needed to help meet the food demands of our growing population, but other aspects need to be re-examined. The first step for us—vegetarians, cooks, and homemakers—is to BE AWARE. By increasing our awareness of how our food is grown and marketed, we can make good choices while shopping, cooking, and eating—and enjoy better health. Most meats and dairy products in our supermarkets contain more harmful chemical residues, artificial colors, and preservatives than fresh produce, legumes, and whole grains do. The less your food choices depend on animal products, the safer your pantry is (and the safer the animals are too).

SEVEN GOLDEN RULES OF THE NEW VEGETARIAN CUISINE OF INDIA

Here are some tips for healthful eating that combine nutrition and food safety with traditional Indian cooking practices.

(1) Use whole grains and flours made from whole grains in your cooking as much as possible. If processed grains or flour (such as unbleached white flour) are necessary for your recipe, make sure they are additive-free. Balance the menu by serving a refined grain dish with a hearty entrée.

(2) Use sweeteners sparingly, especially the refined sugars. Indian treats are notoriously over-sweetened. My repertoire of Indian desserts is limited for this very reason. The desserts in this book are modified and nutritionally upscale.

(3) Use oils and other cooking fats with care and in moderation. (Read about the nutritional aspect of fats on pages 9-10 and using fats for cooking on page 19).

(4) Whenever possible, use fresh, seasonal, and organically grown produce. When buying groceries and spices, make sure that they are additive-free. Fresh produce is more nutritious and tasty than its frozen or canned counterpart. When fresh fruits and vegetables are unavailable, frozen varieties are a better choice than canned. The health virtues of eating seasonal food are emphasized in the Asian health doctrine called *macrobiotics* and in the ancient Indian health science called *ayurveda*. Both disciplines

promote the concept that nature produces certain foods in a particular growing season to create balance, and, therefore, eating seasonal food can be healing. Certain allergies are claimed to be cured by eating seasonal food items. In this book, I have experimented with seasonally grown, local produce to replace imported items unavailable outside of India. Try experimenting with your own locally grown produce in Indian recipes. I also advocate using fresh herbs, such as garlic and chives, in addition to dry spices. Organically grown food may not be available in your community currently. However, growing public awareness regarding the risks of certain chemical food additives has brought many organic foods into our local markets. Shop at your local health food store, food co-op, or farmers' market for fresh and additive-free food. Grow your own food, if possible. How to clean your produce to remove chemical residue is explained on page 78.

(5) Include some uncooked vegetables and fruits in your diet, and do not overcook vegetables. Many vegetable recipes, especially in Indian cookery, call for a longer cooking time than is necessary. In India, most produce is cooked thoroughly or peeled to remove water-based bacteria. For this reason, raw salads are not traditional in India. However, where food is grown in bacteria-free water, leafy, raw vegetables with an Indian salad dressing can be incorporated into an Indian menu. In this book, I have also included some fresh Indian salads. I have also considerably shortened the cooking time of most vegetables to retain good texture and some of the micronutrients which are destroyed with overcooking. Of course, some vegetables, such as potatoes, require a longer cooking time in order to make them fully digestible. Consume fresh fruits in season frequently, and serve them as a snack or dessert in place of sweet Indian treats.

(6) Use salt sparingly in your cooking. Traditionally, salt and pepper shakers are not present at Indian meals, as cooked food is presumed to be flavored correctly. However, many Indian recipes call for too much salt. Over-consumption of salt has been linked with high blood pressure and other illnesses. In this book, salt has been used moderately and can be further reduced. The selective use of spices, as explained in the next section, along with lemon juice, can bring out the natural salts in your foods and thus reduce the need for added salt. Make your own condiments, such as the *chutneys* in this book, instead of buying over-salted, processed varieties.

(7) Know your spices and use them with discrimination. It is the art of using spices that makes Indian cuisine distinctive. *Indian food can be spicy without being hot.* This is a fact many people unfamiliar with the subtlety of Indian food do not know. In proper Indian cooking, spices should enhance the flavors of the food, not blind it. Moderate use of spices can help your appetite and digestion, but overuse can be harmful to your health, according to Indian herbal science.

GRAINS, FLOURS, AND RICE

Rice is a very important food for many people of the world, so much so that the words for food and rice are the same in several Asian languages. To many Western cooks, rice is thought of only as a substitute for potatoes or pasta. This is a gross underestimation of a grain so perfect, it is considered almost a complete food by some people (such as those that practice macrobiotics). In India, there are many colorful varieties of rice, some of them not found in the West. Here is a list of rice you can find easily in your health food store or at an import market:

Brown Rice: Most long-grain rice available in health food stores is suitable for Indian recipes, although locally grown brown *basmati* is the best. Short-grain brown rice, which is slightly more nutritious that the long-grain, can be used in *khichadi* or other bean-based rice dishes.

White *Basmati* Rice: *Basmati* rice, grown in North India and Pakistan, is considered the "queen of rice" by many Asian people. Its unique, nut-like flavor and aromatic fragrance has been attributed to the soil in which it grows. *Basmati* rice grown in other countries lacks that certain flavor. Therefore, when buying white *basmati* rice, get a Pakistani or Indian variety. I have been told that imported white *basmati* has been hand hulled to retain its long kernels. For that reason, it retains some of its nutrients and, unlike, many types of commercial white rice, is not coated with talc. Imported white *basmati* certainly smells authentic when I cook with it, and I have a special craving for it from time to time. In India, *basmati* rice is expensive and considered worth saving for special occasions. Your neighbors would know when you have special guests by smelling the cooking *basmati*.

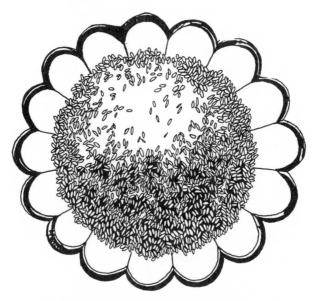

Other White Rice: Most health food books would frown upon white rice, since it is less nutritious than brown rice. But there are times when white rice is preferred, such as when serving to elderly folk or youngsters who cannot digest brown rice as easily. Or perhaps, when you are in a hurry, you do not have the time needed to cook brown rice. In these situations, buy either the above mentioned white *basmati* which is very quick to prepare (about 10 minutes) or the parboiled, converted variety available in most supermarkets. The process of parboiling and converting dissolves some of the grain's nutrients from the outer layer of the kernel into the water and then seals them back. This keeps a lot of the micronutrients, but loses much of the fiber. Converted rice is quicker to cook and easier to digest than brown rice and is more nutritious than unconverted rice. It also does not have talc which most white rice is coated with. Do not buy instant rice; it lacks taste, texture, and nutrients.

Other Whole Grains: In addition to rice, other whole grains such as millet, bulgur (partially cooked, cracked wheat), rye, kasha (buckwheat), and quinoa (a South American grain) can be used instead of rice in dishes such as *pilau* and *birianis*.

FLOURS

There are as many flour mills in India as there are laundromats in Western countries. There, you can take your grains to the mill and have them ground to the consistency you desire. You could ask the mill worker to grind your whole wheat flour finely for *chapatis* or grind your rice coarsely for a dessert dish like *firni*. Now, many people also have their own little flour mill (the size of a computer) so that they can have freshly ground flour everyday. Outside India you have to improvise by mixing various types of flour for a particular recipe.

All flours should be kept in closed containers for no longer than a month, unless they are refrigerated, in which case they can last for several months.

After years of trial and error, I have come up with a good mixture for Indian breads (see page 143); you may come up with your own favorite blend. Here are some flours to stock up on for the recipes in this book.

Whole Wheat Flour: The flour of hard wheat berries (which contains all the nutrients of the grain) is easy to find in your supermarket or health food store. Get one that is finely ground to use for making *chapatis* and other Indian bread recipes.

Whole Wheat Pastry Flour: This flour is milled from light-colored soft wheat berries. It contains less protein and gluten than flour made from hard berries, but it still retains all the nutrients of the whole soft wheat berries. Stock this flour to mix with regular whole wheat flour for *chapatis* and pastry-like dishes.

Unbleached White Flour: This is made from the inside of the wheat berry and is mostly starch—devoid of bran or germ. It is good, however, for obtaining a smooth, elastic texture and is well suited for many thin, delicate confections, such as the outside layer of stuffed *samosas*. I also combine it with regular whole wheat flour and whole wheat pastry flour to get the texture needed for most Indian wheat breads.

OTHER NON-WHEAT FLOURS: There are a variety of grains and their flours that can be enjoyed by people who are allergic to wheat or simply want a variation. Here are some that are easy to find in your health food market.

Cornmeal: Purchase varieties that still retain the germ. Cornmeal can be combined with wheat or the other flours mentioned in the following text when making an alternative to wheat-based *chapatis*.

Rice Flour: Somewhat difficult to find, brown rice or white rice flours lack gluten. Therefore, they need be combined with cornmeal and other flours to obtain the consistency necessary for Indian breads.

Rye Flour: This is the flour of a very nutritious grain and can be a good substitute for wheat flour in Indian cooking. It tastes like Indian millet flour and can be used for a hand-patted Indian bread called *rotla*.

Millet Flour: Indian millet is different in texture and color than the American variety. Both are nutritious. Millet contains more complete protein than either rice and wheat, and it is rich in other nutrients such as iron and calcium. Many village folks consume millet in western India in place of wheat because it is cheaper. Indian millet flour can be purchased from Indian specialty stores. It is mostly used to make *rotla*.

Potato Flour: This is not a grain flour, but it can be used in combination with rye or rice flour to obtain the consistency necessary for making bread or Indian appetizers.

Besan **(Chick-pea or Garbanzo Flour):** Garbanzo flour (*besan*) is also known as chick-pea flour, or *chana* flour, since chick-peas and garbanzos are similar beans and their flours are nearly identical. This is a high-protein bean flour which is suitable for making batter or stuffing. It is too dense for making bread, although it can be added to other flours for this purpose and will enrich the bread nutritionally. Store *besan* in the refrigerator or in a very cool place or else it will go rancid.

BEANS OR *DAL*

Dal, which literally means "split beans," is an important component of Indian meals. The word *dal* generally refers to any soup-like dish served at an Indian meal, although the consistency of *dal* can vary from a broth to a very thick stew. *Dal*-based dishes contribute a significant amount of protein to a vegetarian diet, so it is always, included in a complete, traditional Indian meal. Most health food stores now carry *mung dal* (split mung) and *masoor dal* (yellow lentils). Other popular dals such as *toor dal*, *chana dal*, and *urad dal* can be obtained from Indian specialty stores. Yellow and green split peas, as well as brown lentils, also a make good *dal*. Other beans such as pintos, black beans, and red beans can be used in *dal* recipes. Store the beans, lentils, or *dal* in closed jars. They can keep for a number of months. You can find out more about *dals* in Chapter 6.

NUTS AND SEEDS

Nuts and seeds add protein as well as micronutrients (such as vitamin E) to your vegetarian diet. However, they are densely packed with calories as well as nutrients, so use them sparingly. Traditionally in the Indian diet, nuts and seeds are not consumed by the bowlful like American trail mixes are, but used in small amounts to give dishes a crunchy texture. Stock almonds, cashews, pistachios, peanuts, and sesame seeds in your Indian pantry. Keep them cool or refrigerated.

COOKING FATS

A detailed discussion on the nutritional aspects of dietary fats has been provided in the first chapter. Based on this knowledge, choose the type of cooking oils suited to your life-style. Some flavored oils traditionally used in Asian cooking (such as smoked sesame oil) and others, such as extra-virgin olive oil, already have strong flavors of their own, and, therefore, may not be suitable for Indian dishes. Generally, I recommend the use of unsaturated, bland oils, such as corn, safflower, and canola in my Indian cooking.

For certain recipes, however, specific types of fats work better than other. For example, in making Indian desserts, I may indulge in *ghee*—made from butter, a saturated fat. *Ghee* is actually clarified butter, in which all the milk solids have been removed. Through this process, butter can be saved for several weeks in a pantry. In many parts of India where refrigeration is not available, people prepare *ghee* in large quantities, which they then store in metal containers for months. I will provide instructions on how to make *ghee* on page 33. *Ghee* is a delicious cooking fat favored by many Indian chefs. It should be consumed sparingly by most people and avoided by those who are advised to be on a low-fat diet.

SPICES AND CULINARY HERBS

Well-cooked Indian food is not only nutritious, but visually appealing, fragrant, and delicious. When we are hungry, we desire the sensual delights, not a list of nutrients. The art of blending spices is an important part of the technique of Indian cooking.

Outsiders may find it surprising that people in India do not use curry powder as a flavoring medium. Curry powder is an item packaged for Western cooks who may not be familiar with the subtle nature of the many blends and combinations of Indian spices. A *pakka* or proper Indian cook uses each individual spice at different stages in cooking, as a conductor might introduce various instruments progressively in an orchestra. To prepare a real Indian meal, first acquire some of the basic spices: turmeric, black or brown mustard seeds, cumin, coriander, gingerroot, and garlic. Also, whenever a fresh herb is called for in a recipe, try to get it. Later, you can build up your spice cabinet with the more exotic spices listed in the next section. Various blends, such as tea *masala* (spice blend) and *garam* (hot) *masala*, can also be made, using the instructions given on pages 38-39 instead of buying pre-mixed blends. The amount of spice called for in the recipes in this book will produce a dish which may be considered "mild" to some readers. People who desire their food to be more sensational can add more hot spices, such as cayenne, fresh hot chiles, and ginger. However, those of you who shy away from Indian food because it is usually too hot, can be assured that you can make it spicy without making it hot. You will learn this technique after reading this chapter and using the recipes that follow.

HOW TO BUY AND STORE SPICES: Where you buy your spices and how you store them is as important as learning how to use them. First of all, do not purchase your spices from supermarkets, where they are already packaged in tins or bottles. These spices cannot be inspected by shoppers for their freshness. Instead, buy your spices in bulk from an Indian food store or a health food store. Stores that sell spices in bulk tend to replenish their stock often, and the spices you buy there will be much fresher than packaged spices sold at supermarkets. Another advantage of buying spices in bulk (aside from a cheaper price) is being able to inspect, smell, and even taste a bit of the spice to test its quality, relative potency, and freshness. Buy most of your spices in small quantities (¼ lb. or less), and store them in glass jars in a cool place away from direct sunlight. Dry spices will stay good for months if kept in air-tight containers. Fresh herbs need to be used within few days. Whole spices are often ground before you cook with them. See the section on kitchen equipment on pages 27-28 for advice on what type of spice grinder you may want to invest in.

The following seven basic spices, which are easy to find in any food store, will get you started:

Turmeric (*Haldi*): The poor man's saffron, turmeric is a popular Indian spice, used for its "curry" color as well as its unique taste. Not a relative of the saffron family, turmeric is grown as a root, like ginger, then dried and ground into powder. Used in Indian cooking primarily in its powdered form, turmeric can be stored for over a year. Turmeric can also be used as a natural dye.

Black or Brown Mustard Seeds (*Rai*): These small, black (or smaller, dark brown) mustard seeds are an essential part of Indian cooking, as you will often "pop" them in hot oil for stir-frying many vegetable dishes. The yellow or white ones will *not* do as a substitute. Buy them whole and replenish them every few months.

Cayenne (*Mirchi*): It is cayenne—more than any other spice—that makes Indian food spicy hot. Therefore, use cayenne with discretion. It comes in varying strengths, and too much of the potent powder can mask other flavors. Obtained from dry, hot chiles, this spice can be substituted with any fresh, hot chile (see the section on fresh herbs on page 23). *Kala mirch* or black pepper grows wild in India (as well as white pepper and long pepper of the peppercorn family), but is not as widely used there as cayenne. Whole peppercorns are used in making some Indian pickles and South Indian dishes, as well as in some *garam masala* recipes. However, cayenne is the main "heat" element of most Indian food.

Cumin (*Jeera*): Not to be confused with its look-alikes, caraway or anise seed, these earthy seeds are also used Mexican and Middle Eastern cuisines. For Indian cooking, buy cumin in powder and seed form, as you will be using them both. *Kala jeera*, or black cumin, is a darker variety; it smells a bit different but can be substituted by the more common green variety. *Ajowan* is another look-alike Indian spice which is often confused with black cumin in many Indian cookbooks. Indian cooks know *ajowan* well for its distinctive taste and digestive properties, and will use *ajowan* in bean dishes.

Coriander or Cilantro (*Dhania*): Fresh coriander looks like parsley and is also known as cilantro or Chinese parsley. As a fresh herb, coriander leaves have a strong flavor and are an acquired taste. After the plant flowers, the resulting pods (the seeds) are dried and ground. The ground seeds are more "mild-mannered" and have a flavor much different from the aromatic leaves. The powder can be used liberally even by those who do not like the flavor of the leaves. However, when a recipe calls for the leaves, the powder will not do as a substitute (especially as far as the cilantro lover is concerned). Fresh coriander can be grown in a sunny kitchen window. It can also be found in most supermarkets. It is very perishable, but can be kept in the refrigerator for over a week if the stalks are placed in a jar of water, and the entire bunch (jar and all) is completely covered with a plastic bag. Coriander powder can be stored for months without losing its taste, but some chefs prefer to grind the seeds as they are needed, using a peppercorn grinder.

Gingerroot (*Adu*): Fresh gingerroot is now available in most markets for use in cooking and herbal tonics. Powdered ginger is a poor substitute for the strong, pungent flavor of fresh ginger. Gingerroot may dry out or get moldy after a while. To revitalize dry ginger, soak in warm water. To keep ginger fresh longer, keep it standing in a jar of water in the refrigerator and change the water after several days or store, tightly wrapped, in your freezer. To use ginger for cooking, grate it instead of mincing.

Garlic (*Lasan*): Garlic powder or granules are never the same as the powerful flavor of fresh garlic. It is worth the trouble to peel and mince. Fresh garlic also has many medicinal uses, from curing the common cold to killing bacteria. Buy garlic with big cloves for easier peeling. To peel the clove, smash it with the flat surface of a wide-bladed knife, then mince or chop it. Indian cooks do not use a garlic press, although many chefs use a food processor for mincing garlic in large quantities. (Green garlic is discussed on page 23).

FRESH CULINARY HERBS: When fresh herbs are used as spices in Indian cuisine, they impart a strong fragrance and often a different flavor than their dried counterparts. Many fresh herbs have medicinal value, as well, and are brewed into teas for that purpose. Indian cooks use these herbs to great culinary advantage when the season permits. Some of these herbs, such as scallions (green onions), are available year around. Others, such as green garlic, have a short season. Some, such as curry leaves, are hard to find outside of India. Many herbs can be planted and grown in your backyard or kitchen window. Most fresh herbs keep well in the refrigerator for a couple of weeks. Dry them in the sun to preserve them longer. The fresh herbs used frequently in Indian cuisine, such as cilantro and ginger, have been discussed already. They are so important to daily cooking in India that most cooks start their day shopping for fresh vegetables and herbs—which almost always includes cilantro, ginger, and fresh chiles, often sold together in one small bundle.

Onions and Scallions (*Kanda*): Yellow, red, and white onions can be used interchangeably in Indian cuisine. Green onions (scallions) are preferred by many cooks for their relatively mild flavor, especially for making fresh chutneys. People who have problems digesting onions often do well by using scallions instead. When I cook with scallions, I use most of the green leaves along with the white stem.

Green Garlic (*Lilu Lasan*): Although green garlic has a very short season, it is wonderfully spicy and worth looking for. Use the greens and stems in place of the garlic bulb.

Fresh Hot Chiles (*Mirchi*): Whole books have been written about the passionate character of fresh chiles. There is an incredible variety of fresh, hot chiles available throughout the world. In India, fresh chiles are used everywhere, but each region has its own names for different varieties of chiles, so it is hard to give the reader recommendations on which chile is hot and which is not. Even here, in California, many fresh chiles are known by different names, depending on the farmer who grows them. More perplexing yet is the fact that one batch of jalapeños may be hotter than another batch, even when bought from the same shop or farm. So you just have to try a bit of each chile to find out how potent it is. As a rule, the chiles that are known as jalapeños and serranos in California are hot chiles. The Anaheim chile is somewhere between hot and mild and is very versatile in its culinary use. If you are wary of chiles with too much heat, here is how to "cure" or "tame" a hot chile and still keep its flavor. Cut the chile lengthwise and remove the veins and seeds, where most of the "heat" resides. Mince the chile finely to distribute its flavor. Do not touch your eyes while cutting chiles, and wash your hands thoroughly after you finish.

Mint Leaves (*Phodino*): This aromatic herb is used in making hot tea or is added to a pot of iced tea as a flavoring. Hot mint tea is used as a worldwide remedy for upset stomach. Similarly, a *chutney* (condiment) made out of mint is often served with fried appetizers to aid digestion.

Curry Leaves (*Kadhi patti* or *mitha neem patti*): Leaves of the sweet *neem* tree (not to be confused with the bitter, medicinal *neem* tree) are used in soup-like dishes such as *dal* and yogurt soup (*kadhi*). It is difficult to find the fresh leaves outside of India. The dried leaves can be purchased in specialty stores, but they lack the distinct aroma and flavor of this fresh herb. *Tej patti* or bay leaf (often used as an incorrect translation for curry leaves) is not a substitute for curry leaves, although bay leaf is used in some South Indian dishes.

Lemon or Lime (*Nimu or Limnu*): I wish to include lemons and limes in the herb section, since no Indian meal would be complete without the use of these fruits as fresh spices. Typically, a vegetable, soup, or an appetizer dish will have freshly squeezed lemon juice sprinkled on it as a last step to bring out all the flavors and colors. Wedges of lemon or lime are always served with an Indian meal.

SWEET INDIAN SPICES

Cinnamon (*Taj*): Native to Sri Lanka and South India, cinnamon comes from the bark of a tree and is both a sweet and a hot spice. Much of the cinnamon sold in the West is cinnamon cassia, a slightly bitter but close relative to the real thing. Buy cinnamon in sticks for Indian food, as you will be using it whole or grinding it yourself. Dinner guests can remove the pieces while eating when whole sticks are used.

Cloves (*Loving*): This distinct spice is the dried flower bud of a tropical tree. Buy cloves whole as they are used that way for most Indian cooking and removed before eating.

Cardamom Pods (*Ilaichi*): Cardamom, an exotic, aromatic spice originally from Nepal, is considered the "queen of spices" in Indian cuisine. It is sold as a green or beige pod the size of a pea. Both kinds of pods are good to buy. There is a puffy, white version which is bleached. Do not buy this kind, because the bleach is not healthful, and it ruins the spicy aroma. There is also a darker, bigger pod which is sold more cheaply. This is not true cardamom and lacks the fragrance and sweet taste of real cardamom.

To use cardamom, remove and discard the skin and collect the black seeds. This laborious task is worthwhile, because the flavor of these seeds cannot be matched by any other spice. If you are going to use a lot of cardamom, you can also buy the shelled seeds at Indian shops. Store them in a cool place. Do not buy powdered cardamom, as it is often stale, and the pod is ground with skin and all. Some recipes call for whole pods, which should be removed before eating.

Sweet Spice Mix (*Garam Masala*): Garam masala is a sweet spice mix, made from the three sweet spices listed previously, in equal portion by weight. Some *garam masalas* include as many as 12 to 18 spices. How many spices you mix to make this *masala* depends on the recipe you use. However, two things are common in all garam masala recipes: the mix is made from roasting and grinding the **whole** spices, and it always contains cardamom, cinnamon, and cloves. Instructions for making Basic *Masala* Mix are given on page 38.

Indian Tea Spice Mix (*Chai Masala*): This spice blend can be made in the same manner as *garam masala*. See the instructions on page 39.

OTHER MORE DIFFICULT TO FIND INDIAN SPICES: The spices listed below are more difficult to find where an Indian population is not present. However, they can be purchased through mail order from some of the sources listed in the back of this book. You can consider them optional and use the substitutes when mentioned, although substitutes cannot truly replace the real spices.

Asafetida (*Hing*): *Hing* is obtained from dried resins scrapped from the stalks of a particular East Indian plant. This spice is almost always sold in ground form, as the lumpy, hard resin is almost impossible to grind with an ordinary kitchen tool. *Hing* smells rather strong because it contains natural sulfuric compounds and thus is considered beneficial in releasing stomach gases and flatulence. A pinch of this powerful spice will be enough for a whole pot of soup. Its strong smell dissipates as it is stirred in hot oil. Use hing after acquiring a taste for it and learning how to use it, or omit it, if you prefer (although no Indian chef would cook a dal without *hing*).

Fenugreek (*Methi*): Fenugreek seeds are small, yellow, and slightly bitter in taste. A small amount is used for stir-frying vegetables and in bean dishes. They can be considered optional in most recipes, except in preserved pickles where they are an important ingredient. Fenugreek seeds aid digestion and are also helpful in relieving mucous conditions.

Rose Water (*Gulab Jal*): Rose water is an aromatic liquid made from crushed rose petals. It can be bought in bottles from stores specializing in Indian, Arabic, or French food. It is used mainly to flavor sweets and milk-based drinks. Rose water loses its fragrance after about a month, so replenish it from time to time.

Screwpine Water (*Kevra Jal*): This essence is made from screwpine flowers and is mainly used to flavor sweets. Rose water can be substituted in place of *kevra* water.

Saffron (*Kesar*): Saffron is the most expensive spice in the world. In fact, it costs as much as gold by weight. The high cost of this rare, fragrant, and colorful spice is due to the fact that over 80,000 stigmas of the beautiful crocus plant must be hand picked in order to make a pound of saffron. In addition to its golden color, saffron also imparts a unique fragrance to food. Saffron has been prized for its culinary and folk medicinal values for centuries. It was taken from Asia to Spain by the Arabs in the tenth century where it is cultivated to this day. In fact, the best quality saffron now comes from Spain and Kashmir.

Purchase saffron as threads and not in its powdered form, as the powder may have been adulterated. Also watch out for "fake" saffron which is really safflower that is sold as saffron in some shops. Safflower threads are thicker than those of saffron. They will color the food, but lack the aroma of saffron. Soak saffron threads in hot water or milk for a few minutes to bring out their color; then add the threads and liquid to your dish. You can use saffron sparingly, as its strong flavor will go a long way.

Tamarind (*Imli*): Another exotic spice, tamarind is a fruit resembling fresh peas in a pod. When green, the fruit is very, very sour. It is used in making chutneys and as a spice in South India. When ripe, tamarind possesses a sweet-and-sour taste. The brittle, shell-like skin of the ripe, dried tamarind is removed, and the pulp (flesh) is collected after removing the hard seeds from inside. Tamarind is also sold in another form—a dehydrated, compact brick. After the skin and seeds of the fruit are removed, the pulp is compressed and dried. This form of tamarind is easier to use. However, beware of occasional seeds which may be left in this compact block. Once, I almost broke the glass jar of my blender when making chutney from this "seedless" tamarind. Some ethnic shops also sell tamarind concentrate, a thick paste which can be used in small amounts to flavor a dish. For a sweet-and-sour, tamarind-like substitute, I sometimes recommend lime juice and brown sugar. However, I go out of my way to Indian (or Mexican) shops to get dry pods. To use the whole dry pods, first remove the skin. Soak the dry pods in warm water for few minutes, then remove the seeds before adding the pulp to your recipe. To use bricks of tamarind, break off a small section, and soak in hot water for few minutes before using.

Nutmeg (*Jaifal*) and Mace (*Jaifal Patti*): Nutmeg and mace are two spices packaged naturally in one nut. The outer covering surrounding the shell of the nutmeg is the lacy mace—another spice. Both spices should be bought whole and can be substituted for each other since they smell and taste very similar. Nutmeg is more readily available than mace. It can be stored in its whole form and ground fresh when needed, using the fine teeth of a cheese grinder. In Indian cooking, both nutmeg and mace are used sparingly—mostly for sweets.

White Poppy Seeds (*Khas Khas*): The seeds extracted from ripe poppy pods are gathered as this nutty spice. (These poppies do not contain any narcotic properties—only the unripe poppies do). In North India, they are mainly used to decorate sweets, such as *ladoos*, which are important for ceremonial purposes. Black poppy seeds taste similar but will not produce the same decorative effect.

Fennel and Anise (*Variali* or *Saunf*): I am lumping these two related spices together, because in Indian cooking they are used interchangeably. Known for their digestive properties, a drink made from either herb is often given to colicky babies. The munchies handed out in Indian restaurants near the cashier's counter are also made from fennel seeds and are meant to be eaten after a meal as a breath freshener and/or digestive aid. To make similar munchies at home, roast some fennel or anise seeds with sesame seeds, add some salt and dehydrated coconut flakes, and keep them in a jar.

Pomegranate Seeds (*Anar Dana*): Fresh pomegranate fruits bear juicy seeds which are enjoyed by many Asian people. The juicy seeds are dried and preserved to use as spices, to make chutney with, or to use as a food coloring. Any sweet-and-sour spice mix can be substituted for pomegranate seeds. Use fresh seeds, by all means, when they are in season.

Mango Powder (*Amchoor*): *Amchoor* is made out of dried, unripe, sour mangoes which are normally used for making pickles. It is sold in powder form and keeps indefinitely. In North India, we often use it in place of lemon juice, to give tartness to vegetable dishes. Lime juice can be substituted for *amchoor*.

In this limited space I have tried my best to cover the major spices used in Indian cooking, because it is the art of using spices which makes Indian cuisine so unique. However, the subject of Indian spices is a vast one. India has been influenced by the people of many other cultures, who brought and integrated their own spices into Indian cooking. I am not familiar with many regional spices and the ones which are chiefly used in cooking meat (such as in some Mogulai dishes influenced by Persian cuisine.) Therefore, forgive me if, during your shopping trips, you come across a spice I have not included here. Also, I have only mentioned the medicinal use of some spices when it is widely known, since the discussion of medicinal Indian spices is another field worthy of presenting in a book of its own.

KITCHEN EQUIPMENT

Your kitchen may already be equipped with conventional pots and pans, many of which can be used for cooking Indian food. There is no need, then, to buy special gadgets for your Indian pantry, except for a few useful specialty tools such as those that follow. These items are available in Indian stores; other ethnic food stores may have similar appliances.

Spice Grinder: Since the use of spices is the key to Indian cuisine, it is worth investing in some spice-grinding tools. Buy two mortar and pestle sets, one made out wood or ceramic (such as a Japanese *suribachi*) for crushing seeds and herbs such as garlic. The other one should be a heavier grinder made out of marble or metal (such as stainless steel or brass) in order to grind hard, dry spices such as cinnamon sticks. I also keep a coffee grinder reserved to crush spices and seeds for when I need to grind a lot of dry spices for *garam masala*.

Kadhai or Wok (Frying Pan): The Indian *kadhai* is similar to the Chinese wok. It is a frying pan with a curved bottom which helps distribute both the heat and oil more quickly and evenly as you cook. The *kadhai* is a bit taller and more rounded than the wok, but the later can be substituted easily. If you do not have a wok or *kadhai*, use any shallow pot for frying. If you are a tool collector, buy two *kadhais*, one lightweight wok made out of stainless steel or carbon steel for sautéing and the other a cast iron one for deep-frying.

Tava (**Roasting Pan**): This concave, lightweight, iron or steel pan is used for roasting chapatis, a kind of flat bread. A heavy, cast iron pan or griddle would do fine as a substitute.

Velan (**Rolling Pin**): The rolling pins used in Indian cooking are solid pieces of wood, wider in the middle and gradually tapering off at the end. I think this shape helps to roll the bread into a perfect circle, but any rolling pin will do.

Patli (**Bread-Rolling Board**): Round rolling boards are used in India to facilitate the rolling of round breads such as chapatis.

Jara (**Slotted Spoon**): A slotted spoon for draining excess oil while deep-frying is an easy-to-find tool for your kitchen.

OTHER USEFUL TOOLS FOR INDIAN COOKING: The following kitchen tools are good to have around:

Cast Iron Pot or Dutch Oven: I find that this pot is the most suitable for making perfect brown rice. You will also get an essential micronutrient—iron—by using an iron pot.

Big, Wide Stainless Steel Pot (Dutch Oven): These pots are good for making large quantities of food. Also, they are well suited for creating your own steaming apparatus or for making steamed dishes as described in chapters to follow.

Bamboo or Stainless Steel Steamer Baskets: Most kitchens have folding vegetable steamer baskets which are adequate for steaming some of the appetizers included in this book. Bamboo steamers have covers which can be used with topless woks.

I enjoy collecting kitchen gadgets. However, I have also liked the challenge of creating a cooking tool out of a strange item, such as making rolling pin out of a bottle on a camping trip. If you don't have a proper tool, do not worry. Use your imagination and improvise with what surrounds you. Like my mother used to say: "A good cook can create a feast out of dust with the simplest clay pot. And a bad cook can reduce good food into dirt even with a golden vessel."

CHAPTER THREE
BASIC RECIPES

This chapter will cover the preparation of some basic foods which are unique to the Indian kitchen: yogurt and the popular frying medium, *ghee* or clarified butter, and *paneer*, a kind of homemade cheese.

There are also some innovative, non-dairy substitutes for those people who wish to avoid dairy. Although these non-dairy equivalents may be frowned upon as being not traditionally Indian, they are now sought out even by Indian homemakers who are concerned with excessive dairy consumption and animal rights.

Also included are instructions for making spice blends such as *garam masala*, garlic/cayenne paste, and tamarind paste. Finally, it will include some sauces which can be made ahead of time to incorporate in your menu.

DAIRY BASICS AND THEIR EQUIVALENTS

One reason why the cow is considered sacred in India is the wondrous milk that she provides. Lord Krishna, as a young man, is frequently portrayed in Indian temples in the company of humble cows and milkmaids. Although milk from the goat and the graceful buffalo is available, the cow, by and large, is the main source of milk in India. The nutritional importance of milk cannot be overstated to an Indian vegetarian. Milk is a prime source of protein, calcium, and many vitamins for them. It is a shame, however, that many people, including growing children, cannot afford to drink a sufficient amount of milk, which in India is a luxury for those who can afford it.

In contrast, here in Western countries where milk and dairy products are overabundant, over-produced, and over-consumed, there is a growing concern among many health practitioners about their misuse. On one hand, modern technology and animal husbandry have made milk readily available to all people here; on the other, the profit-motivated dairy industry has mass-produced and over-popularized milk's consumption to such a degree that it is perhaps harmful to our health. Everybody does not need milk and perhaps should not consume milk.

The growing vegan movement calls attention to the fact that dairy products are not only unnecessary for good health, but the production of dairy products is no less harmful or cruel to animals in the modern factory farming industry than their being slaughtered for meat.

The reasons for advocating a dairy-free diet in the modern world are many. First of all, being a vegan is ecologically less taxing to the earth, as the production of food animals often requires use of scarce water and arable land. Secondly, avoiding the unnecessary exploitation of our fellow animals is morally defensible. Third, dairy products can be unhealthful for many of us. Most dairy products are fattening, laden with cholesterol and saturated fats. Dairy products can create difficulties when fighting a virus or cold. Some people are dairy-sensitive or allergic and should not consume dairy at all.

In India, the less technological and perhaps more humane dairy industry is not yet able, for better or worse, to flood the country with a surplus of milk. As a result, milk is mostly organic, unadulterated, and fresh. There is a government-owned dairy which is now expanding to supply milk to towns accessible by train. However, the majority of the Indian population, being rural, still obtains milk fresh and raw from local cows, buffalos, or goats. The milk of Indian buffalos, which are referred to here as water buffalo, is very popular in India. Buffalo milk tastes sweeter, richer, and is more expensive than cow's milk. The least popular milk is goat's milk. Children are told it is good for them. But since adults turn their noses up at this virtuous milk, children in India tend to do the same. Gandhi preferred goat's milk for its health virtues. He considered goat's milk consumption more ethical because, unlike cows and buffaloes, goats are not easily exploited as domesticated animals.

Yogurt and buttermilk are important and extremely popular dairy products throughout India. Yogurt will keep for days without refrigeration. It is easier to digest than plain milk, even by those who are sensitive to milk. Yogurt and buttermilk are very versatile in cooking, for making sauces, and thickening curries. I personally find yogurt very satisfying to cook with, and I enjoy it with my dinner. It is one of the only dairy products I continue to eat.

Ghee, or clarified butter, is another popular cooking medium in India. Although most things are fried in oil, *ghee* gives an added flavor to festive cooking and is almost unavoidable when making Indian sweets. However, many Indians living in America have said to me that they have cut down on their *ghee* consumption for health reasons.

Paneer or homemade cheese is another popular dairy item in the North Indian states such as Punjab, where milk is more abundant. However, the majority of Indian states currently lack the dairy surplus necessary for a large cheese industry. There is one brand of packaged cheese on the Indian market which vaguely resembles a mild cheddar, but one must go to a specialty store to buy it. During certain seasons, animal feed and, therefore, milk is cheaper. At these times, various types of cheese are made at home in different parts of India. However, *paneer* is the only cheese for which modern Indian restaurants have created a daily market. So, at least in city restaurants, you can order *matar paneer* any day. Pre-made *paneer* is difficult to purchase, even in North India. If you like cooking with *paneer*, you have to learn how to make it.

HOMEMADE YOGURT

Once you learn how easy it is to make yogurt, you will probably think twice about spending money on commercially available yogurt which is often made with "fillers" and usually not with organic milk. However, since developing the yogurt culture takes several hours, requiring one to plan in advance, we all break down and buy yogurt from time to time.

Yogurt-making is simple. All you need is milk and a yogurt starter. You boil milk and blend in the yogurt starter after the milk has cooled down a bit. Then you wait until the mixture has thickened.

While the yogurt is forming, it is quite temperamental. During this time, the mixture should not be disturbed or shaken. Also, it should be kept at a constant temperature and humidity. These conditions are often difficult to find in an average kitchen. If it is a clear day and a clear night, with a temperature of 65°F to 70°F, the yogurt will become a creamy milk jelly. But on a cloudy night, the yogurt will come out runny.

Many companies have come up with simple gadgets called yogurt makers which serve as perfect "incubators" for yogurt. All these gadgets do is supply a constant temperature and uniform humidity. This appliance is worth buying if you want your yogurt to come out solid each time. You can also experiment with homemade techniques such as wrapping the container of milk with towels and keeping it near (not on) a radiator, or in an unlit oven while the yogurt is forming. Once you have decided on where you are going to put your yogurt container, proceed to the next step.

1 quart whole or low-fat milk (organic if
  possible)
1 tablespoon of good quality, unsweetened
  yogurt without fillers

Boil the milk in a pot large enough to
ensure that it does not boil over. While the milk
is coming to a boil, blend the starter yogurt with
a tablespoon of warm milk, and set it aside.
When the milk starts to foam up to the top of
the pot, turn the heat off. Now the milk must
cool to room temperature (105°F to 107°F) before
you add the culture. Do not refrigerate the milk
to cool it. Transfer the hot milk into a large
mixing bowl. When the milk is lukewarm to the
touch, you are ready to add the yogurt culture.

For the first few times, you may want to
use a candy (or yogurt) thermometer to make
sure the milk is at the right temperature before
adding the starter. Add the culture and stir
thoroughly with a clean fork. Now transfer this
milk to the container (or containers) in which
it will thicken. If you have a yogurt maker, the
device will come with instructions on how long
it will take for the yogurt to thicken. Generally
speaking, it takes six to eight hours for the
yogurt to solidify. The warmer the weather, the
faster the yogurt culture works.

Keep the yogurt where it will not be
shaken or disturbed while it is forming. At the
expected time of completion, uncover the
yogurt containers and gently giggle to see if it
has set; if not, allow it to stand for another hour
or so. When set, cover the yogurt containers
and refrigerate until ready to use.

VERY LOW-FAT YOGURT
1 quart low-fat milk
1 cup non-fat milk powder
2 teaspoons unsweetened yogurt for starter

Use the same method for making yogurt
as described in the previous recipe. Blend the
liquid milk and milk powder thoroughly with
a whisk or a blender. You also need to stir the
mixture while it is heating to prevent the
powdered milk from sticking to the bottom of
the saucepan. The finished yogurt will be tarter
and less solid than the basic yogurt, but it will
still be very tasty and contain significantly
fewer calories.

BUTTERMILK
In India, there are two types of buttermilk. One
is made by blending yogurt with an equal
amount of water. This drink is similar to
American buttermilk, only a little tarter. It is
like a liquid meal—very nutritious and soothing during the hot summer months. By adding
some ice and sugar or salt to this drink you can
turn it into a beverage called *lassi* (see the recipe
on page 180).

Another type of buttermilk is called *chhash*,
a thin dairy beverage consumed by many poor
people in India. *Chhash* is a by-product of
churning yogurt to retrieve butter from it. In
Western countries, butter is usually made from
sweet, fresh cream. In India, butter is made
from yogurt. The yogurt is mixed with water
and churned vigorously until fatty particles
(butterfat) form on top. This butter is collected
and chilled, while the thin, almost fat-free

liquid is saved and sold for pennies as a drink. *Chhash* is very nourishing and affordable for those Indian folks who cannot buy rich, full-fat yogurt. Outside of India, the only way to prepare a drink like *chhash* is by blending one part non-fat yogurt or buttermilk with four to five parts water.

GHEE

Ghee is butter which has had all the milk solids (and salt, in case of salty butter) removed. The clarified butter used in French cuisine closely resembles *ghee* but is not as pure. You can easily use sweet butter or margarine in many Indian recipes calling for *ghee*, as the fully clarified product is not always necessary.

The process of making *ghee* from butter preserves butterfat at room temperature for long periods of time in semi-tropical regions where refrigeration is uncommon. In the United States, *ghee* makes excellent camping food.

The other advantage of ghee as a frying medium is that it does not smoke and burn as readily as butter. The flavor of *ghee* is also superb. If you like to indulge occasionally in this simply heavenly fat, here is the way to make it.

Take two or four sticks of sweet (unsalted) butter, and place them in a shallow, thick-bottomed saucepan. Melt the butter over low heat, and continue to heat while stirring from time to time. It is important to attend to the *ghee* frequently because it should not be allowed to burn. I usually make *ghee* on the back burner while preparing other dishes. As the butter melts completely, it will bubble and the milk solids will float to the surface. Remove the milk solids using a spoon, and continue to heat the butter. If you continue skimming solids from the surface, the foaming will stop in about 20 minutes and the butter will be almost completely clear, except for some sediment that will be gathering at the bottom of the pot. Turn the heat off and allow the *ghee* to stand for a while at room temperature. Most of the sediment will settle, and any remaining milk solids will float to the top. Remove these floating milk solids, then carefully transfer the *ghee* (while it is still warm and liquid) into a clean jar, leaving the few tablespoons of unclear residue at the bottom of the pot. You can also strain the liquid *ghee* using a cheesecloth. In either case, it is necessary to discard any residue so that it does not cloud the clarified *ghee*.

Ghee can be stored at room temperature for several weeks, because it is the milk solids in butter that spoils. Of course, if you refrigerate *ghee*, it will last for months. *Ghee* solidifies when you refrigerate it, so heat it over a low flame before you use it.

VEGETABLE *GHEE*

In India, *ghee* made from vegetable oil is often substituted for the real thing, not so much for health reasons, but because it is cheaper—much the way some homemakers use margarine due to its lower cost. You can find many brands of vegetable *ghee* in Indian markets.

An Indian family living in New York gave me this recipe for making vegetable *ghee* from margarine. It is remarkably similar to *ghee* in appearance. However, I am not so sure about its dietary superiority over animal fat, since I have learned that when margarine is made, some of the healthful properties of the oil it's made from are lost. One advantage of dairy-free margarine over dairy fat is that it has a lower concentration of chemical pesticide residues than commercial butter does.

MARGARINE *GHEE* OR "*GHEE* GONE VEGAN"

Place two sticks of soy margarine in a heavy-bottomed saucepan, and melt over low heat. Continue to heat while stirring occasionally and removing the solids that float to the top. The clarification of margarine will take place faster than that of butter. Some margarine has a lot of sediment, so you may have to skim off the solids more frequently. In about ten minutes, you will have clear liquid oil, but it has something of a *ghee*-like flavor. Strain the liquid using muslin or cheesecloth, and store in a jar, keeping it in a cool spot or in the refrigerator. Use the margarine *ghee* as you would use *ghee* or butter.

PANEER

Paneer is Punjabi homemade cheese that resembles farmers' cheese or ricotta. It is made using a simple process of separating the milk into curds and whey with the help of yogurt or lemon juice. The curds are then drained and shaped into small balls or cubes and used in making dishes such as *matar paneer* (cheese and peas) or *saag paneer* (spinach and cheese) or sweets like *paneer halva*. If you use whole milk combined with non-fat milk powder, the resulting *paneer* will be low-fat.

1 quart whole milk,
or 3 cups whole milk blended with 1 cup
    non-fat milk powder
Juice of ½ lemon blended with ½ cup plain
    yogurt,
or juice of 1 lemon

If you are planning to make low-fat *paneer* using the liquid whole milk and non-fat powdered milk combination, blend them thoroughly using a whisk, blender, or food processor. Do not add water. Select a heavy-bottomed saucepan, and heat the milk while stirring frequently, so that it does not stick to the bottom.

While waiting for the liquid to boil up to the top, mix the lemon juice and yogurt with a fork. Set up a straining apparatus, using a mesh sieve or a colander lined with cheesecloth set in a large mixing bowl.

When the milk boils, it will rise to the top of the pan. Turn off the heat and immediately add the lemon juice and yogurt mixture. Stir with a wooden spoon, and you should witness the dramatic separation of the milk into spongy curds and thin, watery whey. Once in a while, the milk does not fully separate, and the whey appears more milky. If this happens, first add two more teaspoons of lemon juice, and reboil the milk. The second boil will produce the desired result with a jade-greenish whey. Carefully pour the curdled milk into the straining apparatus. The whey will pass through the cheesecloth, and the curds will collect inside. Save the nutritious whey for using as a soup stock or to cook rice with.

The soft curds can be shaped after the excess whey is drained off. The easiest way to drain off the whey is to hang the cheesecloth above the kitchen sink. When the whey stops dripping, the *paneer* is ready to be shaped and put away.

PANEER BALLS: One way to shape the curds is to transfer them into a mixing bowl, and shape into small beads by rubbing small pieces into your moist hands. Then deep-fry them in hot oil until golden. These *paneer* balls are ready for *matar paneer*.

PANEER CUBES: An alternative, less greasy way of shaping *paneer* is to place the drained curds on a cutting board lined with several layers of absorbent paper or kitchen cloth. Flatten and shape the curds using your hands to form a ½-inch thick rectangle. Then cover this rectangle with four or five more layers of paper towels or kitchen cloth. Pile a pan with six to seven heavy books on top. After an hour, remove the books, pan, and towels, and you will have a nearly solid *paneer* that can now be cut with a knife.

Cut the *paneer* slab into strips first. Then cut the strips into sugar cube-sized pieces. For *matar paneer*, these cubes should be briefly stir-fried using two teaspoons of oil until they are golden brown. The fried *paneer* cubes can be stored in the refrigerator for a few weeks before using.

TOFU CUBES AS *PANEER*: This may sound a bit too unorthodox to people who love *paneer* and do not want yet another substitute for something as unique as Indian *paneer*. However, since *paneer* is time-consuming to make and not available ready-made even in most Indian shops, many cooks I know use tofu as a substitute for *paneer*. Of course, tofu cubes do not taste the same as *paneer*, but their porous, soft consistency is more than adequate to incorporate with the spicy tomato sauce of *matar paneer*. When preparing tofu cubes for *matar* tofu, purchase firm or extra-firm tofu. Cut into sugar cube-sized pieces, and fry in a single layer with a small amount of oil until golden. They will look like *paneer* cubes and act as a perfect vegan substitute for them. The fried tofu cubes can be stored in the refrigerator for five to six days.

COCONUT AND COCONUT MILK

Dairy products are not as plentiful in the south of India as they are in the north. Animal husbandry for the production of dairy products was introduced in the south much later. Even in these modern days, coconut is much more widely used than dairy products in South Indian cooking. Fresh coconut and its milk are used in many southeast Asian cuisines for making refreshments and sauces. Vegans can use coconut milk in place of dairy milk and butter to make all sorts of delicious Indian dishes and desserts.

HOW TO OPEN A COCONUT: Purchase a coconut that feels as though it is full of liquid when shaken. At one end of the coconut there will be two or three soft spots. Puncture the coconut at two of these soft spots using a screw driver or a nail and hammer, and drain out all the coconut liquid. This liquid (which is not coconut milk) makes a good drink, so save and enjoy, if you wish. Now place the coconut on a flat surface, and, using a hammer, break the coconut open. One well-placed blow should split it into two pieces. Then, using a blunt end of a butter knife, carefully pry the white meat loose from its hard, brown shell, and discard the shell. The white meat will still have a thin brown skin attached to it which is edible. Enjoy the fresh coconut in small portions, and refrigerate the rest. (Too much fresh coconut at one time can be difficult to digest).

HOW TO MAKE COCONUT MILK FROM FRESH COCONUT: To make milk from the white meat of a coconut, you have to peel off the inner brown skin using a sharp knife. Collect the skinned white meat, and chop it into small pieces. Then place the pieces in a blender or food processor, adding three cups of warm water per cup of coconut pieces. Blend at high speed until the coconut pieces are shredded into tiny pieces.

Then, using a fine sieve or layer of cheesecloth, strain the coconut liquid. Reserve the liquid "milk" for your recipes, and discard the pulp left in the sieve or cheesecloth.

CANNED COCONUT MILK: If you do not want to make milk out of coconut, canned coconut milk is O.K. However, beware of some brands of coconut milk which contain questionable additives. Make sure you are buying the right consistency. Some varieties of canned coconut milk are too creamy for some recipes.

SPICE BLENDS AND PASTES

Garam masala has been discussed on page 24. It is a spice mixture made by roasting a blend of spices such as cinnamon and cloves. There are many regional varieties of *garam masala*, calling for as few as three to as many as thirty ingredients to be ground together. There are further variations created by individual cooks or households. At any rate, two things are usually consistent in all *garam masala* blends: (1) You always buy these spices whole, not ground; (2) The three sweet spices—cardamom, cloves, and cinnamon are always present. By grinding the whole spices into a powdered blend, you will have fresh *garam masala* which is almost always better tasting than what you would buy from a specialty spice shop. I prefer to keep my *garam masala* simple by grinding equal parts cinnamon, cloves, and cardamom; you can create any blend that you like. Use a heavy mortar and pestle to crush the whole spices into as fine a powder as you can make. I keep an electric coffee grinder in my kitchen just to grind whole spices. With the electric grinder, the process is faster and the product finer.

BASIC *GARAM MASALA*

This is how I was taught to make a basic *garam masala* by my Punjabi chef-teacher. According to him, one can add other spices to this basic *masala* depending on the particular dish it will be added to.

4 oz. each (by weight) cinnamon sticks, cardamom seeds (not pods), and whole cloves

Roast these spices in a heavy iron pan, stirring them from time to time for about 10-15 minutes. Or preheat the oven to 200°F, and spread the whole spices on a cookie sheet. Place them in the heated oven for 15 minutes or so until fragrant and dry. Be careful not to burn the spices while roasting. Grind them using a heavy mortar and pestle or a clean coffee grinder which is used only for spices. Store the ground *masala* in a tightly closed container in a cool place.

BOMBAY *GARAM MASALA*

Here is an elaborate *garam masala* blend I learned in Bombay.

¼ cup cloves (whole)
¼ cup cardamom seeds
5 to 6 three-inch cinnamon sticks, broken into smaller pieces
2 tablespoons cumin seeds
2 tablespoons coriander seeds
1 tablespoon whole black or white peppercorns
1 tablespoon fennel seeds
1 teaspoon ground nutmeg or mace

Place all the spices, except the ground nutmeg or mace, in a heavy frying pan, and toast, stirring frequently, for 10 to 15 minutes. Or place on a cookie sheet, and roast in a preheated 200°F oven for 15 minutes. Cool the spices for a few minutes. Then, using a heavy duty mortar and pestle or a coffee grinder, grind them into a powder. Add the powdered nutmeg or mace, and mix well. Store in a tightly closed jar, and keep in a cool place.

CHAI MASALA

This is a spice blend used to flavor the Indian black tea beverage, called *chai*. Like *garam masala*, *chai masala* can have regional, as well personal, variations, but in most versions, it contains the sweet, warming spices: cardamom and cinnamon. Here is one version.

2 sticks of cinnamon
2 teaspoons cardamom seeds
½ teaspoon whole cloves
1 teaspoon powdered ginger

Toast all the spices, except the ginger, in a warm skillet, shaking from time to time to prevent burning. Cool and grind them using a mortar and pestle or an electric grinder. Add the powdered ginger. Store in a jar placed in a cool spot. Use only a few pinches of this potent *masala* per cup of tea.

HERB PASTES

These pastes are freshly made to flavor dals or vegetables. They are a kind of Indian "pesto," and they often, if not always, contain garlic in some form.

GARLIC PASTE

This is a simple Gujarati recipe available to all people rich or poor. Sometimes called garlic *chutney*, this paste is not served as a *chutney* since it is quite potent.

Garlic paste # 1
4 cloves of garlic, peeled and mashed or
   chopped
1 teaspoon cayenne powder

Blend the garlic and cayenne powder into a smooth paste using a mortar and pestle. As an alternative, you can mash the chopped garlic and cayenne together with a rolling pin on a cutting board, continually scrapping the paste off of the pin and re-crushing the pile. Either way, the oil in the fresh garlic will blend with the powdered pepper to make a smooth paste. Collect all the bits and pieces using a knife, and store in cool place. You will usually only need about ½ teaspoon at a time in any one recipe.

Garlic paste # 2

4 cloves of garlic, peeled and mashed or
    chopped
1 teaspoon cayenne powder, or 1 tablespoon
    finely chopped green hot chile, seeds
    removed
1 teaspoon cumin seeds

This will be a green paste if you use the
fresh chile. The cumin is an added flavor.
Follow directions for paste #1, storing and
using it in a similar fashion.

Garlic paste # 3

4 sprigs of green (spring) garlic
¼ cup chopped, fresh cilantro, thick stems
    removed
1 green hot chile, such as jalapeño (remove
    seeds and core)
1 tablespoon water or oil

Place all the ingredients in a blender or
food processor, and puree to a coarse consistency. As an alternative, you can use a mortar
and pestle to grind the ingredients to a pulpy
consistency. This will not form as fine a paste
as the previous two recipes. This is a tasty
paste, so make it as often as you can while
spring garlic is in season.

TAMARIND PASTE

Tamarind paste has a sweet-and-sour flavor
which is difficult to replace with anything else.
This paste is thin—more like a sauce. It can be
used to make a dip for appetizers like *samosa* or
as a flavoring in a number of dishes.

¼ pound ripe tamarind pods
water

If available, purchase ripened, dry tamarind pods which have a brittle outer shell.
Remove the shell and the stringy fibers surrounding each pod. Rinse the pods and place
them in a bowl with enough warm water to
immerse completely. Let them soak for 30
minutes. By this time, the pods will look
swollen and plump. While rubbing a few pods
at a time right above the bowl, squeeze the
pulpy flesh surrounding the seeds into the
water. When the water turns into a thick sauce
and the pods contain almost nothing but seeds
and membrane, the paste is ready. Discard the
seeds and membrane, and store the paste in a jar.

Even if you refrigerate this paste, it should
be used in few days since it is very perishable.
If you want to preserve tamarind paste for a
longer time, cook it down to about half of its
original volume over low heat, adding a teaspoon of salt as you simmer it. This tamarind
paste will be good for a week or longer. If
tamarind pods are not available, buy a package
of compressed tamarind from an Indian grocery store, and use it as follows.

HOW TO MAKE TAMARIND PASTE USING COMPRESSED TAMARIND: Dried, ripe tamarind pods can be purchased in a compressed, brick-like package. In this form, the tamarind has been shelled and the seeds removed. It is then dehydrated before packing, so you need to soak this type of tamarind a bit longer and in more water than you would with dry pods.

½ cup pieces of tamarind, broken off from the compressed brick
1½ cups warm water

Soak the tamarind chunks in water for 20-30 minutes. Then place the tamarind with its soaking water in a food processor or blender. Make sure no seeds are left. (The "seedless" brick sometimes contains seeds). Blend until pureed into a paste-like consistency. Store in the refrigerator.

SAUCES

Most vegetable and bean dishes will create their own sauces as they cook, deriving liquid from the juices of the ingredients. For example, cauliflower and potato *bhaji* makes a thick sauce from the potato starch and the juices of cauliflower and tomato added at the end. Other times, plain, steamed vegetables can be served with one of the freshly made *chutneys* from pages 64-72, which will serve as a sauce and give the plain vegetables zest and flavor. For some entrees, a special sauce can be made ahead of time and added to the rest of the ingredients right before serving. This makes preparation of the main entrees easier during the bustle of catering or hosting a party.

BASIC TOMATO SAUCE (for *matar paneer* or *matar* tofu)
This sauce can make any steamed vegetable into an "instant curry." It is a must for cheese-and-peas *matar paneer*.

1½ lbs. ripe tomatoes, preferably organic (about 4 cups chopped)
2 tablespoons oil, butter, or *ghee*
1 cup finely chopped onion
2 cloves garlic, minced
1 tablespoon finely grated or minced fresh gingerroot
½ teaspoon Basic *Garam Masala* (see page 38)
¼ teaspoon turmeric powder
⅛ teaspoon cayenne powder, or to taste
1 teaspoon salt
½ cup water (or *paneer* whey)

If using fresh tomatoes, remove their peels by bringing a large pot of water to a boil, and immersing the tomatoes in it. Boil the tomatoes for a few minutes until some of their skins split open. Then remove the tomatoes from the hot water, and transfer them to a bowl of cold water. After a few minutes you will be able to peel them easily with your fingertips. Cut the peeled tomatoes and set them aside. If using canned tomatoes, they are already peeled, so cut them into chunks and set them aside.

In a saucepan, heat the oil, butter, or *ghee*, and add the onions. Sauté the onions until very soft, and then add garlic. Continue to fry for two more minutes, and then add the tomato chunks.

Add all the spices and salt. Cook for 10 minutes, stirring occasionally and breaking the tomatoes apart. Then add the water or whey, and continue to cook until the sauce achieves a gravy-like consistency.

THICK TOMATO SAUCE

Basic Tomato Sauce is for dishes which require a gravy-like sauce. But for dishes such as *kofta* curry or whole steamed cauliflower, this thicker sauce will work better.

2 lbs. fresh tomatoes, preferably organic
(about 5½ cups chopped)
4 tablespoons of oil, butter, or *ghee*
½ cup minced onion
1 tablespoon minced or finely grated
gingerroot
1 fresh, hot green chile, minced after
removing seeds and core

1 tablespoon freshly ground coriander seeds
2 teaspoons freshly ground cumin seeds
1 teaspoon Basic *Garam Masala* (see page 38)
1 teaspoon salt, or to taste
1 tablespoon chopped cilantro

If using fresh tomatoes, remove the skins as described in the previous recipe. Chop the fresh or canned tomatoes, and set them aside. In a saucepan, heat the oil or *ghee*, and sauté the onion until very soft. Then add the grated ginger and the chile. Cook them for a minute, and then add tomatoes. Cook the tomatoes for ten minutes, stirring often and breaking any lumps. Add the salt and the rest of the spices (except the cilantro), and continue to cook the mixture for about fifteen minutes, until it forms a thick sauce. Garnish with cilantro after the sauce has been combined with the *kofta* or any steamed vegetable.

SWEET TOMATO SAUCE

In this sauce, small, Italian-style plum tomatoes mate with sweet bell or pimento peppers to make an interesting, sweet sauce. The optional addition of yogurt turns the sauce into a salmon-colored, sweet-and-sour sauce.

2 lbs. Italian-style plum tomatoes, preferably
fresh and organic (about 5½ cups
chopped)
1 lb. sweet red bell or pimento pepper
1 cup unflavored yogurt (optional),
or ¾ cup water
4 tablespoons oil

½ red onion, finely chopped
1 tablespoon grated gingerroot
1 teaspoon whole cumin
1 teaspoon Bombay *Garam Masala*, page 38-39
½ teaspoon turmeric
Salt to taste

If using fresh tomatoes, peel them as described in the recipe for Basic Tomato Sauce. Chop the tomatoes and set them aside. Roast the bell or pimento peppers over a burner on medium heat, turning them frequently. Then wash them to remove the charred skin. Chop the peppers and place them in a blender or food processor. Add the yogurt or water to the peppers, and puree them; set the puree aside. In a saucepan, heat the oil and cook the onion until translucent. Add the ginger and cumin, and cook for a minute. Then add the tomato chunks, and cook the mixture for 15 to 20 minutes, stirring frequently and breaking any lumps. Then add the pureed pepper, garam masala, turmeric, and salt. Cook the sauce for another 10 to 15 minutes, until it becomes thick and gravy-like.

Note: This sauce can be made without the tomatoes and with twice as many peppers. (Yellow or orange peppers, when in season, can also create an interesting variation of this sauce.)

INDIAN CREAM SAUCE

This is an Indian version of rich white sauce. I am sure it was influenced by the British. As far as I know, cream is not a traditional cooking ingredient in India. However, when I asked a restaurant chef in India the secret of his steamed cauliflower sauce, he gave me this recipe.

¼ cup *ghee* or oil
¼ cup minced green or white onion
½ cup ground cashews, almonds, or
    pistachio nuts (freshly ground to a fine
    meal, using a blender or food processor)
2 cups cream, half-and-half, or low-fat
    buttermilk, left at room temperature or
    heated briefly
½ teaspoon each Basic *Garam Masala* (see
    page 38), turmeric, and cumin powder
⅛ teaspoon cayenne or ground white
    pepper, to taste
1½ teaspoons salt

Heat the *ghee* or oil, and sauté the onion until limp and translucent. Add the nuts and continue to stir-fry for a few minutes until the nuts change color and are fragrant. Then add the cream, half-and-half, or buttermilk. (The buttermilk will make a lower-calorie sauce, but it will impart a somewhat tart taste. You can balance this by adding a teaspoon of sugar or honey.)

Then add the spices and salt. Cook briefly until all the ingredients are well-blended. If the sauce is not smooth, the nuts may have been ground too coarsely. In that case, pour the contents into the blender or food processor, and blend very briefly. Reheat the sauce. Adjust the seasonings to taste. Serve this sauce over any steamed vegetable or *kofta*.

VEGAN VARIATIONS OF INDIAN CREAM SAUCE: For a dairy-free version of the above sauce (1) use 2 cups coconut milk (canned is O.K.), and proceed with the above recipe, or (2) use 1½ cups vegetable stock which has been blended with 2 tablespoons of *besan* (chick-pea or garbanzo flour). The *besan* will thicken the sauce as it cooks, but you have to stir it frequently so that it does not form lumps. This is a good, low-calorie, vegan sauce.

CHAPTER FOUR
APPETIZERS, SNACKS & CHUTNEYS

Snacks or appetizers (known as *farasan* in India) are more than just bite-sized treats. They can be just a tidbit or a feast by themselves, tantalizing to the taste and time-consuming to make. Like the dim sum of China, they can be heart warming gifts to the guests or to the family, and elaborate enough to challenge the best cook. Or they can be simple nibblers, quickly prepared (or gotten from the dry pantry) to be served at tea time or while waiting for the meal to be cooked.

In railroad stations and bazaars throughout India, you are constantly passing by the many *farasan* shops that offer these tempting snacks, each served with a unique condiment known as *chutney*. An office worker may pass up his or her usual lunch and substitute instead one of the many snacks which are available for a few *rupees*. The *farasan* shops are as popular in big Indian towns as pizzerias are in the United States. However, in small villages there are no restaurants or *farasan* shops, and one is dependent on the household cook to spend the extra time it takes to prepare these delicacies. More elaborate snacks may be prepared as a fancy lunch, as the appetizer for an important meal, or as a special holiday treat. Simpler munchies are often prepared during the cook's free time and can be stocked in the pantry for a few weeks. They can also be bought packaged from Indian specialty stores. However, the homemade snacks are almost always tastier, more nutritious, and more satisfying to the palate.

Many of these appetizers are deep-fried and not suited for those people who wish to avoid the extra fat. As an alternative, I have made a special effort to include *farasan* which are not deep-fried. I have also created some not-so-traditional recipes, such as *Samosa* Pie, which is baked.

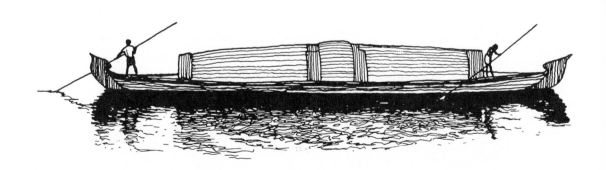

NIBBLERS OR MUNCHIES

CHIVRA

A popular tea time snack, *chivra* can be stored in tight jars for a few weeks in the pantry. (Do not refrigerate). Although this snack is available in packages, homemade *chivra* can be much more nutritious and less salty than store-bought varieties. It is also very quick to prepare.

3 cups pounded puffed rice (*pauva*) or
    unsweetened puffed rice cereal (such as
    Rice Krispies)
1 cup chopped mixed nuts (cashews, peanuts,
    almonds, etc.)
½ cup roasted chick-peas, *sev*, or spicy
    sakkarpara (see pages 47-48)
1 tablespoon dry, unsweetened, shredded
    coconut
1 tablespoon sesame seeds
2 tablespoons yellow (preferably) or black
    raisins
2 tablespoons oil
¼ teaspoon *ajowan* or cumin seeds
½ teaspoon turmeric powder
⅛ teaspoon or less cayenne powder
½ teaspoon salt
Juice of one lemon
2 tablespoons chopped curry leaves or
    coriander leaves (optional for garnish)

In a large bowl, combine the first six ingredients (up to and including the raisins). In a wok or wide saucepan, heat the oil and add the cumin or *ajowan* seeds. Brown the seeds for a minute, then add the turmeric, stir, and quickly add the mixed ingredients from the bowl. Stir-fry continuously for a few minutes, then add the rest of the ingredients except the garnish. Stir-fry until the lemon juice has evaporated, which should take a few minutes. Garnish and serve the *chivra* after it has cooled thoroughly, or pack it away in a tightly closed jar. It should keep well for over a month.

FARALI CHIVRA (dry fruits and nuts)
On religious holidays, some Hindus restrict their diet to fruits and nuts only. This is a type of fast when one does not eat dairy or grains, and *farali chivra*, which literally means fruitarian munchies, come in handy. These munchies are also good as a trail mix.

2 cups mixed dried fruits, such as pineapple
    and papaya (cut into the size of raisins),
    golden or black raisins, currants,
    cranberries, etc.
2 cups of mixed nuts and seed, such as
    cashews, peanuts, sesame seeds, and dry,
    shredded coconut
Juice of 1 lime or lemon
1 tablespoon oil (optional)
Salt and cayenne to taste

Mix the nuts, seeds, and fruits in a bowl. Heat a heavy skillet, using the optional oil (if desired), and stir in the nuts and fruits until fragrant and light brown. Do not burn. Next, sprinkle on the lemon juice, and turn off the heat. Add the salt and cayenne. Stir to cool and allow the juice to evaporate. Cool to room temperature and serve, or stock in a tightly covered container.

Another way to prepare these munchies is by toasting all the ingredients in the oven as carefully and quickly as possible so that you do not burn them.

SEV

Easy to make and store (they'll last on your shelf for a couple of months), these noodles can be combined with the *chivra* on page 46.

1 cup *besan* (chick-pea flour)
1 tablespoon oil
a few pinches of baking powder
½ teaspoon salt
⅛ teaspoon turmeric powder
⅛ teaspoon cumin or *ajowan* seeds (oregano)
1-1½ cups oil for frying

Combine the flour, oil, baking powder, salt, and spices in a bowl. Add water, a little bit at a time, to make a stiff dough. Oil the dough surface and set aside.

Heat the oil for frying in a wok or frying pan. To form and fry these noodles, most Indian households have a handy gadget called a *sev* press. It looks like a giant peppercorn grinder. The container holds the dough inside. To fry the noodles, you hold the press above the hot oil, and crank its handle. The dough presses out in the form of strings and drops into the hot oil, which almost instantly cooks them into golden noodles.

If you do not have this gadget, you can use one of two methods to form the noodles. If you like to play with your dough and have extra little hands who can help, break off the dough into small, walnut-size pieces. Roll into long strings using the palms of your hands, and lay them on an oily surface or wax paper. When you have enough spirals to make about ½ cup, drop them in very hot oil, and fry them, stirring until all sides are golden brown. The second method uses a heavy-duty, plastic freezer bag. Place the dough in the bag, and cut a tiny hole in a corner. Squeeze out the dough, which should extrude in the form of a spiral, and spread it on waxed paper. Collect about ½ cup of these spirals, and then deep-fry them until golden brown. Take out the fried noodles with a slotted spoon, draining the excess oil completely. Place them on a paper towel to further absorb the oil. Serve or store after the noodles have cooled.

SAKKARPARA

This snack is like homemade crackers. Since I am not happy with most store-bought crackers, I often trouble myself to make this delicacy.

1 cup unbleached white flour
½ teaspoon baking powder
½ cup *besan* (chick-pea or garbanzo flour)
4 tablespoons oil
½ teaspoon salt
1 tablespoon black or white sesame seeds,
or ½ teaspoon *ajowan* seeds,
or 1 teaspoon oregano
3 tablespoon water

Sift the white flour and baking powder together. Add the *besan* and other ingredients, except the water; mix thoroughly. Gradually add the water while forming a stiff dough. (You can also mix all the ingredients using a food processor). Roll the dough between sheets of wax paper until fairly thin, but dense enough to cut into small diamonds or squares—about ¾" x ¾". Arrange the crackers in a single layer on a well-oiled cookie sheet. Bake in a preheated 350°F oven for 15 minutes, or until golden. Cool the diamonds to store. Serve hot or cool.

Traditionally these diamonds are deep-fried. However, the baked variety is more nutritious, and I think you will find them equally tasty.

SPICY *SAKKARPARA*: Add 1 tablespoon minced, semi-spicy hot chile (such as the Anaheim).

SWEET *SAKKARPARA*: Instead of water use a half water/half honey mixture to make this mildly sweet variety.

WHEAT-FREE *SAKKARPARA*: Use a mixture of ½ cup of rice flour and ½ cup rye flour instead of the unbleached white flour. Add the rest of the ingredients, and follow any of the above recipes for *sakkarpara*.

PAPAD OR PAPADAM

These crispy, potato chip-like crackers are almost always bought dry in packages, even by the most traditional Indian households. The process of making *papadams* from scratch is very time-consuming and done by skilled people who make it their life's work. The very stiff, glutinous dough is made from lentils and rice, then rolled very, very thinly. I presume that modern appliances are now used to make this process simpler. At any rate, they are readily available in ethnic food markets and even in health food stores, since they are a wheat-free product. Store *papad* in a dry place, not in the refrigerator.

HOW TO PREPARE PAPAD

Dry, packaged *papads* can be prepared in minutes, following either of these directions.

(1) Heat a heavy skillet thoroughly. Separate the *papads* carefully, since these thin, dry wafers are packed very densely. Take one *papad* at a time, and press it onto the hot skillet, using an oven glove or tea towel. Turn it quickly since it only takes seconds to toast it to a brown color. If a few blisters appear, this is fine. Press the blisters down and cook the other side just as quickly. Serve hot or cold.

(2) Heat 1 cup of oil in a wok or frying pan, and deep-fry the *papad*, one at a time. Slip the *papad* into oil, and turn quickly to fry the other side. Remove it from the hot oil using a slotted spoon, draining all of the excess oil. Place on paper towels to remove any additional oil. You may want to deep-fry *papadam* if you have oil leftover from another fried dish. Do not reuse the oil after frying *papads* for another dish, as the *papads* cloud up the oil quickly. These are salty snacks and go well with your tea break. Break them into halves before serving.

HEARTY SNACKS OR APPETIZERS

The following snacks are substantial enough to have alone as a fancy luncheon or serve as a separate course for an elaborate dinner. They are always served with a *chutney* or two and yogurt.

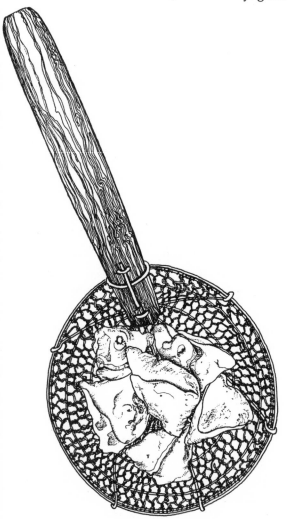

PAKORA OR *BHAJIA*
(DEEP-FRIED VEGETABLES IN BATTER)

Basically, *bhajia* or *pakora* are cut-up vegetables which are dipped into a *besan* batter and deep-fried in oil. In this manner, they are similar to Japanese tempura. The difference is that the batter for tempura is usually made from wheat or rice flour, whereas the *bhajia* batter is made with chick-pea flour. Almost any vegetable can be used, including non-traditional vegetables like mushrooms or asparagus. The main thing to remember is to cut the vegetables thinly, since they are not precooked and will be cooked only for a few minutes in the oil.

2 cups *besan* (chick-pea or garbanzo flour)
½ teaspoon coriander powder,
    or 1 tablespoon minced cilantro
½ teaspoon cumin powder
⅛ teaspoon garlic powder,
    or 2 cloves minced or crushed garlic
¼ teaspoon cayenne
1 teaspoon salt
A few pinches of baking powder
Juice of 1 lemon
1 cup water

Any combination of the following vegetables:
10 thin slices of eggplant (about ¼ of a
    medium eggplant)
12 carrot sticks (cut to the size of a French fry)
A few scallions, trimmed, or a few, thin onion
    rings, sliced and separated
A few spinach or mint leaves, washed and
    dried thoroughly
1 firm banana, peeled and sliced ¼" thick

A few sticks of celery, cut into finger-size pieces

A few cauliflower or broccoli buds

2 cups of peanut, corn, or canola oil for deep-frying

Prepare the batter by mixing the dry ingredients, plus any fresh herbs and garlic, in a bowl. Add the water and lemon juice, breaking up any lumps to make a mixture that is a bit thicker than pancake batter; set this batter aside. Cut the vegetables and towel dry; set them aside. Heat the oil in a wok or frying pan until very hot, but not smoking. When a small drop of batter is placed in the oil and comes to the surface right away, it is ready. Reduce the heat to medium-high, and place a handful of cut-up vegetables into the batter. Cover each piece with the batter as much as possible, and gently drop about six pieces into the hot oil. Turn the *pakora* in the hot oil until they are golden, then remove them from the oil using a slotted spoon, allowing the excess oil to drip back into the pan. Place the hot *pakora* on paper towels to further drain the oil. Fry the remaining vegetables until all of the batter is used up. The leftover batter and/or vegetables can be stored in the refrigerator separately and used another day.

Note: The batter for my *pakora* has become thinner over the years (you can see parts of the vegetables through it), as this method uses more vegetables. For more traditional *pakora*, use less water in your batter. Also, using the leaves is my own invention. Fried leaves with spicy batters are out of this world! They have to be completely dry or else water drops splatter all over in the hot oil and out of the pan.

There is no way to make this recipe without deep-frying.

PAKORA MADE WITH *BESAN* AND CORNMEAL: Use the same ingredients to make the batter, except use ¾ cup cornmeal and 1¼ cups *besan* in place of the 2 cups of *besan*. This variation makes a fluffier and less beany batter. It also helps you stretch out your *besan* if you do not have enough. Follow the rest of the recipe as directed.

CHEESE *PAKORA*: Instead of using vegetables, use hard cheese such as mozzarella, Swiss, or cheddar. Using ¾ cup water instead of 1 cup, make the batter a bit thicker so that the cheese won't ooze out.

PAKORA MADE WITH SHREDDED VEGETABLE BATTER: In this variation, the batter is made with an equal amount of shredded vegetables and *besan*. Use any of the following vegetables which are juicy and shreddable: carrots, zucchini, crook neck squash, sunburst squash, or Indian *opo* squash. Mix the *besan* and shredded vegetables. A bit of additional water may be necessary for a batter which is drier and more dense than my basic *pakora* batter. Or, conversely, you may need to add more *besan* if the vegetables are too juicy. Add the same spices as listed for the basic *pakora*. Place one tablespoon of batter mix into the hot oil, and deep-fry until golden. You can also place a few spoonfuls at a time, which will cool down the oil a little and take a little longer to cook.

UPMA

Upma can be served as a light meal, lunch, or a snack. It is often eaten for breakfast in South India. If you forget to soak the *urad dal* or do not have it, omit it, although traditionally it is present in the recipe.

2 tablespoons melted butter or oil
1 teaspoon *urad dal*, soaked for about ½ hour
    (optional) and then drained completely
⅛ teaspoon black mustard seeds
1 medium onion, finely chopped
1 cup cream of wheat or cream of rice (for a
    wheat-free recipe)
2 cups hot water
A few pinches of turmeric
Salt and cayenne pepper to taste
½ teaspoon brown sugar or honey (optional)
1 tomato, cut up into chunks
Juice of 1 lemon
2-3 tablespoons chopped mixed nuts, such as
    cashews, almonds, walnuts, or peanuts
Chopped cilantro for garnish (optional)

    Place the butter or oil in a wide, heavy pan over medium heat. Add the mustard seeds. When they start popping, add the drained *dal*. Add the onion and stir-fry for five minutes. Stir in the grain and continue to stir-fry, until the mixture turns reddish in color. Lower the heat and start adding the hot water slowly, stirring constantly so that the grain does not lump together. Add the rest of the ingredients, and stir-fry until the liquid has been absorbed. Cover, remove from the heat, and let it stand for a few minutes before serving.

MORE ELABORATE APPETIZERS OR LIGHT MEALS

The following *farasans* are reserved for special occasions or entertaining guests, or they can be served as a complete meal. Most of them take a couple of steps, but with enough planning, they can be made within an hour. Some steps can be prepared ahead of time, and rest of the process finished right before serving.

VADA

    This dish is quick to prepare, although it requires a little planning because the main ingredient—*urad dal*—needs to be soaked for at least five hours. Nowadays, ready-made, ground "*vada* mixes" are available in specialty shops, but I prefer *vada* made from dry *dal*.

1 cup *urad dal*, skinned (white)
1 small, hot chile, minced, or ⅛ teaspoon
    cayenne
½ teaspoon finely chopped or grated
    gingerroot
¼ teaspoon cumin powder
few pinches of baking powder
Juice of one lemon
½ teaspoon salt
½ cup vegetable oil for deep-frying

Soak the *dal* in two cups of water, overnight or for five to six hours. Wash the *dal* thoroughly and drain. Place the *dal* in a food processor or a blender with ½ cup water. (A food processor works better. If you are using a blender, you may have to divide the dal into three parts to avoid gumming up the blades.) Puree the *dal* until it turns into a paste, adding a little more water if necessary, but don't turn it into a batter. Place the pureed *dal* in a mixing bowl, and set it aside. Grind all the spices into a coarse mass using a mortar and pestle or a rolling pin. Add to the *dal* paste. Add the salt, baking powder, and lemon juice. Mix well and set aside.

Heat the oil in a wok or a frying pan. Take one tablespoon of the batter-paste at a time, and drop into the hot oil. You can fry up to six pieces at a time, but don't overcrowd the pan. Fry the pieces until dark brown. Remove the *vadas* from the oil, using a slotted spoon and draining them. Collect them in a single layer on a cookie sheet which has been lined with paper towels. Serve hot with *raita* or plain yogurt.

In South India, *vadas* are usually shaped like a tiny doughnut with a hole in the middle. This takes a lot of practice, however, and the *vadas* don't taste any different than the easily formed, irregularly shaped versions.

Nonetheless, if you are willing to be adventurous, try making doughnut-shaped *vadas* following this method. Start by heating the oil over a moderate heat. After having made the *vada* paste, rub some oil into the palm of your hand. Place a big spoonful of paste on your oily palm, and, using the other hand, shape it into a small doughnut—about an inch in diameter. Carefully slip the wet *vada* into the oil without burning your palm. Increase the heat and turn the *vada* to cook on the other side. You have to keep adjusting the heat because of the time it takes to shape the dough before slipping it into the hot oil. The first few *vadas* may fall apart as they land in the oil. If you get good at this method, you can shape, slip, and fry a few *vadas* at a time. If this method is too much trouble, go back to the easy, lumpy shape described above.

LEAFY *VADAS*: Add a cup of minced spinach, mustard greens, or watercress to your batter for additional taste and nutrients. You need to make the batter thicker since the water released from the leaves may further moisten the mixture. Follow the above instructions for frying golden brown *vadas*.

MIXED *DAL VADAS*: Use equal portions of these three dals: skinned *urad dal*, skinned *mung dal*, and skinned *chana dal*. Soak them together and follow the above recipe to puree and fry.

DAHI VADA

For those people who want to avoid deep-fried food, here is a recipe in which most of the oil from the fried fritters is removed. Then they are soaked in flavored yogurt, making them a truly distinctive delicacy.

1 recipe prepared *vadas* (make them using any one of the previous *vada* recipes)
1 teaspoon oil
¼ teaspoon black mustard seeds
1 dry, hot red chile, cut into pieces
1 cup yogurt blended with ¼ cup water
A few sprigs of cilantro, chopped

To make the yogurt marinade, heat the oil in a small pot, and add the black mustard seeds. When they start popping, add the chile pieces. When the oil is nearly smoking (which will only take seconds), remove from the heat and add to the yogurt-water mixture. When the yogurt cools, remove the chile pieces. Add a few pinches of salt, and set aside.

Prepare the *vada* using any of the previous *vada* recipes. While you are deep-frying them, place a bowl of cold water to one side. As you take the fried *vada* out of the oil, drain them, and place them in the cold water. When you finish cooking the *vadas*, gently take them out of the water, squeezing the water out using the palms of your hands. Don't break them while squeezing the water out. This step removes the water and oil from the *vadas* and prepares them to soak up the yogurt marinade. Place the *vada* on a platter or a shallow bowl, and pour the yogurt marinade on top. Garnish with chopped cilantro, if you wish, and serve chilled.

VEGAN *DAHI VADA*: *Dahi* is the word for yogurt, so it may seem difficult to make this recipe without it. You can modify this recipe by substituting unflavored soy yogurt or silken tofu (both well-blended with water, as in the *dahi vada* marinade).

BATATA VADA

This is another two-step *vada*, but worth the trouble since they are filling enough to make up a one-dish meal. The potato filling can be prepared ahead of time, even a day before. Make the batter when you are ready to fry and serve.

Filling

2 medium potatoes
2 tablespoons vegetable oil
3 tablespoons minced green onion with leaves
1 teaspoon minced, hot green chile,
or ⅛ teaspoon cayenne
½ teaspoon minced fresh gingerroot
⅛ teaspoon turmeric
½ teaspoon salt
Juice of ½ lemon

Batter

1 cup *besan* (chick-pea or garbanzo flour)
½ cup water
1 tablespoon lemon juice
¼ teaspoon each coriander powder, cumin
    powder, and turmeric powder
⅛ teaspoon cayenne
½ teaspoon salt
few pinches of baking powder

About 1½ cups oil for deep-frying

To make the filling, boil the potatoes until they are very soft. Cool and discard the skins. Dice them into small pieces, and set aside. Heat the 2 tablespoons of oil, and add the onion, chile, and gingerroot. Add the diced potatoes and the rest of the ingredients for the filling. Stir while mashing the potatoes. After a few minutes, turn off the heat and transfer the filling to a bowl. After the potatoes have cooled, mold them into small, firm balls (the size of a small lemon) with oiled hands. Add a bit of water if the potatoes are too dry to form balls; add a little flour if they are too wet. Set them aside.

Make the batter by mixing all the ingredients and breaking up any lumps of *besan*. Set the batter aside. Heat the oil in a wok or frying pan. Place about five potato balls in the batter. Coat them thoroughly with the batter, and put them in the hot oil. Turn the balls as they get bigger, and cook them until golden brown. Remove them from the oil using a slotted spoon, and place them on a platter lined with a paper towel. Finish coating and frying the balls. As the oil gets hotter, you can fry 8 to 10 at a time. Regulate the heat so that the oil does not start to smoke. Serve them hot, with a sweet-and-sour *chutney* such as raisin, tamarind, or date *chutney*.

SAMOSA

This is everyone's favorite appetizer. My students cannot wait to learn how to make them. I will show you the traditional, deep-fried version first and then my baked, less oily version, which I call "*samosa* pie." For either recipe, prepare the same filling first.

Filling

4 medium potatoes, peeled and cubed

1 carrot, grated or chopped finely

½ cup fresh peas or frozen, thawed peas

2 tablespoons vegetable oil

3 tablespoons finely chopped green or regular onion

⅛ teaspoon each cumin seeds, turmeric, *garam masala*, and grated or minced gingerroot

½ teaspoon salt

½ cup water

Juice of ½ lemon

A few sprigs of cilantro (optional)

Dough for Deep-Fried Samosa

½ cup unbleached white flour

1 tablespoon oil

½ teaspoon salt

3 to 4 tablespoons water

2 cups oil for deep-frying

DEEP-FRIED *SAMOSA*

To prepare the filling, heat 2 tablespoons of oil in a frying pan, add the onion, and sauté for a few minutes. Add the cumin seeds and brown them, then add the vegetables and stir to mix. Add the spices and stir-fry for about seven minutes until the spices are well blended. Add the water and salt, cover, and cook over low heat for about 10 to 15 minutes, until the potatoes are soft but not mashed. If after this time some water is still left, uncover the pot and stir to evaporate the liquid. Add the lemon juice and optional cilantro, and set the filling aside. Allow the filling to cool while preparing the dough.

Mix the flour with 1 tablespoon oil and salt. Slowly add the water as needed to form a stiff, but smooth dough. Knead the dough until it is smooth and forms a ball. Oil the ball and set aside. This dough is now ready to be rolled out into about 10 triangular or half-moon shaped *samosa* jackets.

Break off a lemon-sized piece of dough, and flatten out with your palms. Oil the rolling surface and sprinkle a little flour on top. Using a rolling pin, roll the dough out into a circle four inches in diameter. Roll out circles until the dough is used up. Take one circle at a time, and place about 2 tablespoons or less filling on half of the circle as illustrated. Fold the dough over the stuffing to form a half circle. Close the open sides by pinching the dough, using a bit of oil to help seal the edges. Alternatively, to make triangle-shaped *samosa*, cut the circles into halves. Fill half the space of the half circle with stuffing, and fold one pointed end of the half-circle over to meet the other pointed end, ending with a quarter-circle shape. Press the edges together to seal them closed. Fill all the *samosas* and set them aside, covered with a damp cloth.

To deep-fry the *samosas*, heat the oil until very hot, and add only one *samosa* at a time to start with. Cook the *samosa* while turning until both sides are light brown. Take out using a slotted spoon, and drain it completely. Place on a platter lined with a paper towel. Now the oil should be hot enough to deep-fry three to four *samosas* at a time. When you are finished frying, serve them while piping hot, or save them on a cookie sheet so that they can be reheated in an oven before serving. Serve *samosas* with yogurt and a *chutney* or a *raita*.

SAMOSA PIE

1¾ cups unbleached white flour
6 tablespoons chilled margarine or oil
3 to 4 tablespoons chilled water
½ teaspoon salt

Prepare a pie dough by combining the above ingredients. You can use this recipe or your favorite pie crust recipe, if you prefer. If you have a food processor, place the flour and margarine or oil into the processor bowl, and blend for a minute. Then gradually add enough water to form a pie crust-like dough. If you do not own a food processor, mix the flour and margarine or oil first. Then add the water gradually while mixing.

Knead the dough briefly to form a uniform ball, but do not overwork. Refrigerate the dough for a few minutes, then divide into two parts, and roll into two very thin pie crusts, either between sheets of waxed paper or using whatever method works for you.

Grease a pie plate and place one of the pie crusts in it gently. Fill the pie plate with *samosa* filling. (If the filling is too dry, mix in a little water.) Cover with the top crust. Pinch the edges of the two crusts together carefully to seal the pie, and prick the top crust several times with a fork. Place small pieces of margarine on the top crust or brush with oil, and place in a preheated 350°F oven for about one hour or little longer, until the pie looks golden brown. Serve with lots of *chutney* and/or yogurt.

DHOKLA

This is a typical Gujarati appetizer made with a variety of grain mixtures. First, the cream of rice and cornmeal mixture (or its variation) is soaked with yogurt or buttermilk, but water and lemon juice will work too. Spices and vegetables are added next, then the batter is poured onto a pie plate and steam cooked. Steamed *dhoklas* are cooled a bit, then cut into squares or diamonds and served while still hot with a *chutney*. Or the pieces are briefly stir-fried with a bit of oil and more spices and then served. (People who wish to avoid the extra oil can skip the last step, although the stir-frying step makes them extra tasty, in my opinion).

1 cup uncooked cream of rice
1 cup cornmeal
1 cup non-fat or low-fat plain yogurt mixed
    with ½ cup water,
  or ¾ cup buttermilk blended with ¾ cup
    water
(for a non-dairy version, mix 3 tablespoons
    lemon juice with ¾ cup water—you may
    need to add more water right before
    cooking to make a pourable batter)
¼ cup *besan* (chick-pea or garbanzo flour), or
    unbleached white flour
1 teaspoon salt
A few pinches of baking powder
¼ teaspoon turmeric
Cayenne-garlic paste made with ⅛ teaspoon
    cayenne powder and 2 cloves of garlic
½ cup of any of the following grated
    vegetables: carrots, zucchini, Indian
    squash, or shredded, dry coconut

1 tablespoon corn, safflower, or canola oil
¼ teaspoon black or brown mustard seeds

Mix the cream of rice, cornmeal, flour, yogurt, and water mixture (or the water and lemon juice) thoroughly. Cover and soak for at least two to three hours or overnight. After soaking, the mixture will be thick. Now add the *besan* or wheat flour, salt, and baking powder. Set aside and soak for a few minutes while setting up the steamer. An Asian steaming basket works well for this recipe. Alternatively, take a wide Dutch oven or wok with a tight-fitting lid, and place two cups of water in it. Place a vegetable steamer upside down in the pot. The pie plate with the dhokla mix will sit on the steamer so that the steam can go up from all around the steamer. Heat the water over medium heat.

To make the *dhokla* batter, prepare a garlic and cayenne paste by grinding the minced garlic with the powdered cayenne using a rolling pin or a mortar and pestle. Add bits of this paste, the grated vegetable of your choice, and turmeric to the *dhokla* batter. Add a few more tablespoons of water to make the batter pourable. Oil the pie plate and pour on enough batter to fill the plate halfway. (Leftover batter can make the second *dhokla* pie). Carefully place the pie plate on top of the steamer, and cover. Cook for about 20 minutes, until the batter looks dry and a fork poked through it comes out clean. Cool for a few minutes, then cut into squares or diamonds, and serve with a chutney. Alternatively, you can pan-fry as follows. Place the oil in a frying pan, and heat it over medium heat. Add the mustard seeds; when they start popping, place the *dhokla* pieces in, and stir-fry for five minutes. This last step makes the *dhokla* taste great served hot or cold. Serve with a *chutney* of your choice.

Variations:

(1) Mix ½ cup cream of wheat, instead of cream of rice, with an equal portion of soaked and ground *chana dal* or yellow split peas (Soak the peas for four to five hours, then grind them using a food processor or an electric blender).

(2) If you do not wish to wait for the long time of soaking, briefly soak 1½ cup of *besan* with ½ cup cornmeal in the same liquids as the main recipe, adding ½ teaspoon of baking powder and ½ teaspoon salt. Set aside for ½ hour. Follow the remaining directions.

DOSA

A *dosa* is a thin, crisp, crêpe-like snack that is served with a hot broth called *rasam* or a *dal* called *sambhar*. You can also pack a *dosa* for lunch by itself. In South India, *dosas* are extremely popular, almost like a national snack or a brief meal—like pizza is here in The U. S. Many hours are spent in the South Indian kitchen grinding and pulverizing the grain mix, using a heavy grinding stone in order to achieve the ideal paste necessary for the perfect *dosa*. Thin, crisp dosas are made with a fine paste which still has some texture. I have been reasonably successful using a blender or food processor in place of a grinding stone. The perfect *dosa* will take some practice and patience, after you determine which utensils work best for you.

1 cup skinned (white) *urad dal*
1 cup uncooked white rice (parboiled preferred)
1 teaspoon salt
oil for greasing the skillet

In two separate bowls, soak the rice and *dal*, using enough water to cover them completely. Set them aside and soak for five hours or overnight. When ready to prepare the *dosas*, wash the dal thoroughly and drain. Place in a food processor or blender with ¼ cup water. Grind the *dal* into a smooth paste, adding a bit more water if necessary. Transfer the *dal* puree into a mixing bowl. Place the drained rice in the food processor or blender with ½ cup water, and blend to the consistency of a wet cream of rice—in other words, a bit grainy. Add to the *dal* puree. Add the salt and mix thoroughly using a fork. Allow the mixture to sit for another hour, which will allow the mixture to ferment and foam up. Once this has happened, add more water to make an easily pourable batter.

Heat a heavy, well-seasoned frying pan or any non-stick pan. (I prefer a non-stick pan for this recipe). Add a teaspoon of oil, and spread it quickly, tipping the pan from side to side. Mix the batter well, ladle out ½ cup, and pour it into the skillet. Using the back of the ladle, spread it into a circle. The art of spreading the *dosa* batter lies in your ability to make a circle out of the batter as quickly as possible so that the partial batter does not start hardening before the circle is finished. Also, try to spread the batter as thinly as possible. Some of the best *dosas* I've had were paper thin, but this will require a certain amount of expertise. Cook the dosa for about five to six minutes, and then flip it over using a spatula. Cook the other side until brown. (Many times, the first *dosa* will not come out successfully since the skillet may not be hot enough yet, but the second one will be easier). Finish making the *dosa* and stack them on a cookie sheet. Rewarm them before serving with a *rasam*, using the recipe on page 122. Or make the potato stuffing using the recipe the next page, and serve as *masala dosa*.

MASALA DOSA

This is a spicy filling for *dosa*. Make *dosa* as instructed in the preceding recipe, then make this potato filling.

4 medium-sized potatoes (about 1 pound), cut into quarters, but not peeled
2 tablespoons vegetable oil
½ teaspoon black mustard seeds
½ cup finely chopped onion or scallion with some greens
1 hot chile pepper, minced after removing core and seeds
¼ teaspoon cumin seeds
½ teaspoon turmeric
¾ teaspoon salt
1 tablespoon minced fresh cilantro leaves, or ¼ teaspoon coriander powder
Juice of 1 lemon

Boil the potatoes in a big pot of water. When they are soft, remove the potatoes from the water, and peel and cut them into large chunks; set them aside. Heat the oil in a frying pan, and add the mustard seeds. When the seeds begin popping, add the onion or scallion and the chile pepper. Saute them together for two minutes, and add the potatoes, cumin, turmeric, salt, and cilantro or coriander powder. Stir-fry for five to seven minutes until all the ingredients are well blended. Transfer to a platter and spread it out to cool. Squeeze lemon juice on top, and use the filling in *dosa* as instructed.

Prepare the *dosa* and place three to four tablespoons of filling in the center of each crepe. Fold two ends of the *dosa* over the filling to form a tube, or fold the dosa as you would a tortilla for burritos. Serve hot or store in a wide casserole dish, and rewarm in a 300°F oven for a few minutes before serving.

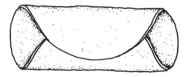

IDLI

Idlis are steamed, round dumplings which resemble Jewish matzo balls. They are served alone or with a clear broth called *rasam* (see page 122) or with a more substantial soup called *sambhar* (see recipe, page 125). *Idlis* with *sambhar* makes a meal in itself. When I was traveling in Madras and sometimes got tired of the spicy food, I would resort to ordering a platter of *idlis* for safety.

1 cup white rice
½ cup skinned (white) *urad dal*
½ teaspoon salt
A few pinches of baking powder
Water as needed

Soak the rice and *dal* in separate bowls of water, with enough liquid to cover the grains completely. Soak them for four to six hours or overnight. Then discard the soaking water, and wash and drain the *dal* thoroughly. Place in a blender or food processor with ½ cup water, and grind it to a fine paste. Transfer it to a bowl. Then place the washed, drained rice in your blender or food processor with 1 cup of water, and grind it to a coarse consistency. (It will look like wet cream of rice). Add the rice to the *dal* puree, and mix them together. Allow the mixture to soak for ½ hour or longer in a warm (but not hot) place in your kitchen. Then add the salt and baking powder, and set the batter aside while preparing the steaming apparatus.

In India, you can buy an *idli* steamer, which is a pot that comes with a round plate containing cup-like compartments in which you would pour the *idli* batter to steam. If you do not have such an *idli* maker, select a large pot (such as a Dutch oven) or a wok with a tightly fitting lid. Place two to three cups of water in this pot. Then set a vegetable steamer or a metal plate with holes in the pot. Find small metal or heatproof glass bowls (such as used in poaching eggs) to pour the *idli* batter in. A round muffin pan would be perfect to use here. Oil the bowl or containers, and pour three tablespoons of *idli* batter in each. Then place the batter-filled containers in the vegetable steamer basket or the steamer plate. Cover the pot (or wok), and steam the *idli* for about 30 minutes, or until the dumplings are solid. After they have been cooled a bit, take the *idlis* out and refill to prepare the next batch. Serve the *idlis* hot or cold with or without *sambhar* or *rasam*.

PATRA

Patra is a popular street snack sold all over India, but it is seldom found on the menus of Indian restaurants in other parts of the world. This is also a nutritious snack that is not deep-fried, so it is worth the trouble of making. It is substantial enough to turn into a one-course meal. Traditionally, the leaves of taro plants (which are not edible uncooked) are used to make this dish, but any large, edible leaf such as chard, spinach, kale, and collards can be used. Cabbage greens, however, should not be used for this recipe.

This is a three-step recipe, and each step can be done separately. First, make the chick-pea flour batter, and spread it on leaves, one at a time. Stack the battered leaves and then roll them into a log. The rolls are steamed and then sliced into rounds and fried.

4 to 6 large taro leaves, or 8 green or red chard
    leaves, or 8 collard green leaves
2 cups *besan* (chick-pea or garbanzo flour)
1 cup water
¼ teaspoon each ground turmeric, cumin,
    coriander, and cayenne powder
½ teaspoon minced or crushed fresh garlic,
or ⅛ teaspoon garlic powder
1 to 1½ teaspoons salt
Juice of 1 lemon or lime

For Frying
3 tablespoons peanut or corn oil
½ teaspoon black or brown mustard seeds
1 lemon or lime

Wash the leaves well and pat dry with towels. Cut them in half, lengthwise (as shown), and set them aside. Make the batter by thoroughly mixing the flour, spices, lemon juice, salt, and water. On a flat work surface, place half a leaf and spread two tablespoons of batter evenly over it. Place a second leaf on top, and spread the batter. Continue to stack the leaves in this manner until eight halves have been used. Carefully roll the leaves together like a jelly roll, making it very compact, as shown in the illustration. (If some batter falls out, that is O.K. You can spread it on top of the next roll later). Make the second and third rolls (if enough batter and leaves are left) in the same fashion. Using a brightly colored thread, tie the rolls to keep them together; set them aside. The rolls may feel wet and not so compact right now, but the next step will solidify them.

To steam the rolls, you will need a big, wide Dutch oven or a wok with a tightly fitting lid in which a steamer will rest easily. Put two cups of water in the pot, and carefully place the steamer with the rolls in it. (Make sure the water does not touch the rolls.)

Over medium heat, steam the rolls for about 30 minutes until they are solid to the touch. Take the basket out carefully (it is very hot!), and let it rest for ½ hour. Then the rolls will be cool and firm enough to handle. Place them on a cutting board, and allow them to cool completely. Then snip and remove the thread. With a sharp or serrated (bread) knife, cut the rolls into thin slices, each about ½ inch wide. Set the slices on a platter. Some people would serve them just like this with lemon juice sprinkled on top. But the final stage makes them more delicious. For this last step, heat 1 tablespoon oil in a wide frying pan (cast iron will do fine) over moderate heat, and add the mustard seeds. Allow the seeds to

pop, and then place as many *patra* slices in the frying pan as you can fit in a single layer. Cook them for a few minutes until they are browned on the bottom. Turn them over and cook the other sides. Repeat with the remaining *patra*— any seeds left in the pan from the first batch will cook into the remaining batches.

Transfer the *patra* to a platter, and squeeze fresh lemon juice on top. Serve the *patra* with a *chutney* dip, such as tamarind or mint *chutney*. To make *patra* ahead of time, steam, cool, and refrigerate. When you are ready to eat, slice them and warm them up in the oven, or fry them as described above, and serve.

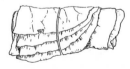

CHUTNEYS AND PICKLES

In most parts of India, one person—usually a woman—spends the majority of the day planning, shopping for, and cooking the family's meals. A typical day might start with shopping for the produce, lighting the wood stove, and preparing a fresh *chutney*. Dry goods may be gotten from the pantry, but the menu is usually prepared around the fresh vegetable(s) of the day. Even the simplest meal must have a bread (or rice), a vegetable, and a *chutney*. Perhaps it would be just a snack and a *chutney* if one was in a hurry.

Chutneys are similar in concept to Western condiments such as mustard, relish, and catsup. They are used to add flavor and as an appetite stimulant. *Chutneys* are served in very small quantities, but no Indian meal can be considered complete without at least one *chutney*. *Chutneys* are usually very spicy and not to be considered as a side dish. Usually only a teaspoon (or so) of chutney is placed at the edge of a plate or in an individual little dish to complement an Indian meal. People unfamiliar with Indian food should be forewarned about *chutney* before they sample it, lest they take too much.

Two types of *chutneys* will be described here: the simple fresh *chutneys* which are made for daily use, and the more complex, preserved *chutneys*, which are made seasonally and known as pickles in India. The pickles (or preserved *chutneys*) are often made using seasonally abundant items, such as green mangoes and chiles, to put away for later. Small work parties may be organized by the women folk to make mango pickles, inviting expert older aunts or grandmothers. Many of these recipes require complicated procedures taking as long as two weeks to prepare, and some of the ingredients are unavailable out of India. Fortunately for us, some of these skilled grandmothers got jobs preparing pickles at "Gandhi shops," a type of cottage industry supported by the Indian government. Thus, preserved pickles imported from India are now readily available in the West. If they are unavailable in your locale, they can be ordered by mail from one of the places listed at the end of this book. A few recipes for simple preserved pickles are given here after the fresh *chutney* recipes. Preserved pickles can keep for many months.

FRESH CHUTNEYS

These *chutneys* can be made fresh every day in a few minutes' time with the aid of a blender or food processor, although, if you wish, feel free to use the more traditional grinding stone or a mortar and a pestle. In a refrigerator (which is still a novelty in India), these *chutneys* can keep for a few weeks. One word of caution when using an electric gadget to make *chutneys*. Allow the ingredients to settle down for a few minutes after they have been pureed and before you open the lid. The air inside the jar becomes filled with the hot essence of the spices, and it can be very irritating to your eyes.

When serving, the *chutney* bowl can go in the center of the dining table to be passed around, so that each person can take a little bit of it on his or her plate.

RAISIN *CHUTNEY*

An easy-to-make sweet-and-sour chutney.

1 cup raisins
1 tablespoon grated or minced fresh
    gingerroot
¼ teaspoon cayenne
½ teaspoon salt
4 to 6 tablespoons warm water
Juice of 1 lemon

Combine all the ingredients in a food processor or blender. Blend until well pureed, adding a bit more water as necessary. Empty out and serve or refrigerate. This *chutney* will keep for several weeks if refrigerated soon after each use.

CURRANT *CHUTNEY*: Substitute 1 cup of currants in place of the raisins

DRIED APPLE *CHUTNEY*: Substitute 1 cup of dried apples in place of the raisins

SPRING CLEANSING *CHUTNEY*: Combine ½ cup pitted, chopped prunes with ½ cup raisins. Follow the above recipe. (This *chutney* serves as a mild laxative and is tastier than having to eat plain prunes.)

PEANUT *CHUTNEY*

1 cup shelled, roasted skinless peanuts
½ cup fresh coriander leaves
1 tablespoon chopped fresh gingerroot
2 fresh, hot green chiles, seeds and veins
    removed and chopped,
or ½ teaspoon cayenne and 1 bell pepper
    chopped
½ cup plain (unsweetened) yogurt,
or ½ cup water blended with 2 tablespoons
    lemon juice
1 teaspoon sugar
½ teaspoon salt

Place all the ingredients in a blender or food processor, and mix until it attains a consistency similar to crunchy peanut butter. Let it sit for a few minutes, then serve.

This *chutney* is substantial enough to be used as a sandwich filler.

VARIATIONS:

(1) Use a combination of roasted cashews and peanuts in place of just the peanuts to create a peanut-cashew *chutney*.

(2) Use cashews alone to make cashew *chutney*.

TAMARIND *CHUTNEY*

Tamarind *chutney* is best when made with dry, ripe tamarind pods, which are readily available in stores specializing in Latin American and southeast Asian food. The dehydrated and compressed pulp available in Indian markets can be used when the ripe, dry pods are unavailable.

This *chutney* has a thin consistency, like a sauce. It can be used as a dip for snacks, such as *samosa* and *patra*.

½ pound fresh, dry tamarind pods,
or ½ cup compressed, seeded tamarind pulp
1 cup warm water
1 tablespoon finely grated gingerroot
3 tablespoons honey or sugar
¼ teaspoon ground cayenne
½ teaspoon salt

Peel off the brittle outer shells of the tamarind pods. Then remove the stringy fibers surrounding the pod. Rinse the pods and place them in a bowl of warm water. Let them soak for about 30 minutes. Then, by rubbing the tamarind with your fingers right above the bowl, draw out as much of the pulp into the water as possible. (Wear rubber gloves if handling the pulp feels uncomfortable). When the water attains a thick, sauce-like consistency and the pods are left with only a thin membrane surrounding the seeds, the *chutney* is ready to be spiced. Discard the seeds along with the skin that sticks to them. Mix the rest of the ingredients into the tamarind. Adjust the seasonings to taste, chill, and serve.

If you are using preserved, compressed tamarind for this recipe, first break apart the pulp into smaller chunks. Remove any seeds and fiber (even the so-called seedless, compressed tamarind often has seeds). Soak the tamarind chunks in warm water for a few minutes. Then transfer the tamarind with its water to a blender or food processor. Add the rest of the ingredients, and blend until well pureed. Add more water, if necessary, to form a sauce-like *chutney*. Chill and serve.

CORIANDER *CHUTNEY*

Here is a *chutney* for the cilantro lover. If you are not one, use parsley in place of cilantro (which is not a fair substitute, of course!)

1 cup washed and finely chopped fresh
    cilantro (coriander) leaves, with large
    stems removed
1 large Anaheim chile, or 1 small jalapeño
1 tablespoon minced or grated fresh
    gingerroot
1 teaspoon sugar or honey
½ teaspoon salt
Juice of ½ lemon
A few tablespoons water as needed

Place all the ingredients in a blender or food processor, and mix them well, using the on/off button to allow the leaves to catch on to the blades. Add a little water to make a sauce-like *chutney*, but be careful not to add too much as the leaves will slowly add more moisture to the mix.

DATE *CHUTNEY*

1 cup chopped, pitted dates
Juice of 1 lemon blended with 4 to 6
    tablespoons water
or ½ cup tamarind sauce (see Tamarind
    Chutney, page 67, for directions on how to
    prepare this sauce)
½ teaspoon cayenne
1 tablespoon grated gingerroot
1 teaspoon salt

If you are using tamarind for this sweet-and-sour *chutney*, read the Tamarind *Chutney* recipe first for directions on how to make the tamarind sauce. If using lemon juice, blend it with the water. Combine all the ingredients in a food processor or blender, and mix well. Serve cold.

SHANTA'S TROPICAL *CHUTNEY*

I am proud to have created this recipe in California where dried tropical fruits are abundant.

1 cup chopped, dried tropical fruits—a
    combination of any of these: mangoes,
    papaya, pineapple, or guavas (peaches and
    apricots are also good additions)
1 cup hot water
1 cup yellow raisins (sultana)
2 tablespoons fresh, grated gingerroot
Juice of 1 large lemon
½ teaspoon cayenne
1 teaspoon salt
More water as needed

Soak the tropical fruit pieces in hot water, and set aside for ½ hour. Alternatively, if you are in a hurry, cook them for a few minutes until the dry fruit softens. Then combine all the ingredients, including the water in which tropical fruits were soaking (or cooking), in a blender or food processor, and puree, adding more water if needed to form a thick, pudding-like consistency. Allow to stand for few minutes. Serve or refrigerate. This *chutney* makes a delicious gift!

GREEN GARLIC *CHUTNEY*

Green garlic (also known as spring garlic) has a short season, so take advantage of this wonderful herb while it lasts.

8 to 10 sprigs of green garlic, trimmed but
    most greens included, and chopped
1 bunch fresh cilantro or parsley, stems
    removed and chopped
2 fresh, hot green chiles, seeds and veins
    removed,
or 1 chopped bell pepper and ¼ teaspoon
    cayenne
1 teaspoon salt
Juice of 1 lime
2 to 3 tablespoons of water

Mix all the ingredients in a blender or food processor, except the water. Using a tablespoon of water at a time, blend until pureed to a sauce-like consistency. Let it sit for a few minutes and serve.

GARLIC *CHUTNEY*

This is a dry *chutney* which looks like a paste when it is done, instead of a puree or a sauce. In Gujarat, a small lump of this *chutney* or paste is often used as a part of the stuffing for a vegetable, or it is used as a spice blend, ready to be added to a recipe. The proportions of the ingredients can vary in this recipe depending on the individual tastes of the cook. In some South Indian recipes, coconut is added to this paste.

3 to 5 cloves of fresh garlic, peeled and
    chopped
2 teaspoons cayenne powder
½ teaspoon cumin powder
½ teaspoon coriander powder,
or 1 tablespoon fresh, minced cilantro

    Mix all the ingredients in a mortar and pestle. Grind them until a smooth lump is formed. You can also use a wooden board or any cutting board to make this paste. Place all the ingredients on a board and, using a rolling pin, grind them together. The juice of the garlic will blend with the dry spices, making the mixture stick to the rolling pin or the pestle. Gather together the sticky paste, and keep on piling on spices until a uniform mound is formed. Store the paste in a jar, and use sparingly as it is very hot! Only a small portion of this paste is added to a dish while cooking. The rest can be refrigerated and saved for several weeks.

    VARIATIONS:

    (1) When making this paste to flavor *pakora*, use green garlic with stems when in season.

    (2) Add a tablespoon of fresh or dehydrated coconut to the ingredients

    (3) Add two tablespoons of roasted chickpeas (available in Indian markets) and 2 tablespoons of yogurt to make this *chutney* into a puree. (Use an electric blender or food processor for this variation.)

MINT *CHUTNEY*

1 cup firmly packed fresh mint leaves (thick
    stems removed)
½ cup chopped green onions, including most
    of their greens
1 tablespoon chopped or grated gingerroot
1 or 2 fresh, hot chiles, seeded, deveined, and
    chopped
1 teaspoon salt
½ cup plain yogurt, blended with
    2 tablespoons water,
or (for a dairy-free recipe) try one of the
    following two substitutions:
½ cup water blended with 2 tablespoons
    lemon juice,
or ¼ cup tofu and ¼ cup water blended with
    2 tablespoons lemon juice

    Place all the ingredients in a blender or food processor. Blend until it becomes a smooth, thin puree, the consistency of a runny sauce. Keep covered and let stand for few minutes before serving.

    Note: If fresh, hot chiles are unavailable, mix 1 small, chopped bell pepper with ½ teaspoon cayenne powder, and follow the rest of the recipe.

COCONUT *CHUTNEY*

The use of coconut is abundant along the southern coast of India, so many variations of this chutney can be found there. Here are two.

COCONUT *CHUTNEY* # 1

This is a popular *chutney* for serving with *dosa* or *idli*. It requires a two-step process. First, you will grind a group of ingredients into a smooth puree, and then you will make a *vaghar*, in which the hot oil and mustard will be blended with the yogurt and added to the puree.

1 cup coconut shreds obtained from a fresh
    coconut as described on page 36,
or 1 cup dehydrated coconut shreds soaked in
    ½ cup water for few minutes
¼ cup roasted Indian chick-peas or *sev* (both
    available in Indian markets, or homemade
    sev prepared with the recipe on page 47)
1 teaspoon cumin seeds or powder
1 teaspoon coriander seeds or powder
1 teaspoon salt
2 tablespoons compressed tamarind (soaked for
    ½ hour),
or 1 teaspoon *amchoor* powder (available in
    Indian shops)
or the juice of 1 lemon blended with
    1 tablespoon sugar
½ teaspoon cayenne powder

For the Vaghar
1 tablespoon oil
¼ teaspoon black or brown mustard seeds
a pinch of *hing*
½ cup yogurt, well-blended with
    2 tablespoons water

    Place all ingredients, except the ones for the *vaghar*, into a blender or food processor. Puree to a smooth consistency. Set aside in a mixing bowl. Then heat the oil for the *vaghar* in a small pot, and add the mustard seeds. When the seeds start popping, add the pinch of *hing* and the yogurt mixture. Blend well using a fork or a wire whisk. Pour the yogurt mixture over the coconut puree. Mix well and serve.

COCONUT *CHUTNEY* # 2

1 cup coconut shreds obtained from a fresh
    coconut as described on page 36,
or 1 cup dehydrated coconut shreds soaked in
    ½ cup water for few minutes
Juice of 1 lemon
1 tablespoon brown sugar or honey
2 fresh, hot green chiles, seeds and veins
    removed
1 teaspoon salt
1 cup fresh cilantro (coriander) leaves, thick
    stems removed

    Place all the ingredients in a food processor, and blend until a fairly smooth puree is formed, adding a little water when necessary. This green *chutney* is a colorful compliment to yellow appetizers such as *samosa* or *pakora*.

COOKED *CHUTNEYS*

TOMATO *CHUTNEY*

I suggest you use organically grown tomatoes in this recipe because, among all fruits, tomatoes have the most superior flavor when grown without chemicals. When I made this *chutney* with homegrown tomatoes, before organically grown produce was available on the market, I realized how and why this *chutney* tasted so much like the one back home!

4 large or 6 medium-size ripe tomatoes, preferably organically grown
2 tablespoons sesame or other vegetable oil
½ teaspoon each mustard seeds and cumin seeds
4 cloves of garlic, crushed and mashed or minced
2 dry, hot red chiles, cut into 4 to 6 pieces, seeds mostly removed
two pinches of *hing*
1 tablespoon grated gingerroot
¼ teaspoon each cayenne and turmeric powder
1 teaspoon salt

Peel the tomatoes by placing them in a pot of rapidly boiling water for a few minutes. When the skins of the tomatoes appear broken, remove them from the boiling water, one at a time, using a slotted spoon, and immediately place them in a bowl of cold water. This will cool the tomatoes, and the skins will peel off very easily. Cut the peeled tomatoes into chunks, and set aside.

Over a moderate to high temperature, heat the oil in a saucepan, and add the mustard seeds. When they start popping, add the cumin and chile. As soon as the chiles start smoking, (don't burn them too much), add the *hing* quickly. Add the tomato chunks and cover the pan right away. Reduce the heat, cover, and cook for a minute. Then add the rest of the ingredients, and stir-fry the mixture while crushing the tomato chunks with a wooden spoon. Remove the large chile pieces if you want the *chutney* to be mild. Cook the *chutney* for 8 to 10 minutes to form a smooth sauce, stirring and removing fibers, if any. Serve after the *chutney* cools.

CRANBERRY *CHUTNEY*

During the Thanksgiving holidays, we usually go to a friend's house to celebrate and have a big festive dinner. And, of course, they all expect me to bring my vegetarian specialties with me. One of the things that I bring to the Thanksgiving dinner table is my cranberry *chutney*. As far as I know, this is my own invention, inspired as an alternative to traditional American cranberry sauce.

3 cups fresh or frozen cranberries, thawed and drained
1 cup water
2 cups of honey,
or 2½ cups sugar or fructose
1 tablespoon finely grated, fresh gingerroot
½ teaspoon each ground cinnamon, cloves, and cardamom
¼ teaspoon cayenne powder (optional)

Chop the cranberries coarsely using a food processor, blender, or knife. Don't over-chop. Transfer them to a pot with the water, and cook for a few minutes until soft. Then add the sweetener and spices, and cook for 10 to 15 minutes, until the *chutney* looks jam-like and glazed. It will further solidify as it cools. The cayenne can be omitted if you wish to make this *chutney* milder, so that you can serve it to young people. Even without any oil or salt added to this *chutney*, it will keep for months in the refrigerator.

GREEN TOMATO *CHUTNEY*

This is a tangy and beautiful *chutney*, similar to salsa verde, but with its own ethnic identity. Preparing this *chutney* is also a good way to use up your green garden tomatoes, which may never turn red if you happen to grow them in a fog belt (such as San Francisco!).

4 to 6 green tomatoes
2 tablespoons vegetable oil (unflavored sesame oil is preferred, but any vegetable oil will do)
½ teaspoon cumin seeds
2 to 3 cloves of garlic, mashed and chopped finely or minced
A pinch of *hing*
1 or 2 fresh, hot green chiles, minced finely
3 tablespoons chopped coriander (cilantro) or parsley leaves
1 teaspoon salt
A few dry, crumbled curry leaves, or three fresh chopped curry leaves (optional)

Boil the tomatoes for 3 minutes, and then dunk them in cold water to loosen their skins. Peel, then cut the peeled tomatoes, and set aside.

Alternatively, remove the skin of the tomatoes by roasting them over a hot burner, using metal thongs for turning so you don't burn yourself. Or you can use a metal screen which sits over the burner, and the tomatoes can roast on them. Turn the tomatoes carefully so that they don't fall apart but the skin becomes charred. Cool them for a few minutes, and the skin will come off by rubbing the surface. Cut the roasted tomatoes into chunks, and set aside. Roasting is a skilled task, but it gives the *chutney* a unique, barbecue flavor. (When mastered, you can use this skill for other recipes described later in the book.)

Heat the oil in a pan, and add the cumin seeds and garlic. When the garlic turns brown, add the *hing*, chiles, and coriander, and stir-fry them until fragrant. Then add the tomato chunks and salt. Some people add brown sugar or honey to balance the tangy flavor, but I personally like this *chutney* to be tart. Add the optional curry leaves if you have them. Cover and let the *chutney* stand for half an hour to settle the flavors. Remove the curry leaves if you have used them, and serve.

PICKLES

Due to the elaborate process involved in making preserved pickles and because good quality bottled pickles are available at import stores, I am only including a few pickle recipes here. I also reserve these pickles for an occasional dinner since they are—unlike the fresh *chutneys*—a bit greasy and salty. The first two preserved pickle recipes that follow are a short cut from traditional family recipes. They are authentic enough, but these pickles would last for only few months, whereas pickles preserved using more elaborate methods and executed by experts will keep for years. The next two pickle recipes are for ready-to-eat pickles. You do not have to wait for days to eat them, and usually they will not keep beyond several weeks even when refrigerated.

HOT CHILE PICKLES

Here are some pickles for a sheer hot sensation! Buy any variety of hot green chiles in season or mix a few varieties. Anaheim chiles are medium-hot and make these pickles moderately hot. Make sure the chiles are fresh and crisp.

¾ lb. fresh, hot green chiles, such as cayenne,
    Anaheim, or serrano
¼ cup salt
1 teaspoon *amchoor* powder,
or ¼ teaspoon ascorbic acid powder (vitamin C)
1 cup mustard or sesame oil
1 tablespoon each whole, black mustard seeds
    and fenugreek seeds
1 teaspoon turmeric powder

Wash, dry, and cut the chiles into big pieces. Small chiles can be used uncut. Place them in a mixing bowl. Sprinkle salt all over the chiles, and set aside for at least two hours or overnight. Then rinse them and drain. Add the powdered *amchoor* or substitute ascorbic acid for a dry tartness. Mix well and set the chiles aside. Heat the oil in a pot, and add the whole mustard and fenugreek seeds. Allow the mustard seeds to pop, then turn off the heat. When the oil is still warm, but not hot, add the turmeric and the chiles. Bottle the mixture in a jar with a lid. Set it aside on your pantry or shelf for a week before eating. Shake to mix the chiles from time to time during this period. After a week, the pickles are ready to serve. They will keep for at least a month if you refrigerate the unused portion.

MANGO PICKLES

The mangoes used for making pickles are raw, green mangoes. They are not meant to be eaten without pickling, and they are not sweet. In fact, some varieties of mangoes are particularly bred as pickling mangoes, as they are very hard and sour and will never ripen. Outside India, purchase any green or unripe, hard mangoes for making pickles.

6 raw, unripe, small mangoes
¼ cup salt
4 tablespoons each black or brown mustard
    seeds and fenugreek seeds
2 cups mustard or sesame oil
1 tablespoon each turmeric and cayenne
    powder
½ teaspoon *hing*

Wash the mangoes and lay them on a cutting surface. Cut each unpeeled mango lengthwise into strips, leaving the seed and the hard core and fibers surrounding it. These can be discarded. Cut the strips into bite-size chunks, and place them in a bowl. Sprinkle salt all over, mix well, and set aside to soak overnight.

The next day, rinse the mangoes briefly, and let them drain. Using a mortar and pestle, a food processor, or a coffee grinder, coarsely grind the mustard seeds and fenugreek seeds. (You can also buy these spices ground to a coarse consistency in Indian specialty stores.) Place this spice mixture in a stainless steel mixing bowl.

Add the rest of the spices to this bowl, and set the spice blend aside.

Heat the oil until very hot over medium heat for about five to eight minutes, until hot vapors of oil appear on the surface, and then turn off the heat. When the oil cools slightly (about five minutes), pour it over the spice blend. This will bubble up the mixture and make the kitchen smell very good. If you allow the hot oil to become too cool, it will not cook the spice blend. But if you add the oil while it is still very hot, it will burn the spices, so the temperature of oil to be poured on the spices needs to be just right. Allow the spice and oil mixture to cool completely to room temperature. Pour the mixture onto the mango pieces and mix well, using a clean spoon.

Transfer the mango pieces to a wide-mouth jar, and tie a cheese cloth or muslin over the top. Place the mango pickles in a sunny window or outside in a safe, sunny place for about two weeks, bringing it back inside the house at night and shaking it a few times to mix the spices well. Do not refrigerate it during these two weeks. After this period, the pickles are ready to eat, although aging them for few more weeks in a cupboard will make the mangoes softer and the pickles tastier. (Do not put the pickles back out in the sun after the two weeks are over). When the mangoes become tender and the skin seems soft enough to eat, the pickles are done. Now you can serve them and refrigerate them for future use.

FRESH PICKLES

Here are some pickles that do not need much aging or preserving.

CARROT PICKLES

4 carrots
1 teaspoon salt
Juice of 1 lemon

Scrape the carrots clean and cut lengthwise into thin strips. Place them in a mixing bowl, and sprinkle with the salt and lemon juice. Mix well and allow to stand for 1 or 2 hours at room temperature before serving. Refrigerate the unused pickles. They can be used for a week.

CUCUMBER PICKLES

4 regular or 8 pickling cucumbers, peeled and
     cut lengthwise into strips
1 teaspoon salt
½ teaspoon turmeric
1 tablespoon lime or lemon juice

Place the cucumber strips in a bowl, and mix the rest of the ingredients. Keep at room temperature for a couple of hours (while cooking other dishes), stirring to mix a few times. These pickles are meant to be eaten within a day or two.

GINGER PICKLES

¼ lb. fresh gingerroot, peeled and cut into
     ¼" slices
1 tablespoon salt
1 tablespoon turmeric powder
Juice of 2 to 3 limes or lemons

Mix all the ingredients in a bowl, and then place them in a glass jar with a lid. Cover and leave the jar at room temperature for a day or two, shaking every now and then to distribute the salt and lemon juice. At the end of 12 to 20 hours, the spices will have marinated the gingerroot, turning it into a sour, salty pickle which has lost its original strong, hot spiciness. You can serve it immediately. Keep any leftover pickle in the refrigerator; it should keep for several weeks.

RAITA

Another accompaniment to Indian snacks and appetizers, the *raitas* are served in a little bit bigger portions than the *chutneys*, and they are usually made with uncooked vegetables (or fruits). *Raitas* will be covered on pages 107-09 with the vegetable and salad dishes.

CHAPTER FIVE
VEGETABLES, VEGETABLE-BASED
DISHES, AND SALADS

Vegetarians tend to be more familiar with the world of vegetables and how they can be prepared than are non-vegetarians. Or, at least, this is what my American students who have become vegetarian report to me. They say they are now more conscious of various vegetables in the supermarket and on the menus in restaurants than they were when they ate meat. They are also more eager to try out various vegetables and different methods

of preparing them. It is as though the change of diet has caused a reawakening of the taste buds.

It has also been brought to my attention that many people in America got their introduction to the world of vegetables through canned peas and carrots. Many children grew up disliking vegetables because they were forced to eat these poor-tasting, non-nutritious canned vegetables. Vegetables, to them, were like bad-tasting medicine that they had to take. These same people, after discovering real vegetables, now enjoy preparing and eating them. They also understand that the nutritive value of vegetables will be preserved by not overcooking them. Even city folks are now starting to realize the relationship between the taste of vegetables and how they are grown, thanks to organic and farm-fresh produce available to them at farmers' markets.

Many, if not most, of India's people are vegetarians, meaning that they do not eat any flesh whether it comes from a cow, fish, or fowl. Since dairy products are not abundant in that very populated country, vegetables, beans, and grains constitute a major portion of the diet for India's vegetarians. Every town in India has a large produce market where, from sunup to sunset, endless varieties of vegetables are displayed. One member of the family will start his or her day by going to the produce market where they discuss, bargain, and argue over the prices of various vegetables being purchased. Occasionally a cow or goat will sneak its head among the women's saris and snatch away a vegetable or two, much to the chagrin of the merchant. Small children may pretend to cry so that a sympathetic vendor will offer them a fruit to dry away their tears. It is quite a colorful scene—the vegetable market—charged with energy and emotion. In India it is as entertaining to purchase vegetables as it is to cook, serve, and eat them.

The idea of a main dish is not employed in Indian menu planning. Rather, a grouping of equally important dishes are served on a *thali*, a round metal plate with small *katories* (cups or bowls) filled with vegetables, *dal* (beans), rice, bread, and a *chutney*. This combination would be considered a simple, but complete, *thali*. A more elaborate or festive *thali* would contain a similar variety of each dish, as well as some sweets. When I was a little girl, my grandmother would sometimes put me to sleep with a bedtime story. My favorite part in this story was when a lavish dinner was served containing "32 types of sweets and 36 different vegetable dishes." On the other hand, a quick meal may contain fewer items than the basic *thali*. In any case, a menu is often planned around the choice of vegetable dish(es). Unlike a meat-centered diet where vegetables play second fiddle, vegetables play center stage in India. These days in many Indian cities (and abroad at specialty shops), sweets can be purchased ready-made, but the preparation of different vegetables displays a cook's special touch.

In this chapter, I have included tradition-al methods of preparing Indian vegetables (with my special touches), as well as recipes for some non-Indian vegetables, such as mushrooms and celery. Use fresh vegetables that are grown organically without the use of chemicals, whenever possible. If commercial produce is used, wash it thoroughly and scrub gently with a vegetable brush to remove chemicals which may have been sprayed on its surface. You can also use a mild soap solution (Tamcon, etc.) to remove any coating, such as wax, from your produce. This step is important when you cook vegetables such as cauliflower, which tends to accumulate sprayed chemicals deep within its textured surface. Avoid using canned vegetables. If a vegetable called for in a recipe is not fresh, use a frozen one or substitute with something similar that is in season. Most of the vegetables in the following recipes are available in American supermarkets. If not, shop around in ethnic grocery stores such as Chinese or Mexican shops.

The following vegetables are used commonly in Indian dishes. Here are some tips on how to select and prepare them for cooking.

CABBAGE: A poor peoples' staple around the world, green and red cabbage can be used in Indian dishes. The quick stir-frying method given in the recipes to follow preserves its crisp texture and taste. Cabbage can stay fresh for weeks in the refrigerator. Remove a couple of the outer leaves if they are limp.

CAULIFLOWER: A very popular vegetable throughout India. Select cauliflower that is white with the individual buds tightly compacted, since this indicates freshness. Organic cauliflower may be more yellow (which actually tastes better to me than its white commercial counterpart). Broccoli is not grown and used in India, but it works fine as a substitute or as a colorful companion to cauliflower in a stir-fry recipe.

EGGPLANT: Probably the most popular and widely used vegetable in India. Even in a small Indian market, you will find a number of varieties in different shapes, colors, and sizes. In Western countries, two varieties are available: the big, globe-shaped eggplant, and the long "Japanese" variety. Japanese eggplants are preferred in most Indian recipes, since this type is seedless and, thus, is not bitter. Some big eggplants are seedless and very tasty, but it is hard to know this until you open it. Also, when you want to prepare Indian-style stuffed eggplants, you will need the "Japanese" variety. When you prepare eggplants for an Indian recipe, remove the stem before cooking, but do not peel.

OKRA: Okra is also known as "ladies' fingers" and is a popular soul food in America. In India, it is one of the most favored vegetables available during the monsoon season. Many people in the West do not like okra, because when it is cooked with water or a sauce like in American "gumbo," it has a slimy consistency. But if you cook okra using one of the recipes in this chapter, you will be delighted with the crispy, tasty pods. Buy okra when it is small and bright green. The large pods tend to be stringy.

POPULAR INDIAN SQUASHES: *DOODHI, GALKA, and KARELA*: In South India, some big winter squashes such as pumpkin are used. But squashes which are tender and cook quickly (unlike winter squashes, which usually need to be baked) are grown and sold year around throughout India.

DOODHI (also known as *opo* in Asian markets): This is a large, gourd-shaped squash. It is light green outside and white inside. The thick skin must be removed before cooking. A *doodhi* is fresh if you can easily penetrate its surface with your fingernail.

GHISODA: This vegetable looks like a cucumber with a bumpy skin. The skin should be thoroughly removed before cooking the white flesh. It is also available in Chinese and Filipino neighborhood stores. Fresh *ghisoda* should be firm and not limp.

GALKA is very similar in taste and appearance to small, young zucchini.

Western substitutes: Doodhi, ghisoda, and galka can be substituted by using zucchini, yellow crook neck squash, or other quick-cooking summer squashes, such as sun burst and patty cake squash. These quick-cooking American squashes do not have to be peeled, especially if they are organically grown. If they are not organic, wash and scrub them gently using a vegetable brush to remove anything coating them.

KARELA: Karela is a vegetable not easily liked by everyone, especially among children, because it is very, very bitter. However, *karela's* natural properties as a medicinal food are outlined both in Ayurvedic literature and in Chinese herbal texts. Therefore, *karelas* are sought out during their season by adults and are prepared in many ways to make them tasty. However, the real *karela* lover likes it as it is, cooked but bitter. There is no equivalent or substitute for *karela*.

SOME NOTES ON COOKING VEGETABLES

In India, *subji, shak, tarkari,* or *bhaji* all mean "cooked vegetables." Vegetables cooked Indian-style are loosely labeled as "curries" outside of India. I have organized the recipes by dividing these Indian cooking methods into four groups. In addition, I will add another grouping of "uncooked" vegetable recipes. The first group employs a quick, stir-fry method: *suki bhaji*. Vegetables are stir-fried with spices quickly, producing a dish without sauce. In the second method, the vegetables are stir-fried first and then cooked slowly with water or another juicy vegetable, such as tomato, to produce a dish with a sauce. In the third group, vegetables are cooked first and then blended with already prepared sauces. In the fourth grouping, vegetables are stuffed with spices and other ingredients and then cooked with water, yogurt, or coconut milk. You will also find more ways of cooking vegetables in other chapters, such as cooking rice and vegetables together (*biriani*) in Chapter Seven and cooking vegetables with batter (*pakora*) in Chapter Four. All vegetables need to be rinsed and drained before cooking. Some vegetables, such as eggplants and potatoes, will discolor if you don't keep them soaking in water after you cut them up for a recipe. Just drain thoroughly before stir-frying. Read the introduction to each cooking method before trying a recipe.

SUKI BHAJI (DRY VEGETABLES)

Most vegetable dishes of this type will have enough juice of their own to cook quickly without any additional liquid. In fact, if you overcook these vegetables, all the liquid will be brought out, rendering them limp and soggy. One exception to this rule is vegetables cooked with potatoes, which do need water. In this case, potatoes will be parboiled ahead of time before stir-frying with other vegetables. A wok or shallow saucepan is ideal for this method, since their shape allows liquid to evaporate while stir-frying. Unlike the Chinese stir-fry method, (high heat all the time), an Indian *suki bhaji* is usually prepared over medium heat. Most quick-cooking vegetables are served with freshly squeezed lemon or lime. This brings out the flavors and colors of the vegetables.

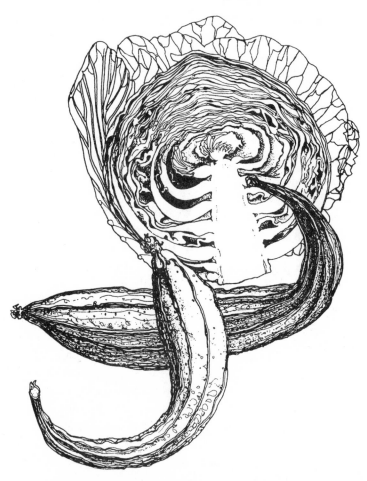

FRIED ZUCCHINI, *GHISODA, GALKA,* OR OTHER SUMMER SQUASH

6 medium-sized zucchini or Indian *galka* or *ghisoda*
2 to 3 tablespoons corn, safflower, peanut, or canola oil
½ teaspoon black or brown mustard seeds
2 chopped scallions, or 2 tablespoons of finely chopped onion (optional)
1 clove of garlic (minced or crushed), or a few pinches of garlic powder
1 teaspoon or less salt
½ teaspoon each cumin, coriander, and turmeric powder
¼ teaspoon cayenne
Juice of ½ lemon

Wash the zucchini or *galka*, and cut them into thin slices. If using *ghisoda*, peel thoroughly; remove the scaly skin before slicing. Set the slices of vegetables aside. Heat the oil in a wok or saucepan over medium heat, and add the mustard seeds. When the seeds start popping, add the onion and fresh garlic. Stir-fry for 30 seconds or a bit longer until the spices are well roasted. Then add the vegetables. Sauté them for two minutes, then add the powdered spices and salt. Continue to cook while stirring frequently. Be gentle while stir-frying to keep at least some of the slices intact. In about 10 or 12 minutes, the squash slices should be well flavored and cooked al denté, which is the way I prefer it. If you like your vegetables to be softer than this, by all means cook them a few minutes longer; you will have a more traditional version of this dish. Sprinkle lemon juice on top, and mix well before serving. This dish can be reheated in the oven at 350°F for five minutes or on the stove by stir-frying for a minute.

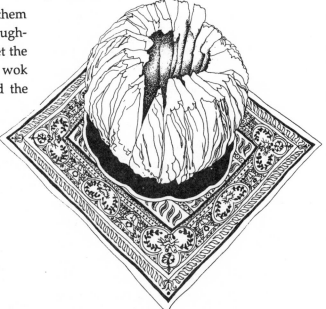

POTATO *BHAJI*

5 medium potatoes (about 2 pounds)
3 tablespoons oil
½ teaspoon black mustard seeds
¼ cup finely chopped onion
2 cloves of garlic, pressed or minced
½ teaspoon each turmeric and cumin
     powder
¼ teaspoon cayenne powder
Juice of 1 lemon
2 tablespoons cilantro or parsley leaves,
     chopped
Salt to taste

Place the unpeeled potatoes in a large pot of water, and boil them until they are tender but not too soft. Then remove them from the water, and allow them to cool enough to handle. Peel the potatoes and cut them into large pieces; set them aside. Heat the oil in a pot, and add the mustard seeds. Allow them to pop for a few minutes, then add the onion and stir-fry it for a minute. Add the garlic and fry for another minute. Then add the parboiled potatoes, and sauté for five minutes. Add the powdered spices and continue to stir-fry for a few more minutes until all ingredients are well-mixed. If the potatoes seem too raw at this point, add a few tablespoons of water, and continue to cook them for a few more minutes until the potatoes are well-cooked but still mostly intact. Add the lemon juice and salt to taste. Garnish with cilantro or parsley, and serve. This dish is also good served at room temperature or cold.

INDIAN POTATO SALAD: Cool the *bhaji* to room temperature. Then whisk one cup of low-fat or non-fat yogurt in a mixing bowl, and add to the cooled potatoes. Adjust the seasonings to taste. For a dairy-free version, whisk 1 cup of soy yogurt or blend ¾ cup soft tofu with 2 tablespoons of water, and mix with the potatoes. Chill and save until ready to use.

VARIATIONS: (1.) Add 1 cup of fresh string beans, cut up into ½-inch pieces, or 1 cup of celery, cut into small cubes or slices, to the parboiled potatoes, and follow rest of the recipe.

(2.) Add 1 cup of fresh snow peas, cut into one-inch pieces, or 1 cup of fresh peas (or frozen peas, thawed and drained), and add to the stir-frying potatoes for the last five minutes of cooking.

SPINACH *BHAJI*
OR OTHER GREEN LEAFY *BHAJI*
This simple but delicious preparation of spinach may change some spinach haters. A combination of two types of greens makes this dish interesting and is a good way to use a quantity of greens when they're in season. Since spinach is mild in flavor, it mixes well with other greens which may be stronger by themselves.

2 bunches of spinach, washed, drained
     thoroughly, trimmed with thick stems
     removed, and chopped
or a combination of 1 bunch spinach and 1
     bunch other greens (such as watercress,
     chard, collards, or kale)

3 tablespoons oil
3 cloves of garlic, finely chopped
3 tablespoons onion, chopped
¼ teaspoon cumin seeds
Salt to taste
A few pinches of cayenne
1 tablespoon freshly squeezed lemon juice

Heat the oil in a frying pan over moderate heat, and add the garlic, onion, and cumin seeds. Allow them to sauté for a minute or so until fragrant. Then add the completely drained, chopped greens. Stir-fry for a minute and add the salt and cayenne. Sauté for 10 minutes or longer until almost all the liquid produced by the leaves has evaporated. By now, the leaves have shrunk considerably. Mix in the lemon juice and serve.

OKRA
4 tablespoons oil
¼ teaspoon black mustard seeds or cumin
   seeds
A few pinches of *hing*
1 pound small, fresh okra
¼ teaspoon each turmeric and coriander
   powder
3 tablespoons of yogurt, or 1 tablespoon
   lemon juice
Salt and cayenne to taste

Okra pods are best cooked without water, since the addition of water makes them gummy. In fact, to clean okra pods for cooking, do not wash them. Instead, sponge them clean with a damp kitchen towel, then remove the tops. Cut the okra either into ¼" wide rounds or lengthwise, forming four long strips out of each pod; set aside. Heat the oil in a heavy pan, such as an iron skillet, and add the mustard (or cumin) seeds. When the mustard seeds stop popping (the cumin seeds don't pop), add the optional hing and immediately stir in the okra. Fry the okra, stirring frequently, over medium to low heat for several minutes. Then add the turmeric and coriander powders, and stir-fry for another five minutes, making sure the okra doesn't burn. Now add the yogurt or the lemon juice, which will make the okra somewhat wet. Stir-fry for few minutes until all the moisture has evaporated. Add salt and cayenne. Adjust the seasonings to taste, and serve.

HOT & SPICY OKRA: Add one finely chopped jalapeño pepper (after removing seeds and central core) instead of the cayenne.

OKRA WITH GREEN TOMATO: Use one small, green tomato, cut up into small chunks, instead of the yogurt or lemon juice, and add to the cooking okra from the very beginning. The tomato will secrete some juice, so more frequent stir-frying may be necessary to get a final product that is dry.

ALU MATAR

Alu matar (potatoes and peas) is a popular North Indian dish.

3 to 4 tablespoons of oil
½ cup finely chopped onion
2 cloves of garlic, minced
1 cup chopped fresh tomato
¼ teaspoon *garam masala*
¼ teaspoon each cumin, turmeric, and
    coriander powder
⅛ teaspoon cayenne (or less)
1 teaspoon salt
1 pound red or yellow potatoes, cut up
    into ½" cubes
1 cup of water
1½ cups shelled fresh peas, or frozen peas,
    thawed and drained
A few sprigs of chopped cilantro for
    garnish (optional)

In a heavy saucepan, heat the oil over moderate heat, and cook the onion and garlic until light brown. Then add the chopped tomato and all the spices, including the salt, and sauté for about five minutes until the ingredients form a well-blended paste. Add the potatoes and fry for 2 minutes until well-mixed. Then add the water, cover, and cook for about 10 minutes. Add the peas and stir-fry for a minute to mix the ingredients. Lower the heat, cover, and cook for another 10 minutes.

At this time, both the potatoes and peas should be cooked but not mushy. If the potatoes taste raw and the mixture needs more water, add a few tablespoons of water, and cook a little longer. Conversely, if the mixture is well-cooked but has too much liquid, stir-fry uncovered for few minutes to evaporate. Adjust the seasoning to taste. Garnish with cilantro if you please, and serve.

MATAR GHOBI (PEAS AND CAULIFLOWER)

2 tablespoons oil

¼ teaspoon black mustard seeds

¼ teaspoon cumin seeds

1 medium head of cauliflower (about 1 pound), stem removed and cut into flowerettes (buds)

1 cup peas, fresh and shelled, or frozen, thawed, and drained

½ teaspoon each turmeric and coriander powder

¼ cup water

Juice of 1 lemon or lime

Salt and cayenne to taste

Few sprigs of chopped cilantro for garnish

In a wok or a frying pan, heat the oil and add the mustard seeds. When they begin popping, add the cumin seeds. Then add the cauliflower buds, and sauté for five minutes. Add the turmeric, coriander, and peas, and stir-fry again for another five minutes until all is well-blended. Then add the water, cover, and cook for about 5 to 10 minutes, until all the liquid is gone and the vegetables are well-cooked but tender. Add the salt and cayenne, and serve with the optional garnish.

BROCCOLI WITH CARROTS: A colorful contrast to the above dish. Use 1 pound of broccoli buds instead of the cauliflower and 1 cup of carrot cubes in place of the peas. Follow the above recipe.

ASPARAGUS WITH MIXED VEGETABLES

I can't wait for the spring crop of asparagus. The stalks look so elegant and smell delicious while cooking. They remind me of an Indian vegetable called "drum sticks," which look like asparagus but taste quite different. Although asparagus is not traditionally Indian, this *suki bhaji* recipe preserves its delicate flavor which is destroyed by overcooking.

2 cups asparagus stalks, cut into 1 to 1½" long pieces after removing the thick ends
1 cup sliced mushrooms
1 cup sliced carrots
1 cup sliced zucchini or sunburst squash
1 tablespoon oil
2 tablespoons green garlic or scallions, chopped finely with its leaves
¼ teaspoon each sesame and cumin seeds
Juice of ½ lemon
Salt and pepper to taste

Trim off the bottom part of the asparagus stems by snapping them off. Set the long stalks aside with the other vegetables. Place the oil in a frying pan, and add the chopped green garlic, if available, or the scallion, and fry them for a minute. Add the cumin and sesame seeds, and stir-fry for a few seconds. Then add all the rest of the vegetables, and fry them for five minutes, stirring frequently. Cover and cook over moderate heat for five to seven more minutes, being careful not to burn the vegetables. If they were fresh, the vegetables' juices will be sufficient to steam them without having to add any water. If they look too dry and the asparagus still tastes bitter, add a few tablespoons of water, cover, and cook for a few more minutes. Add the lemon juice and the salt and pepper to your taste. Stir and serve hot.

FRIED CABBAGE

Cabbage is nutritious but many people do not like over-cooked, watery cabbage stew. The following method of cooking cabbage produces a crunchy, savory dish.

2 to 3 tablespoons oil
½ teaspoon black or brown mustard seeds
2-3 cloves minced or crushed garlic
½ green or red bell pepper, finely chopped
A few pinches of *hing* (optional)
½ head green cabbage (or combination of red and green), shredded after removing the center core
½ teaspoon each turmeric, cumin, and coriander powder
1 teaspoon salt or to taste
1 tablespoon lemon or lime juice

In a heavy frying pan or wok, heat the oil and add the mustard seeds. When they have been popping for a while, add the garlic and stir in the bell pepper. Cook this mixture for five minutes until the pepper pieces are limp. Add the optional *hing* and stir in the cabbage. Continue stirring while adding the spices and salt. Cook the cabbage for 10 to 15 minutes, stirring every few minutes. When fully cooked, the cabbage will shrink down quite a bit but should still taste crunchy. Cook a bit longer if you desire the finished dish to be less crunchy. Add the lemon or lime juice, and serve.

FRIED CABBAGE WITH POTATOES: Peel and cut 3 medium potatoes into about ¼" cubes. Add them to the hot oil after the mustard and bell pepper have been roasted. Sauté for about seven minutes before adding the cabbage. Follow rest of the recipe. Add chopped tomato at the end instead of the lemon juice for more moisture.

DRY *KARELA*

This is an untamed *karela* recipe—very bitter— a *karela* lover's delight.

2 tablespoons oil
¼ teaspoon cumin seeds
4 cloves of minced garlic
3 medium *karelas*, sliced into thin rounds
    after the rough skin has been peeled
¼ teaspoon turmeric powder
Juice of ½ lime or lemon
Salt and cayenne powder to taste

Heat the oil in a skillet, and add the cumin seeds and garlic. After few minutes, or when the garlic turns golden, add the *karela* slices and cook for 10 minutes or a bit longer, stirring frequently. When done, the rounds will look somewhat limp. Add the turmeric powder, lime or lemon juice, salt, and cayenne, and stir-fry again for two minutes. Serve hot with bread and/or rice.

KARELA WITH TOMATO: Add 1 cup of chopped tomatoes with the *karela* rounds to make a less bitter recipe. Do not add the lemon or lime juice.

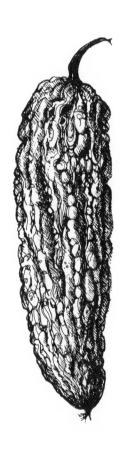

SAUTÉED MIXED SQUASHES
FOR HOLIDAYS

This is my recipe creation for American holidays such as Thanksgiving and Christmas. This recipe uses autumn produce and looks and smells very festive.

1 tiny pumpkin,
or ½ small pumpkin
1 tiny acorn or butternut squash
1 large yam or sweet potato
1 large carrot, sliced into ½" rounds
3 tablespoons oil or butter
Water as needed
A few pinches each of ground cinnamon,
    cloves, cardamom, and cayenne
Juice of 1 lemon
Salt to taste

Wash the squash and pumpkin, and cut into four pieces using a sharp knife or a cleaver. Remove all stringy fibers and seeds, and rinse with warm water. Then cut into large, bite-sized pieces, but do not peel. Set them aside. Clean and cut the yam or sweet potato into ½" slices but do not peel. Set them aside with the carrots. Heat the oil or butter over medium heat in a heavy pan. Add the pumpkin and squash pieces, and stir-fry for two minutes. Then add ½ cup of water, cover, and cook, for about seven minutes. Then add the yam or potato pieces, the carrots and ½ cup water. Cover and cook for another five to seven minutes. If the vegetables are not cooked by now and no liquid is left, add a few more tablespoons of water, and cook for another five minutes. Then add the powdered spices, lemon juice, and salt. Mix well and serve hot. Instruct your dinner guests that it is O.K. for them to remove the squash peels as they eat; the skin is easily separated from the flesh with a spoon or a fork.

RASADAR SHAK
(VEGETABLES WITH SAUCE)

In this group of recipes, you will produce hearty entrees with a "curry-like" sauce. As with "dry" cooking, the vegetables are usually stir-fried first, and then covered and cooked with some water, resulting in a soft, stew-like dish. Many recipes in this group use slow-cooking vegetables, such as eggplants and cauliflower, in combination with sauce-producing vegetables—such as tomatoes and potatoes—and water. Often a quickly-made spice mix, such as garlic and cayenne paste, is added to make this sauce zesty.

EGGPLANT WITH BOILED POTATOES

3 tablespoons vegetable oil

½ teaspoon black or brown mustard seeds

1 pound thick-skinned (russet) potatoes,
   boiled, peeled, and cut into 1" cubes

1 medium unpeeled eggplant (about 1 lb.),
   cut into about ½" cubes

1 teaspoon each turmeric, cumin, and
   coriander powder

1 teaspoon salt

½ teaspoon garlic paste #2 (see page 40)

1 tomato, chopped

1 tablespoon chopped cilantro for garnish

Heat the oil over moderate heat in a saucepan, and add the mustard seeds. When the seeds start popping, add the potato and eggplant pieces. Stir-fry the mixture for a few minutes, and then add the powdered spices and the salt. Continue to fry for several minutes so that all the spices are well-blended. Then mix in the prepared garlic paste, and sauté while breaking down the garlic lumps. Add ¾ cup of water, and lower the heat. Cover and cook the vegetables for about 15 minutes, until they are soft and swimming in the colorful sauce. Add the tomato pieces and cook for two minutes to blend the mixture. At this point if the vegetables look too dry or uncooked, add ¼ cup of water and cook a bit longer. Adjust the seasoning to taste, and keep the pot covered for a few minutes before serving. Garnish with cilantro if you wish, and serve.

VARIATION: Instead of using thick-skinned russet potatoes, use thin-skinned red, yellow, or purple potatoes. Do not boil them. Cut the potatoes smaller, about the size of sugar cubes, and follow the above recipe. The sauce will be thinner and the resulting dish quite different from the above version.

CAULIFLOWER WITH PARBOILED POTATOES

3 tablespoons oil

½ teaspoon black mustard seeds

3 cloves of garlic, finely chopped or pressed

1 pound potatoes, parboiled until tender (not very soft), then cut into 1" cubes

1 medium cauliflower (about 1 pound), cut into small sections, discarding the thick center core

½ teaspoon each turmeric, cumin, and coriander powder

¼ teaspoon cayenne powder

1 teaspoon salt

1 to 1¼ cups water

Juice of 1 lemon or lime

Heat the oil in a pot over moderate heat, and add the mustard seeds. When the seeds begin to pop, add the garlic and allow it to brown a bit. Then add the potatoes and cauliflower pieces, and stir-fry for a minute to mix. Add the powdered spices and salt, and continue to cook, stirring frequently, for five minutes. Then add the water and turn the heat down. Cover and cook for 15 minutes. Then uncover and check to see if the vegetables are cooked and if there is enough sauce. If there is not enough liquid, add ¼ cup water and cook for five additional minutes, while stirring to make sure that the potatoes do not stick to the bottom. Sprinkle the lemon juice on top, and serve hot.

CAULIFLOWER WITH PARBOILED POTATOES AND TOMATO: Chunks of one green or ripe tomato can be added to the pot along with the cauliflower and potatoes. Omit the lemon or lime juice if you choose to use tomato.

BROCCOLI WITH PARBOILED POTATOES AND TOMATO: Substitute the broccoli flowerettes in place of the cauliflower and follow the above recipe. It takes a few minutes less to cook the broccoli than the cauliflower.

CAULIFLOWER AND EGGPLANT WITH THIN SAUCE

This vegetable dish produces a light, spicy, tangy sauce, suitable to serve along with a hearty *dal*.

1 medium cauliflower (about 1 lb.), cut up into small buds
1 unpeeled eggplant (about 1 lb.), cut into ½" cubes
½ teaspoon garlic/cayenne paste #1 (see page 39)
4 tablespoons oil
¼ teaspoon cumin seeds
½ teaspoon each turmeric and coriander powder
1 teaspoon salt
1 to 1¼ cup water
1 tomato, chopped into chunks
2 tablespoons fresh pomegranate seeds, or 1 tablespoon freshly squeezed lemon juice for garnish

Prepare the garlic paste and set it aside. Heat the oil in a pot, and add the cumin seeds. Sauté them for a minute, then add the cauliflower pieces. Stir-fry the mixture while adding the turmeric, coriander, and salt. After having stir-fried them for about five minutes, add ¼ cup of water, mix well, and lower the heat. Cover and cook for five to seven minutes to soften the cauliflower. Then uncover the pot, add the garlic paste and eggplant cubes, and stir-fry the mixture until well-blended. Add ¾ cup of water, raise the heat to medium, cover, and cook for another 10 minutes. By now the vegetables should be cooked. If they are swimming in too much water at this point (this sometimes happens when the vegetables are extremely fresh and juicy), stir-fry them for a few minutes to evaporate some of the excess liquid. (Conversely, if the vegetables are cooked but too dry at this point, add ¼ to ½ cup water, cover, and cook at low heat for five more minutes.) Turn off the heat, add the chopped tomato, and keep it covered for five minutes before serving. Adjust the seasoning to taste, and garnish with fresh pomegranate (when in season) or the lemon juice, and serve hot or at room temperature.

EGGPLANT WITH SNOW PEAS OR STRING BEANS: Use either of these two vegetables in place of the cauliflower in the above recipe. Cut beans into 2" pieces, and add them to the pot at the same time as the eggplant (since this combination will probably cook for the same amount of time). Trim the snow peas, but leave them whole, and add them to the pot for the final five minutes of cooking eggplants.

GHISODA OR *DOODHI*
OR ANY TYPE OF QUICK-COOKING
SQUASH WITH TOMATO

This recipe can use the bumpy, scaly squash called *ghisoda* or the large, long, light green gourd called *doodhi* or *ghia* in India. Any American summer squash, such as zucchini or sunburst squash, can also be used for this recipe. The tamarind used in this recipe makes a light sweet-and-sour sauce.

1 medium *ghia* or *doodhi* (about 1 lb.), top removed, peeled, and cubed into ½" pieces,

or 3 *ghisoda* (about a pound) tops removed, peeled, and cut into ½" cubes,

or 4 small zucchini or crookneck squash, tops removed, scrubbed cleaned, and cut into ½" cubes

1 tablespoon tamarind paste prepared from compressed tamarind or 1 tablespoon of fresh tamarind paste (see pages 40-41)

or a mixture of 1 tablespoon each brown sugar and freshly squeezed lemon juice

3 tablespoons of oil

½ teaspoon black mustard seeds

4 garlic cloves, finely chopped

¼ teaspoon each cumin, coriander, and turmeric powder

½ to ¾ cup water

1 small tomato

cayenne and salt to taste

Cut the squash according to the instructions in the list of ingredients at left. Set them aside. Soak and prepare the tamarind according to the directions given on pages 40-41. Set it aside. Heat the oil in a saucepan over moderate heat, and add the mustard seeds. When the seeds start popping, add garlic and brown it lightly. Immediately add the squash pieces, and stir-fry continuously for about three minutes. Add the powdered spices, the well-blended tamarind pulp (or the sugar and lemon juice mixture), and ½ cup water. Cover and cook for 10 minutes until the squash is soft and some sauce has formed. If the water is almost absorbed, add an additional ¼ cup of water, and cook for one more minute. Add the tomato pieces, salt, and cayenne. Adjust the seasoning to taste, and serve hot.

NORTH INDIAN *NAVARATAN SHAK* AND
SOUTH INDIAN *AVIYAL*

This mixed vegetable dish is an excellent
choice for a festive occasion or party, since it
contains a colorful variety of vegetables. And
everyone is sure to find something they like
in this dish. In the North, I believe, restaurants
popularized this dish by coining it *navaratan*
which literally means "nine jewels," although
the number of vegetables do not really count.
In the South, a similar mixed vegetable dish,
called *aviyal*, is prepared with fresh coconut.

NAVARATAN SHAK

1 cup potatoes, cut into ½" cubes
1 cup eggplant, cut into ½" cubes
1 cup cauliflower or broccoli flower buds,
    separated from the stems (thick stems
    can be cubed too)
1 cup celery, sliced
1 cup carrots, cut into ½" cubes
1 cup string beans or snow peas, cut into
    1" pieces
1 large tomato, cut into small chunks
½ large onion, chopped finely
5 cloves of garlic, minced
1 large red or green bell pepper, finely
    chopped
¼ cup oil, or less if you wish
1 teaspoon black mustard seeds
½ teaspoon each turmeric, coriander,
    cumin, and *garam masala* (or more for a
    spicier dish)
1 tablespoon grated gingerroot
1 to 1½ teaspoons salt

Juice of 1 lemon or lime
2 tablespoons chopped cilantro sprigs for
    garnish

Cut all the vegetables as instructed in the
list of ingredients. Set them aside *separately* as
they will go into the pot at different stages.
In a large pot, heat the oil and add the mustard
seeds, stirring until they pop. Add the onion
and garlic, and sauté for several minutes until
they turn translucent. Add the bell pepper and
stir-fry for another minute. Now the orchestra
of vegetables will start. The potatoes are stir-
fried for a minute, then the cauliflower or
broccoli pieces and the eggplant. The mixture
is stir-fried for few more minutes, this time
with the addition of ¼ cup of water. Next, the
heat gets reduced to low, and our vegetables
simmer quietly, covered for ten minutes or so.
Then the pot opens and the rest of the vegetables (except for the tomato) go in to play
their parts. Dress them all up by sprinkling the
powdered spices, grated gingerroot, and salt.
Add 1 cup of water. Cover and cook them
again for a full fifteen minutes. Then add the
tomato chunks, and gently stir all the
vegetables until well blended. Adjust the
seasoning to taste. Accent the dish by
sprinkling on lemon juice and throwing some
cilantro sprigs on top before serving.

NAVARATAN CREAMY SHAK: A creamy
sauce is produced for this dish by using 1 cup
of yogurt in place of the tomato chunks and
cooking a few minutes longer for the yogurt
to blend in. (Omit the lemon juice.)

SOUTH INDIAN *AVIYAL*

In the south of India where root vegetables flourish, regional vegetables add a flavor to this mixed vegetable dish. A distinct variety of locally grown and seasonal root vegetables (such as turnips or sunchokes) can be used to make your version. In this recipe, vegetables are cooked in larger pieces than in North Indian *navaratan*.

2 medium yams, scrubbed or peeled and
    cut into ¾" pieces
2 carrots, sliced into ½" rounds
2 russet potatoes, peeled and cut into
    ½" cubes
2 turnips, rutabaga, or beets, cut into small
    ¼" cubes
1 cup string beans or snow peas, cut into
    1" long pieces
2 zucchini or yellow crook neck squash,
    sliced into ½" rounds
1 cup fresh peas, shelled, or frozen peas,
    thawed and drained
¼ cup vegetable oil
½ cup onion, finely chopped
1 teaspoon each turmeric and salt
3 to 4 tablespoons water
2 fresh hot chiles, center core and seeds
    removed, then minced
½ cup fresh or dry, grated unsweetened
    coconut
1 cup water
Curry leaves to garnish (optional)

Place all of the yam, carrot, potato, and turnip pieces in a steamer basket, and cook them until soft but not mushy. Set them aside. Cut the remaining vegetables, and set them aside separately. In a large pot, heat the oil over moderate heat, and cook the onion until translucent. Add the second group of vegetables to the pot, and stir-fry for a few minutes, adding the turmeric and the salt. Add a few tablespoons of water, cover, and cook over low heat for five minutes. Then uncover, add the steamed root vegetables, and stir-fry for a minute. Add the minced chiles, coconut, and remaining water. Cover and slow cook for about ½ hour, checking after the first 15 minutes to see if more liquid is required to give the *aviyal* a nice, thick sauce. Adjust the seasoning to taste, and serve with a few fresh curry leaves as a topping, if available.

BAKED EGGPLANT WITH YOGURT SAUCE
(*OLA*)

1 large globular eggplant (about 1 lb.),
or 4 small, Japanese-style eggplants (about
  1 lb.)

¼ cup unflavored yogurt or soy yogurt,
or 2 tablespoons lemon juice

¼ cup water

¼ teaspoon each of turmeric, cumin, and
  coriander powder

⅛ teaspoon cayenne powder

3 tablespoon oil

4 cloves of garlic, minced

A few pinches of *hing*

1 teaspoon salt

2 tablespoons of chopped cilantro or
  parsley for garnish

Preheat the oven to 350°F. Bake the large eggplant for about 40 minutes until the skin looks all wrinkled and the eggplant has lost its shape. Japanese eggplants will only take 20 to 25 minutes to bake. Small eggplants can also be roasted over an open burner while turning, until all sides are charred and the skin can be easily peeled. Check to see if the inside of the eggplant is baked enough by piercing the flesh with a fork. Remove the baked eggplant from the oven carefully using an oven mitt, since it may pop open while you are handling it. Set the baked or roasted eggplant aside, and allow it to cool.

In a mixing bowl, blend the yogurt (or the soy yogurt or lemon juice) with the water. Set the mixture aside. If the eggplant is cool enough to handle by now, peel the charred skin off, and remove the green top. Place the eggplant in a bowl, and mash it with the powdered spices using a fork until it becomes a smooth pulp. A tough eggplant may need to be cut up into small pieces using a knife before mashing. (Do not use a blender or food processor to do this.)

In a heavy, shallow frying pan, heat the oil and add the garlic. Stir until light brown and then add the optional *hing*. Stir in the eggplant pulp, and sauté for five minutes. Add the salt and the yogurt/water mixture, and continue to stir-fry for a few more minutes. Then cover and cook at a low heat for 10 minutes. By now the eggplant will be well blended with the sour ingredients. Adjust the seasoning to taste, and serve lots of cilantro or parsley as a garnish.

PRECOOKED VEGETABLES IN A SAUCE

I have included in this grouping a few recipes in which the sauce for the vegetables is cooked separately and combined with the vegetables later. The sauce can be made ahead of time and the vegetables assembled right before serving. Breaking the process into two steps like this makes it more practical for busy homemakers, although in India the sauce is usually made the same day due to a general lack of refrigeration.

First, prepare the recipe for the sauce you are choosing (from Chapter Three). Prepare the vegetables just before you're ready to assemble them.

STEAMED CAULIFLOWER WITH CREAM SAUCE

This is a restaurant-style recipe which I learned from a chef on my trip to Udaypur, a picturesque city in North India. The sauce (the secret of this recipe) is found on page 43 and can be used for other steamed vegetables, such as a small head of broccoli.

1 small head of cauliflower (about ½ lb.)
2 cups or more of Indian Cream Sauce
    (see page 43), depending on the size of
    cauliflower
Few sprigs of cilantro or parsley for
    garnish

Remove the outer leaves and 1" from the bottom stem of the cauliflower. Place in a small pot with one cup of water. Cover and cook for only 10 minutes, so that it is half cooked and the buds are not falling apart. You can also use a large vegetable steamer to do this, but a covered saucepan will work fine. Set the cauliflower head in a pretty bowl that is ovenproof. Then make the cream sauce. Pour it over the cauliflower so that it is almost all covered. Keep the bowl covered until ready to serve. Bake the cauliflower at 350°F for a few minutes if it is not cooked through enough. Garnish with cilantro and serve the cauliflower head uncut; it will look beautiful. Instruct your dinner guests to cut the dish as they share it.

SQUASH *KOFTA* WITH TOMATO SAUCE

Koftas are small balls (from cherry-sized to as big as a walnut) made with shredded or minced vegetables and chick-pea flour, or a dough made from *dal* (split beans). Then, the balls are usually deep-fried. Vegetables that blend well with *besan* are shredded carrots and zucchini or minced leafy greens. Deep-fried *kofta* can be served piping hot as an appetizer with a *chutney* or a *raita*, but this sauce makes them an elegant entree.

½ lb. *doodhi* (*opo*) squash or zucchini
1 cup *besan* (chick-pea or garbanzo flour)
⅛ teaspoon *ajowan* or cumin seeds
¼ teaspoon cayenne,
  or 1 small, hot chile, seeds and veins
    removed and then minced
Juice of ½ lemon
½ teaspoon salt
1 cup of oil for deep-frying *kofta*
2 cups of any tomato sauce
For a garnish, either 1 tablespoon chopped
    cilantro or parsley,
  or 1 teaspoon sesame seeds,
  or 2 fresh scallions, minced with their
    greens and white tops

If you are using the Indian *doodhi* for this recipe, peel it thoroughly and then shred using a cheese grater. The zucchini does not need to be peeled before shredding. Mix the shredded vegetables with rest of the ingredients for *kofta*. Knead the *kofta* mixture into a dough by adding more bean flour and/or by squeezing out some of the liquid from the vegetables. Then moisten your hands with oil. Take one small piece of dough at a time and, using the hollow space of your palms, form the dough into a ball. Repeat the process until all the dough is used up. Set aside on a platter. Then heat the oil in a small pot or a wok, and deep-fry a couple of balls until they are golden brown on all sides. After a few minutes, the oil will be hot enough so that six to eight balls can be easily fried at once. Remove the fried *koftas* from the oil using a slotted spoon. Drain and set them aside. When ready to serve, heat the sauce and add the *kofta*. Cook over a low heat for a few minutes, stirring carefully so as not to break too many *koftas*. Garnish with your choice of toppings and serve.

CARROT *KOFTA*: Make the *kofta* using ½ pound of carrots in place of the zucchini

SWEET & SOUR *KOFTA*: Combine ¼ cup shredded, coconut, 1 tablespoon tamarind paste (see page 40), and ½ cup watercress with 1 cup of *besan* to form the *kofta*.

DAL *KOFTA*: Soak ⅓ cup each **skinned** *mung dal*, *masoor dal*, and *chana dal* in two cups of water in separate bowls for at least five hours. Then rinse and pulverize them, using enough water to form a thick, wet, cornmeal-like batter. Use this batter in place of the water and *besan* mixture. Then add 2 cups of shredded vegetables and spices, and make the *kofta* balls. You may have to add a few tablespoons of any kind of flour to make the balls stick together. Follow rest of the recipe.

PANEER AND KOFTA CURRY

This is an elegant dish impressive enough to delight any dinner guests, although it requires a four-step process to prepare. You first need to make the *paneer* (or purchase tofu, to cut down on one step and make it vegan). Next, make the tomato sauce. Then make the *kofta* balls, and fry them. Cook the balls with the sauce briefly, and serve.

2 cups of Basic Tomato Sauce (see pages 41-42)
½ cup *paneer* curds (see page 35),
  or ½ cup firm tofu, crumbled and mashed
½ cup *besan* (chick-pea or garbanzo flour)
½ cup cornmeal
⅛ teaspoon *ajowan*, caraway, or cumin seeds
3 cloves of garlic, minced
1 minced hot chile, seeds and central core removed
1 teaspoon salt
1 cup oil for deep-frying *kofta*
2 tablespoons chopped parsley or cilantro

Prepare the tomato sauce and keep it warm in a pot. Have the crumbled and mashed *paneer* or tofu ready in a mixing bowl, then add *the besan*, cornmeal, spice seeds, garlic, chiles, and salt. Knead briefly and form into compact, lime-sized balls, using the oiled palms of your hands. Set them aside. Heat the oil in a saucepan or wok, and deep-fry the balls until they are golden on all sides. Remove the fried balls and drain completely. Set them aside. (The balls can also be served now as an appetizer or as a tea snack with a thin chutney.) Add the balls to the sauce, and cook gently for about five minutes until the balls swell and become porous. Sprinkle on the garnish and serve the *kofta* hot.

MATAR PANEER

Matar paneer can be roughly translated as "peas and cheese." It is made with peas, a homemade cheese called *paneer*, and spicy tomato sauce. Although cheese is not a common food item outside the northern Punjabi region of India, most Indian people love to order when dining out in fancy restaurants, where it is almost always served. In America, this entree is hearty enough to be accepted as a "main dish" among meat-eaters, so I serve it with any dinner I cater when the crowd is not vegetarian.

1 cup *paneer* cubes or balls (see page 35)
2 cups Basic Tomato Sauce (see pages 41-42)
1 cup fresh shelled peas, or frozen peas, thawed and drained
Few sprigs of cilantro for garnish

First, make the *paneer*. While the *paneer* is setting, prepare the tomato sauce. Shell or thaw the peas, and set them aside. Add the fresh peas to the sauce, and cook for five minutes. Then, add the prepared *paneer* to the sauce, and cook for a few more minutes until all the ingredients are well mixed, but do not mash the cheese or peas. If using frozen peas, add them to the sauce at the same time as the *paneer* pieces. Garnish and serve hot. This dish can be easily reheated in an oven at 350°F for a few minutes before serving.

MATAR TOFU

Faster to make than *matar paneer*, this vegan dish can be made within an hour, especially if frozen peas are used. With all the pungent spices going into the sauce, you are unlikely to miss the cheese.

1 tablespoon oil
1 cup firm tofu, cut into ½" cubes
2 cups Basic Tomato Sauce (pages 41-42)
1 cup fresh shelled peas, or frozen peas, thawed and drained
A few sprigs of cilantro, for garnish

Heat the oil in a frying pan, and fry the tofu cubes, turning frequently to cook them until light brown. This brief cooking will help the tofu keep its shape while cooking in the sauce. Set them aside. Make the sauce and add the fresh peas; cover and cook them for five to seven minutes. Then add the tofu cubes, and cook the mixture for a few more minutes until all the ingredients are well-mixed with the sauce. If you are using frozen peas, add them to the sauce at the same time as the tofu. Garnish with the ciiantro and serve.

MATAR PANEER OR *MATAR TOFU* WITH POTATOES: Parboil one potato. Peel and cube and add to the *matar paneer* at the same time as the *paneer* or tofu. The potatoes will help extend the dish if you don't have enough tofu or *paneer*.

STUFFED VEGETABLES

Indian-style stuffed vegetables are somewhat different from the stuffed vegetables you may be familiar with. In the following recipes, the vegetables are not hollowed out when stuffed with the reserved pulp going in the stuffing. Rather, spices and flour or seeds are combined, the vegetables are split open, and the seasoned mixture is spooned inside the vegetables to expand their cavity. Some of these stuffed vegetables turn out "dry," and some are cooked with liquid, in which case the overflowing stuffing mixes with the spices and vegetable juices and makes a deliciously thick sauce.

STUFFED MUSHROOMS

4 tablespoons oil
¾ cup *besan* (chick-pea or garbanzo flour)
¼ teaspoon black mustard seeds
¼ teaspoon each cumin, coriander, and cayenne powder
1 or 2 finely chopped garlic cloves, or a few pinches of garlic powder
1 teaspoon salt
1 tablespoon lemon juice
¼ teaspoon turmeric powder
3 to 4 tablespoons water
24 to 30 large button mushrooms

To prepare the stuffing, toast the *besan* with some of the oil and spices; this is tricky because it is easy to burn it or make it lumpy. Choose a heavy iron pan, and heat 2 tablespoons of oil. Add the mustard seeds and when they have finished popping, add the *besan* and turn the heat to low. Stir the flour continuously with a wooden spoon, adding the powdered spices and the salt. When the flour begins to turn reddish in color, it is cooked enough for stuffing. Immediately transfer it to a mixing bowl, since the very hot pan will continue to cook and burn the flour. When the *besan* is cooled enough to handle, add the lemon juice and turmeric, and mix well. Then add the water, one tablespoon at a time, breaking any lumps that may have formed until you have a crumbly, moist stuffing.

Wash and clean the mushrooms, and then dry them. Remove the stems from the mushrooms to create the cavity for stuffing. (The stems can be used in other vegetable or *dal* dishes). Fill each mushroom with ½ teaspoon or less of stuffing, and set them upside down on a platter.

Heat the rest of the oil in a frying pan, and gently place the mushrooms in with the stuffing facing upwards. Try not to over-crowd the mushrooms. Cook the mushrooms for a few minutes, stirring gently. Then turn the mushrooms so that the side with the stuffing can get cooked. If they seem too dry, sprinkle a few spoons of water on the mushrooms as they are cooking. Cook the mushrooms for few minutes until the stuffing side is light brown.

STUFFED MUSHROOMS WITH READY-MADE TOASTED GARBANZO FLOUR: Some health food stores or ethnic shops sell already toasted and spiced garbanzo meal for making hummus or falafel. If you happen to find this ingredient, it can be used for making the stuffing by adding a bit of water and oil without toasting or adding any spices.

STUFFED OKRA

1 pound fresh okra
½ cup *besan* (chick-pea or garbanzo flour)
¼ teaspoon each coriander, cumin, and
   cayenne powder
¼ teaspoon dry garlic granules,
or 3 cloves minced fresh garlic
½ teaspoon salt
4 tablespoons oil
½ teaspoon mustard seeds
2 tablespoons yogurt or lemon juice
½ teaspoon turmeric powder
¼ teaspoon salt

Clean the okra using a moist towel instead of washing them under running water. Then pat them dry. Remove the tops from the okra. Place the *besan* in a mixing bowl with the powdered spices, garlic, salt, and two tablespoons of oil. Mix the ingredients until they are well-blended and look like a moist, flaky stuffing. Take the okra, one at a time, and make a lengthwise slit down through to the center of the pod to form a "pocket" for the stuffing. Hold the okra open by inserting a thumb in the pod with one hand (as shown in the illustration) while stuffing with the other hand. Do not overstuff the okra or they will break in half. Set the okra pods aside.

Heat the remaining 2 tablespoons of oil in a heavy frying pan or a griddle, and add the mustard seeds. When the seeds start popping, add the stuffed okra and allow them to cook over a low heat while turning them from side to side to cook the entire surface of the pods. After cooking for about 10 minutes, add the yogurt or lemon juice, turmeric, and salt. Stir-fry for 7 to 10 minutes or longer until all the liquid is used up and the okra look browned and somewhat wrinkled. Serve the okra hot. Okra can be reheated in an oven preheated to 300°F for a few minutes before serving.

OKRA STUFFED WITH SESAME SEEDS: Make a stuffing blending ¼ cup coarsely ground sesame seeds with the above spices. Use less stuffing for each pod, and follow the above recipe.

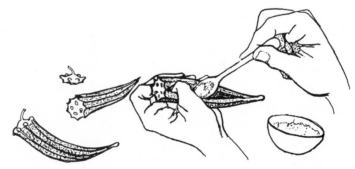

STUFFED EGGPLANTS: *GUJARATI* AND SOUTH INDIAN-STYLE

Here is a popular Indian dish made two different ways, creating entirely two different "curries." In the Gujarati-style recipe, small eggplants are stuffed with garbanzo flour and spices. In the southern style, they are stuffed with coconut, tamarind, and other spices.

GUJARATI-STYLE STUFFED EGGPLANTS

Stuffing

1 teaspoon garlic paste #2 (see page 40)
¾ cup *besan* (chick-pea or garbanzo flour)
1 teaspoon salt
2 tablespoons oil

Eggplant and Other Ingredients

4 to 5 long, Japanese-style eggplants, with
    tops removed
3 tablespoons oil
½ teaspoon mustard seeds
¼ teaspoon each turmeric, cayenne, and
    cumin powder
1½ cups water, well blended with 1
    tablespoon lemon juice (for the dairy-
    free version),
or 1 cup water, well-blended with 1 cup
    unflavored yogurt
½ teaspoon or to taste salt
Few sprigs of cilantro for garnish

Have the garlic paste ready according to the directions given on page 40. Place all the ingredients from the first group in a mixing bowl. Blend them well and set the stuffing aside.

If the eggplants are longer than six inches, cut them in half through the widest part (*not lengthwise*). Then slit each eggplant (or eggplant half) up to the center as illustrated. Hold the slit open with one hand (see illustration) while using the other hand to fill each piece with a teaspoon of stuffing. Do not overstuff or else the eggplant will split. Set the stuffed eggplants and the leftover stuffing aside.

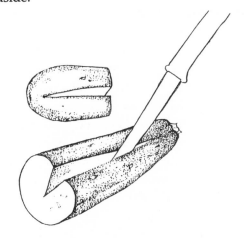

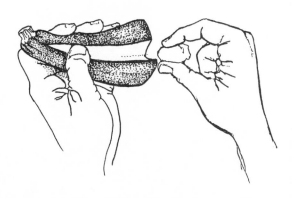

Heat the 3 tablespoons of oil in a saucepan, and add the mustard seeds. When they pop, add the stuffed eggplant but not the leftover stuffing. Stir the stuffed eggplants gently, or cover and shake them from time to time. Cook in this manner for five minutes. Then open the lid and add the powdered spices and the salt, and stir-fry for another minute. Add the water and lemon juice mixture for the dairy-free version, or the yogurt and water mixture. Add the leftover stuffing, cover, and cook for five minutes. Then open and stir the mixture thoroughly. The *besan* tends to stick to the bottom of the pan, so you need to stir this dish every five minutes or so. Cook for 20 to 25 minutes or longer, or until the eggplants look cooked and limp but not broken apart and the sauce has formed a nice, thick gravy. Garnish with sprigs of cilantro and serve.

You can also bake this dish, which will tend to make the eggplants softer. Follow the recipe as above up to the step where you would add the leftover stuffing. Then transfer the dish into an oven-proof casserole with a cover. Bake it in an oven preheated to 350°F for 20 to 25 minutes, checking every few minutes to see that the stuffing does not stick to the bottom.

STUFFED *GUJARATI* EGGPLANTS WITH ZUCCHINI, CROOKNECK SQUASH, AND PEPPERS: Use 2 small Japanese-style eggplants, 2 small zucchinis, 2 small crookneck yellow squash, and 1 small red, green, or yellow bell pepper. Remove the tops from the eggplants and the squashes. Cut the peppers into halves, and remove the core and seeds. Fill vegetables with stuffing as described above, and follow rest of the recipe.

STUFFED EGGPLANTS, SOUTH INDIA-STYLE

Stuffing

½ cup fresh, shredded coconut,

or ½ cup dry, unsweetened, shredded coconut, soaked in soaked in 2 tablespoons of warm water for 10 minutes

2 tablespoons tamarind paste (see page 40)

½ teaspoon each cayenne, cumin powder, and salt

1 teaspoon sugar or honey

1 teaspoon oil

2 to 3 cloves of minced garlic

Eggplants and Other Ingredients

4 to 5 small, Japanese-style eggplants, tops removed

3 tablespoons oil

½ teaspoon brown or black mustard seeds

½ teaspoon each turmeric, cayenne, and salt

½ cup water

1 teaspoon or more sugar or honey (opt.)

Fresh cilantro for garnish

Have the shredded coconut and tamarind paste ready in advance. Combine all the ingredients listed in the first grouping for the stuffing in a mixing bowl, and set aside. Cut the eggplants into two pieces the wide way, and slit each eggplant piece lengthwise up to the center as illustrated on page 103. Then hold the slit open with one hand, while using the other hand to fill each piece with a teaspoon of the stuffing. If the stuffing seems too wet, squeeze the excess liquid out, and reserve it for cooking the eggplants.

Place the 3 tablespoons of oil in a saucepan over moderate heat, and add the mustard seeds. When they start popping, carefully add the stuffed eggplants. Gently stir them for five to seven minutes. Then add the turmeric, salt, cayenne, and water. Also add the reserved liquid from the stuffing, if any. Cover and cook for 15 to 20 minutes, checking frequently so that nothing sticks to the bottom and there is enough liquid left in the pot to allow for sufficient sauce. Add a few more tablespoons of water, if needed, and cook a few minutes longer. Within half an hour or so, the eggplants should be soft and ready, but not falling apart. Taste the sauce to adjust the seasoning. Add a bit of sugar or honey if it is too tart for you. Transfer the eggplants to a serving dish, garnish with cilantro, to taste, and serve.

STUFFED *KARELAS*

Karelas are an acquired taste, since they are very bitter. Some Indian children pride themselves in being old enough to enjoy this "adult" food. *Karelas* are considered very health-promoting in Indian food folklore. Therefore, numerous ways to tame them have been developed in different regions. Here is one.

6 to 8 *karelas* (bitter melons)
2 teaspoons salt for "curing" the *karelas* (most of this will rinse off later)

Stuffing
1 pound potatoes, boiled until soft, and peeled
4 tablespoons oil
¼ onion, chopped
¼ teaspoon each cumin, coriander, cayenne, and turmeric powder
½ teaspoon salt
A few pinches of garlic powder
Juice of 1 lemon
3 tablespoons brown sugar or honey
3 tablespoons water

Remove the bumpy scales from the *karelas* by peeling them thoroughly. Then cut a slit lengthwise up to the center of each *karela*, and scoop out most of the seeds and some of the fibers from the center. Sprinkle the salt all over the inner cavity and the outside of the *karela*. Do not worry about the amount of salt used here; most of this will rinse off later. Set the *karelas* aside while preparing the stuffing.

Boil the potatoes, then peel and mash them completely. Heat 2 tablespoons of oil, and add the onion. When onion is translucent, add the mashed potatoes, cumin, coriander, cayenne, turmeric, and salt. Set the stuffing aside.

Rinse the salt off the *karelas* by washing them thoroughly under running water. Wring out the liquid from each *karela*, and dry them. Stuff each *karela* with a tablespoon of potato stuffing. Tie each karela with a sewing thread so the stuffing does not fall out, and set aside. Heat the remaining 2 tablespoons of oil in a wide saucepan. Place the stuffed *karelas* in the pan, and fry them gently for five minutes, turning them from time to time. Sprinkle the garlic powder, lemon juice, brown sugar, and water on top of the cooking *karelas*. Then cover the pot and cook the *karelas* over low heat for 10 to 15 minutes, until they appear soft and most of the liquid is used up. Remove the threads and serve.

RAITAS AND OTHER RAW VEGETABLE SALADS

Raitas are some of the only traditional Indian dishes that contain raw vegetables. Serving raw produce is uncommon in India, because cooking is one of the main ways of ridding food of harmful bacteria. A *raita* is a yogurt-based dish that is usually served to accompany and impart added flavor to a snack or a main dish. It is not an entree by itself. It is generally served in a small container—about ½ cup per person—a slightly larger portion than a *chutney*.

Most *raitas* contain *rai* (mustard seeds), yogurt or sour cream, and a vegetable or fruit. Traditionally, a powder of black (or brown) mustard seeds, which is available in Indian grocery shops, is used as the main spice for *raita*. For me, any good quality dry or wet mustard, such as Dijon mustard, works well. I have also created some non-dairy *raitas* using soft tofu. Here are some quick *raita* recipes perfect for all occasions. They are especially delightful on a hot day.

CUCUMBER *RAITA*

This is the most common of all *raitas* found on restaurant menus. Outside India, be creative and use other local and seasonal cucumber-like vegetables, such as zucchini, crookneck squash, and celery.

2 cups unflavored yogurt
½ cup water,
or a blend of 1 cup yogurt and 1 cup buttermilk
1 large or 2 small cucumbers,
or 2-3 pickling cucumbers
½ teaspoon salt
⅛ teaspoon mustard powder,
or ½ teaspoon wet Dijon mustard
¼ teaspoon cumin powder
2 teaspoons minced cilantro
A few pinches of cayenne (optional)

Beat the yogurt with water (or buttermilk), and set aside. Peel the cucumbers and cut them into slices. Cut most of the slices into small cubes, reserving a few rounds for a garnish. In a mixing bowl, combine the beaten yogurt, cucumber cubes, salt, mustard, and cumin. Transfer to a serving bowl; decorate with the cucumber circles, and garnish with cilantro and the optional cayenne. Chill and serve.

VEGAN *RAITA*: Puree 1 cup of soft silken tofu with 3 tablespoons of oil using a blender or food processor, and substitute for the yogurt mixture.

EXTRA CREAMY *RAITA*: Beat 1 cup of buttermilk with 1 cup of sour cream for a *raita* with an extra-rich flavor.

RADISH *RAITA*

Here is one *raita* that does not need the *rai* (mustard) because the spiciness of the grated radish is similar to that of mustard.

1 cup grated radish (either the long, white Indian variety or the common red radish)
2 cups unflavored yogurt
¼ teaspoon cumin
1 teaspoon salt
A few radish slices and chopped radish leaves for garnish

Grate the radishes, saving some for a garnish. Blend the yogurt with the cumin and salt, and mix in the grated radish. Transfer to a serving dish, and decorate the surface with slices of radish and a few radish leaves. Chill and serve.

CARROT AND CABBAGE *RAITA*

This is a colorful combination of green cabbage and orange carrot shreds swimming in a pool of white yogurt, slightly tanned by the mustard—a kind of Indian coleslaw.

3 cups plain yogurt blended with ½ cup water
1 cup grated carrot
1 cup shredded green cabbage
⅛ teaspoon each cumin, cayenne, and mustard powder,
or ½ teaspoon wet mustard
1 tablespoon cilantro or parsley leaves for garnish

Combine all the ingredients in a mixing bowl, and blend well. Transfer to a serving bowl, garnish with cilantro or parsley, and chill before serving.

BANANA *RAITA*

2 cups unflavored yogurt blended with ½ cup water
1 or 2 ripe bananas, peeled and sliced thinly
⅛ teaspoon mustard powder,
or ½ teaspoon or less good-quality wet mustard
½ teaspoon salt
A few pinches of cayenne

Combine all the ingredients in a mixing bowl. Chill and serve.

RAITA WITH COOKED POTATOES

2 cups of potatoes, boiled, peeled, and cut
    into 1" cubes
2 cups of yogurt, well-blended with ¼ cup
    water
¼ teaspoon or less mustard powder,
or ½ teaspoon wet mustard
1 teaspoon or less salt
½ teaspoon cumin powder
1 tablespoon chopped cilantro for a garnish

Allow the potato pieces to cool completely. Then mix all the ingredients in a bowl, and chill. Top with cilantro and serve.

VARIATION: Another way to make this *raita* is to make a *vaghar* first by placing 1 tablespoon oil in a pot and frying ½ teaspoon whole cumin seeds. Add a few teaspoons minced onion, and cook for a few minutes, then add the boiled and cubed potatoes. Fry for a few minutes, and set aside to cool completely. Then add the yogurt, mustard, and salt. Mix thoroughly, chill, and top with the cilantro to garnish.

KACHUMBER

Kachumber is the Indian version of salad—vegetables prepared to serve raw. Leafy green salads are not part of traditional Indian menus.

2 big tomatoes, cut into wedges
1 large cucumber, peeled and sliced
6 scallions, chopped with their greens
Juice of 1 lemon or lime
Salt and freshly ground black pepper

Mix the vegetables in a salad bowl. Sprinkle the lemon juice and add the salt and pepper to taste. Serve cold.

VARIATION: To deviate slightly from this traditional *kachumber*, add a few carrots and celery sticks.

CHAPTER SIX
DALS AND BEAN-BASED DISHES

The word *dal* (also spelled *daal, dahl,* or *dhal*) literally means "split lentil," but it has come to include the important, soup-like preparation that is made from split or whole lentils or beans. No Indian meal would be complete without a *dal. Dals* contribute greatly to the Indian vegetarian diet, since they are a great source of protein, vitamins, and minerals.

Split beans and lentils cook much faster than whole beans, which is why, perhaps, this particular method of milling was invented. Also, split beans make a creamier soup and blend well with the vegetables and spices that they are often prepared with. Sometimes, the lentils (or beans) are available without skins, so you can buy split mung with or without the skin, depending on the recipe you need it for. Uncooked beans, lentils, and their flours (such as *besan*) are also used for making batter, dough, and for stuffing in Indian cooking.

Red lentils, known as *masoor dal* in India, and split mung beans (*mung dal*) are easily found in health food stores or in the ethnic food section of large supermarkets. Whole brown lentils, split green or yellow peas, and whole mung beans can also be used for *dal* preparations. Visit Indian specialty stores for other popular Indian *dals* and beans such as *chana dal,* (split garbanzo beans) *toor dal, urad dal,* and others.

One word of warning regarding imported lentils. All beans should be carefully looked through to remove any foreign objects such as stones, twigs, and the like. In India, women often make a social gathering out of this task after purchasing a quantity of *dal*. The ladies gather around in a circle with a *thali* full of *dal* on their laps, cleaning the *dal*, while exchanging gossip or singing a folk melody. Nothing spoils the flavor of a cooked *dal* more than nearly breaking a tooth on a pebble that was left in it.

The consistency of prepared *dal* varies according to its use in the menu, as well as from region to region and kitchen to kitchen. A *dal* can be like a clear broth as in South Indian *rasam* or a thick gruel like Punjabi *chole*. Often is it more like a hearty soup as in *sambhar*. Choose the *dal* recipe that will complement other items in your menu. Some *dals*, like *masoor dal*, can be served as a light entree, whereas the others, such as *dal dhokali*, can be hearty enough to make a meal by itself. Use a varying amount of water to create the consistency you desire. At any rate, unlike other bean dishes which require hours of soaking and cooking, most *dals* can be prepared in about an hour from beginning to end. The *dal* can be simmering on the back burner while you are making the rest of the meal. Or the *dal* can be prepared way ahead of time, since reheated *dal* tastes as good as fresh *dal*.

Prepared *dals* are usually served in individual bowls so that each person can decide how much *dal* he or she wants to mix with each dish. Mostly, *dal* is eaten in combination with other foods, however, the order in which the *dal* is eaten during a meal depends on regional

custom, the menu plan, and individual preference. For example, in many Gujarati homes, rice and *dal* are served as a second course, after the vegetables and bread course. In the South, *dal* is often served together with vegetables and rice. The *dal* can also be eaten straight from the bowl and served as a first course, much in the same manner as soup.

The last step in *dal* making, known as *vaghar* in Indian cookery, sets this dish apart from most other soup-like preparations. In a very small pot (a metal measuring cup or a butter warmer will work fine), a teaspoon of oil is heated with black mustard seeds. When the seeds start popping, whole dried chiles are added. Soon the hot oil will begin to smoke. Very quickly, a pinch of *hing* (asafetida) is added to this oil, the contents of the small pot are added to the *dal*, and the soup pot is covered right away. The whole process is done very quickly, in a minute or so. Adding the smoky oil to the *dal* pot releases vapors of the hot chiles, so it is important not to open the soup pot for a few minutes, so the *vaghar* can "settle" into the *dal*. The "choom" sound of the hot oil hitting the soup pot contents announces to everyone that the *dal* is done.

Before serving, the *dal* is stirred thoroughly to mix in the *vaghar* spices. The whole dry chile pieces can be removed at this point, because they are very hot to bite into. Alternatively, keep the chiles in the dal if you want a spicier dish, but instruct your dinner guests to remove the chiles from their individual portions.

MASOOR DAL

This bright, orange-red lentil is easily found in many ethnic stores. Red lentils cook quickly into a creamy *dal* within 35 to 45 minutes.

1 cup red lentils (*masoor dal*)
5 cups water
1 teaspoon salt
¼ teaspoon each turmeric, coriander, and cumin powder
1 tablespoon finely grated gingerroot
1 teaspoon hot green chile (such as jalapeño or Anaheim), minced after removing the core and seeds
1 tablespoon oil
½ teaspoon black mustard seeds
2 dried hot red chiles, broken in half and most seeds removed
Pinch of *hing*
Juice of ½ lemon or lime
1 tablespoon chopped fresh cilantro leaves

Wash the lentils and drain; set aside. Boil the water and add the lentils. After the water starts to boil again, cook the *dal* uncovered for five minutes. Then turn the heat down to moderate, cover, and cook for about 15 minutes. Next, add the salt, the powdered spices, gingerroot, and minced chile. Cook for another ten minutes until the lentils are quite soft. You may use a whisk to break down the beans at this point. Cook the *dal* over low heat while preparing the next step.

To make a *vaghar*, heat the oil in a small saucepan. Add the mustard seeds. When they finish popping, add the broken chile pieces.

Add the pinch of *hing* and quickly add this oil mixture to the pot of *dal*. Cover the lid right away, so that the vapor from the smoky, hot oil does not fill up the kitchen. Turn off the heat. Keep covered for at least five minutes; this will allow the hot oil to settle on the surface of the *dal*, leaving a spicy veneer. Then uncover, add the lemon or lime juice, and adjust the seasoning to taste. Serve with chopped cilantro. The whole, dried chile pieces can be removed before serving, since you do not want your dinner guests to bite into them; they are very hot. You can also instruct them to remove the chile pieces from their individual portions.

KHATA MUNG (SOUR MUNG)

Mung beans are one of the world's oldest foods. When Buddhist monks journeyed to China from India to spread the teachings of Buddha, they took mung beans with them so that they would be able to maintain a vegetarian diet in a foreign land. Even today, mung beans play an important role in Chinese and other Asian cuisines.

4 cups water
1 cup whole mung beans or unskinned split mung, washed and drained
1 cup yogurt or buttermilk, blended with 1 cup water,
or 2 cups of water blended with 2 tablespoons freshly squeezed lemon juice
½ teaspoon garlic/cayenne paste #1 (see page 39)
1 teaspoon salt
½ teaspoon turmeric and cumin

Boil the water and add the well-rinsed mung beans. Cook uncovered over moderate heat for 10 minutes, skimming off the foam that floats to the surface. Then lower the heat, cover, and cook for the next 20 minutes.

In a mixing bowl, blend the yogurt or buttermilk and water, or the lemon juice and water. Add the garlic paste, salt, turmeric, and cumin to this mixture; using a whisk or a fork, blend the ingredients.

If the mung beans feel very soft when pressed between two fingers, they are ready for the spices. If not, cook a few minutes longer. Then add the contents of your mixing bowl, and stir the *dal* thoroughly. Cook the mung beans uncovered for 20 minutes or longer, stirring frequently until the *dal* turns creamy. Serve hot!

MUNG DAL (DRY)

In this recipe you will create a *dal* that is a dry entree, suitable to serve along with a saucy vegetable dish. Skinned, split mung beans work best here, but split mung with the skin will do the job.

1 cup *mung dal*, preferably without skins
3 cups water
1 teaspoon salt
1 tablespoon vegetable oil
2 tablespoons finely chopped scallion or onion
3 to 4 cloves of garlic, minced or crushed
1 tablespoon minced or grated gingerroot
¼ teaspoon each turmeric, *garam masala*, and cumin powder
1 tomato, chopped
Chopped cilantro for garnish (optional)

Wash the *dal* thoroughly and drain. In a soup pot, bring the water to a boil, and add the *dal* and the salt. Simmer briskly for the first ten minutes, using a slotted spoon to skim off some of the foam that comes to the surface. A lot of the skins will be removed along with the foam if you are using *dal* with the skins. Cover and cook over moderate heat for 15 to 20 minutes. The beans should be very soft and almost all the liquid evaporated. If not, uncover and cook a little longer. Transfer the *dal* into a large bowl, and set it aside.

Clean and dry the soup pot. Heat the oil in that pot, and add the onion, gingerroot, and garlic. Stir-fry for a few minutes until well roasted, and then add the *dal*. Sauté for another minute and add the turmeric, *garam masala*, cumin powder, and chopped tomato. Continue to stir-fry for several minutes until all the ingredients are well-blended and the *dal* is thick enough to stick to a serving spoon. Transfer to a serving bowl, and garnish with cilantro, if you wish.

FOR A THINNER MUNG *DAL*: Use the recipe for *masoor dal* from pages 112-13 to create a soupy *mung dal*.

DRY MUNG *DAL* WITH SPINACH: Add 1 to 2 cups of chopped spinach to the *mung dal* in place of the chopped tomato, and stir-fry until most of the liquid evaporates. The *dal* will turn green and will be more wet.

MUNG DAL WITH SPRING HERBS

This recipe is wonderful to prepare when green garlic is in season. Green garlic is more flavorful and rich, yet less hot, than the more mature garlic bulb. If you cannot find green garlic, a combination of scallions and regular garlic would be an adequate substitute.

5 cups water

1 cup whole or split *mung dal*, washed and drained

2 tablespoons oil

1 cup finely chopped green garlic, with its green leaves,

or ¾ cup chopped scallions with their greens and 6 cloves minced garlic

1 cup chopped cilantro (or parsley), thick stems removed

½ teaspoon cumin seeds

2 hot green chiles (such as jalapeño or serrano), minced after removing seeds and core

1 tablespoon freshly squeezed lemon juice

1 teaspoon salt

Boil the water and add the *mung dal*. Vigorously simmer the *dal* uncovered for 10 minutes, then lower the heat and cook at low to moderate for 30 to 40 minutes, until they are very soft. Whole *dal* will take longer to cook than split *mung*.

In a separate frying pan, heat the oil and add the green garlic, chopped cilantro (or parsley), and minced chiles. Stir-fry them for five minutes. When the herbs have wilted, add the cumin seeds and fry the mixture for another minute. Add these fried spices to the cooking *dal*. Add the lemon juice and salt. Cook the soup for 10 to 15 more minutes, stirring frequently, until it is creamy and well-blended.

TOOR DAL

Toor dal is the most widely used *dal* in India. This *dal* is usually sold with a coating of oil which is used to preserve it. This oil is a safe preservative, but is probably very old by the time you buy the *dal*. Therefore, the oil should be thoroughly removed before cooking the *dal* by rinsing it with very hot water or soaking it in hot water for ½ hour, then rinsing it.

1 cup *toor dal*
6 cups of water
1 teaspoon salt
½ teaspoon each turmeric, cumin, and
    coriander powder
1 hot green chile (such as jalapeño or
    serrano), minced after seeds and veins
    are removed,
or ½ green bell pepper, minced and blended
    with ¼ teaspoon cayenne
1 tablespoon fresh gingerroot, finely grated
1 tablespoon oil
½ teaspoon black or brown mustard seeds
1 dry red chile, broken into two pieces,
    seeds shaken out
Pinch of *hing*
1 large tomato, cut up into chunks,
or 6 cherry tomatoes, halved
Juice of ½ lemon or lime
Chopped cilantro for topping (optional)

Boil the water in a large pot. Soak the *dal* in hot water for ½ hour, then rinse thoroughly. If you are in a hurry, boil the *dal* in a separate pot of water briskly for two minutes, then rinse and drain. Add the rinsed *dal* to the boiling water, cover, and cook for 10 minutes. Then lower the heat and cook for 30 minutes. Uncover, add the salt and the powdered spices, and cook for 10 more minutes. By now the *dal* should be pulverized. Use a whisk to break down the *dal* if you need to. In India, a bowl of *dal* is taken out at this point for the children, before adding the hot spices. Add the minced green chile or bell pepper and gingerroot, and continue to cook for a few more minutes.

To prepare a *vaghar*, heat the oil in a small saucepan, and add the mustard seeds. When the seeds finish popping, quickly add the dry chile pieces and a pinch of *hing*. Add this mixture immediately to the cooking *dal*, and cover the lid right away, so that the vapor from the smoky, hot oil does not fill up the kitchen. Turn off the heat. Do not open the lid for five minutes. Then uncover, add the tomatoes, and cover again for a few minutes or until ready to serve. Right before serving, add the lemon juice and adjust the seasoning to taste. Remove the hot chile pieces, or instruct your dinner guests to do so from their individual servings. Serve with the optional topping.

VARIATIONS: There are many regional variations of this basic *toor dal* throughout India:

(1) Instead of using tomato and lemon juice for the sweet and sour flavors, use 2 tablespoons shredded coconut (fresh or dehydrated) along with a tablespoon of tamarind paste after having soaked it in water.

(2) Make this *dal* thicker by starting with 4 cups of water.

(3) Add 2 cups of shredded carrots or zucchini along with the powdered spices.

CHANA DAL

Indian *chana* taste the same as chick-peas or garbanzo beans. Yellow split peas look like *chana dal* and are adequate as a substitute here, but they will not produce the same flavor.

7 cups water
1 cup *chana dal* or dry yellow split peas
1 teaspoon salt
½ teaspoon each turmeric, cumin, and
    coriander powder
1 tablespoon compressed tamarind, soaked
    in ¼ cup warm water blended with 1
    teaspoon sugar,
or 1 tablespoon lemon juice blended with
    1 teaspoon sugar or honey
1 tablespoon oil
1/2 teaspoon black mustard seeds
2 cloves minced garlic

Begin by boiling the water in a large pot. Rinse the *chana dal* thoroughly, and add to the boiling water. Continue to boil for five more minutes. Then turn down the heat, and simmer for the next 40 minutes.

After the beans have become very soft (which can take about an hour or longer for tough *chana*), add the salt and the powdered spices. Then add the tamarind with the water it was soaking in and the sugar. Break up the *dal* using a whisk if it does not look nearly pureed at this point. Simmer the *dal* while preparing for the next step.

In a small pot, heat the oil and add the mustard seeds. When the seeds start popping, add the garlic and cook until the garlic turns golden. Then add this oil mixture to the simmering *dal*, and cover the pot. Keep covered for five minutes, adjust the seasoning to taste, and serve.

URAD DAL

Urad is a small black bean. When skinned and split, *urad* becomes a dusty white *dal*. This *dal* is used in soups such as this one. In addition, *urad dal* is also soaked and ground into a puree to make other dishes, such as *dosa* and *vada*. It is a popular protein source in South India, much the same way garbanzo flour is used in the North.

5 cups water
1 cup *urad dal*, washed and drained
¼ teaspoon turmeric powder
1 teaspoon salt
½ teaspoon garlic/cayenne paste #2 (see
    page 40)
1 tablespoon lemon juice
Fresh cilantro leaves for garnish

Boil the water and add the *urad*. Bring the mixture to a boil, uncover, and simmer it at a low heat for about 45 minutes. Prepare the garlic paste and set it aside. At this point, if you can easily crush a bean between your fingers, it is ready to be pureed. Using a fork, whisk the *dal* for few minutes. Then add the garlic paste, salt, turmeric, and lemon juice; cover and cook for another 15 minutes. Adjust the seasoning to taste, top with cilantro if you wish, and serve.

URAD DAL WITH YOGURT: For a creamier dish, add 1 cup of yogurt whisked with ½ cup water after the first 30 minutes of cooking.

PANCHA DAL (FIVE BEAN DAL)

This is a colorful holiday dish that uses five different beans, cooked in one pot. The different *dals* are added to the pot in succession, depending on how long it takes each to be cooked.

8 cups water
½ cup each *chana dal, toor dal, urad dal, mung dal*, and *masoor dal*
½ teaspoon each turmeric, cumin, and coriander powder
¼ teaspoon *garam masala* (see page 38)
1½ teaspoon salt
1 tablespoon oil
¼ cup finely chopped onion
1 tablespoon minced or grated gingerroot
1 or 2 hot green chiles, minced after seeds and cores are removed
1 tablespoon dry, unsweetened, shredded coconut

For the Vaghar
2 teaspoons oil
½ teaspoon mustard seeds
2 dry, hot red chiles, broken into large pieces
2 pinches of *hing*

Juice of 1 lemon or lime
Chopped cilantro for garnish (optional)

Boil the water in a large pot. Wash each *dal* separately and keep them in separate bowls. The *toor dal* must be washed in very hot water a few times to remove the oil coating from its surface. Alternatively, *toor dal* can be soaked in very hot water for half an hour and rinsed thoroughly. Soaking will also make the cooking time shorter. Drain each *dal* and set them aside.

Add the *toor* and *chana dals* to the boiling water, and simmer them for 15 minutes. Next, add the *urad* and *mung dal*, and cook the mixture for another 10 minutes. After that, add the *masoor dal*, and cook them all together for another 10 to 15 minutes, stirring often. When all the beans are soft, add the powdered spices, including the *garam masala*, and the salt. Turn the heat down to low, and cook the *dal* while preparing for the next steps.

Heat the tablespoon of oil in a frying pan, and add the chopped onion, gingerroot, and chiles. Stir-fry them until the onion is very soft, then blend in the coconut. Add this mixture to the pot of cooking *dal*. To prepare the *vaghar*, heat the two teaspoons of oil in a small saucepan, and add the mustard seeds. When the seeds finish popping, add the broken pieces of dried chiles. When the chiles start smoking, add the *hing*, and pour the hot oil mixture immediately into the *dal*. Quickly cover the *dal*, so that the vapor from the smoky, hot oil does not fill up the kitchen, and keep it covered for five minutes. Then add the lemon juice, and adjust the seasoning to taste. Top with the optional cilantro, and serve.

SABAT MAAHAN (WHOLE BLACK LENTILS)
The small, black *urad* bean is known as *maahan* in the northern state of Punjab, where this particular preparation of *urad dal* is considered an essential component of a wedding feast. The whole *urad* is quite tough and takes about two hours to cook. Soak the beans in water for several hours to shorten the preparation time.

8 cups water (only 5 cups of water are needed for soaked and drained beans)
1 cup whole *urad* beans, washed and drained (or soaked and drained)
A few pinches of baking powder or baking soda
½ teaspoon each turmeric powder and *garam masala*
1 teaspoon salt
3 tablespoons butter, *ghee*, or oil
½ cup onion, finely chopped
3 to 4 cloves of garlic
1 tablespoon grated gingerroot
1 or 2 hot green chiles, minced after seeds and core are removed
Few pinches of hot pepper flakes or cayenne for additional spiciness
Fresh chopped cilantro for garnish

Boil the eight cups of water, and add the *urad* beans. (If the beans were soaked for at least six hours or overnight, use only five cups of water). Continue to boil the mixture for the first 10 minutes. Then turn down the heat, and cook the beans over moderate heat for about an hour, or until the beans are very soft. (The soaked beans will take less time). Add two pinches of baking soda or powder to speed up the cooking process—if the beans were soaked, the addition of soda is not necessary. After the beans have become soft, add the turmeric, *garam masala*, and salt. Stir the beans well to mix all the ingredients. Then cover and cook for another 30 minutes or so, stirring frequently. By this time, the beans should be broken down. Lower the heat and simmer for a few minutes while preparing the next step.

In a frying pan, heat the *ghee*, butter, or oil. Add the onions and stir-fry until they become translucent. Then add the garlic, gingerroot, and chile. Fry all the ingredients for five minutes, and add to the simmering beans. Stir and cook for a few more minutes to allow all the ingredients to mix and for the *dal* to become creamy. Taste to see if you need more hot pepper or salt. Garnish with chopped cilantro and serve.

PUNJABI CHANA

There is a slight difference between the Spanish variety of garbanzo bean and the Indian *chana* or Middle Eastern chick-pea. The garbanzo is a little larger than the *chana* or chick-pea. Any of these beans can be used for this recipe, and they all take a couple of hours to cook, even after they have been soaked overnight. The canned garbanzo or ceci beans (as they are sometimes labeled on containers) can be used for this dish. However, I think if you start this recipe from scratch using the dry beans, the flavor of the finished product will be superior.

In this recipe, the *dal* will not come out soupy. It is rather like a porridge which you can serve along with a saucy vegetable dish and rice.

8 cups of water (4 cups for soaking and
    4 cups to cook with)
1 cup dry *chana* (chick-peas) or garbanzo
    beans
1 teaspoon salt, or to taste
2 tablespoons *ghee*, butter, or oil
½ cup finely chopped onion
1 finely chopped green or red bell pepper
3 cloves garlic, minced or pressed
1 teaspoon minced gingerroot
½ teaspoon each turmeric, cumin, coriander,
    and *garam masala*
⅛ to ¼ teaspoon cayenne
Juice of 1 lemon
Chopped cilantro or mint leaves for garnish

Soak the beans in four cups of water, overnight or for at least five hours. Then rinse, drain, and set aside. Boil the other four cups of water, and add the rinsed beans. Boil the mixture for 10 minutes, and then lower the heat. Cover and cook the beans over medium to low heat for 40 minutes, checking from time to time to make sure they have enough water. Tough *chana* may use up all the water in half an hour; if so, add 2 more cups to finish the cooking. When the beans are very soft, add the salt. Cook for a few more minutes until almost all the water is used up. Turn off the heat and set the pot aside.

In a separate frying pan, heat the *ghee*, butter, or oil, and fry the onions until they are limp. Then add the bell pepper, and stir-fry for five minutes. Next, add the garlic and ginger-root, and sauté for another minute. Add the fried ingredients to the pot of beans. Return the pot of beans to the stove, and add the powdered spices. Cook over low heat for a few minutes, stirring frequently. Add the lemon juice and stir. Adjust the seasoning to taste, adding as much cayenne and/or salt as you like. Top with chopped cilantro or mint leaves, and serve.

RASAM

In South India, *rasam* is served often, with meals, with *dosa*, or even in the morning as a hot, breakfast drink with a plate of spongy dumplings called *idlis* (see page 61).

½ cup *toor dal*

½ teaspoon salt

⅛ teaspoon turmeric powder

2 teaspoons shredded coconut, fresh or dry
    (unsweetened)

1 tomato, diced

2 dry tamarind pods, or 1 teaspoon dry,
    compressed tamarind

(if tamarind is not available, use a mixture of
    the juice of 1 lemon and ½ teaspoon
    sugar)

1 tablespoon corn or peanut oil

¼ teaspoon black mustard seeds

⅛ teaspoon cumin seeds

1 dry, hot chile, cut into pieces (seeds
    discarded), or ⅛ teaspoon cayenne

a pinch of hing

Wash the *dal* with very hot water to remove the oil it was coated with, and soak it in more hot water. Boil three cups of water with the salt, and add the drained *dal*. Cook over moderate heat for about 30 to 40 minutes until the beans are soft enough to be easily crushed between your fingers. (You can speed up the softening process by adding a few pinches of baking soda). Prepare the tamarind by removing the outer shell and seeds from the pod. Soak the remaining meal in ¼ cup water, and set aside. If using the compressed, seedless variety of tamarind, break it into smaller pieces and then soak.

When the beans are soft, add two cups of water, and cook them for few more minutes. If necessary, use an egg beater to blend the *dal*. Add the turmeric, coconut, and tomato. Add the soaking tamarind with its water or the lemon juice and sugar mixture. Continue to cook for a few more minutes while preparing for the last step. In a separate small pot, heat the oil and add the mustard seeds. When they start popping, add the cumin seeds, chile pieces, and the pinch of hing. Immediately add this smoky spice-oil mixture to the *rasam*, and cover quickly. Turn off the heat, and do not open the lid for a few minutes. Open the pot, stir, and serve. Remind the diners to remove the chile pieces. (If cayenne is used instead of the chile, add it later, after opening the lid.) Serve the rasam with *dosas, idlis,* or by itself as a warming first course.

MOTH (ADJUKI BEANS) COOKED WITH
COCONUT AND TAMARIND

This is a simple Maharashtrian bean recipe
from Central India. It is best cooked with fresh
coconut, but dry, shredded coconut blended
with some canned coconut milk or water will
suffice. The small, brown, mung-sized adjuki
beans used in Japanese cuisine are the same as
Indian *moth* beans. These small beans take a
little longer than an hour to cook.

1 tablespoon dry, compressed or fresh,
    seedless tamarind pulp
4 cups of water
1 cup *moth* (adjuki beans), washed and
    drained
3 to 4 cloves garlic, minced
2 tablespoon fresh gingerroot
½ cup fresh, shredded coconut, blended with
    ½ cup water (see page 36),
or ½ cup dry, unsweetened coconut, blended
    with ½ cup coconut milk or water
Salt and cayenne to taste
Springs of chopped cilantro as garnish

Prepare the tamarind by following the
directions on page 40. While the tamarind is
soaking, cut the coconut if you are using fresh
coconut (see page 36). Boil the water and add
the adjuki beans. Boil them for 15 minutes, then
simmer at low heat for the next 45 minutes.
Place the tamarind, garlic, gingerroot, and fresh
coconut and water (or the dry coconut with
coconut milk or water) in a blender or food
processor, and puree thoroughly. Add the
puree to the soft beans, and cook for an
additional 15 to 20 minutes, stirring often so it
does not stick to the bottom of the pan. Add the
salt and cayenne to your taste. Serve the *dal* hot,
topped with fresh cilantro.

DOODHI-CHANA-NU-SHAK

(*Chana dal* cooked with summer squash)
In this recipe, the *dal* is soaked, boiled, and then cooked with any of the quick-cooking summer squashes, such as *doodhi* or *ghisoda* to make a soup. Zucchini or other summer squashes, such as sunburst or crook neck squash, also work well here. The sweet-and-sour sauce created by adding the tamarind and sugar mixture (or lemon juice and sugar) is the essential flavor in this *dal*.

5 cups water
1/2 cup skinned *chana dal* or yellow split peas
4 cups *doodhi* squash, peeled and cut into small cubes,
or 4 cups zucchini, washed and cubed
3 tablespoons oil
¼ teaspoon black mustard seeds
¼ teaspoon each cumin, turmeric, and coriander powder
1 teaspoon salt
1 tablespoon tamarind paste, blended with 1 teaspoon sugar (see page 40),
or 1 tablespoon lemon juice, blended with 1 teaspoon sugar
½ teaspoon garlic/cayenne paste # 2 (see page 40)
Chunks of 1 large tomato

Soak the *dal* or yellow split peas in two cups of water for about three hours. Then drain them and set aside.

Prepare the squash and set aside. Prepare the tamarind paste and set aside. Make the garlic/cayenne paste and have it ready.

Boil 2½ cups of water in a pot, and add the beans or peas. Cook them over medium heat for 30 minutes; then turn the heat down, and continue to simmer. In a separate pot, heat the oil and add the mustard seeds. When they finish popping, add the squash cubes and stir-fry for a few minutes. Then add the beans or peas along with the liquid in which they were simmering. Next, add the powdered spices and salt. Cook the mixture for a few minutes, then add the tamarind paste and sugar mixture (or the lemon juice and sugar). Mix in the garlic/cayenne paste, and cover the pot. Cook the *dal* over moderate heat for ten minutes. Add the tomato chunks and adjust the seasoning to taste. The *dal* should have plenty of sauce, but it should not be thin when done.

SAMBHAR

Sambhar is a typical South Indian dish in which a variety of vegetables are cooked with *dal*, creating a hearty, one-pot meal. Nowadays, different versions of *sambhar* can be found in other regions of India using local vegetables and blending different spices.

6 cups water
½ cup *toor dal* preferred, but *masoor dal* (red lentils) will do
½ teaspoon each coriander and turmeric powder
1 teaspoon gingerroot root, minced
1 to 2 hot chiles, minced after seeds and cores are removed
1 teaspoon salt
l tablespoon tamarind paste (see page 40)
l tablespoon oil
¼ cup finely chopped onion
1 cup each carrots, eggplant, and celery or zucchini, cut into ½" pieces
1 cup cauliflower pieces, separated into buds
1 tablespoon dry, shredded, unsweetened coconut
8 to 10 cherry tomatoes, cut into halves
Chopped cilantro for garnish

For Vaghar
2 teaspoons oil
½ teaspoon black mustard seeds
⅛ teaspoon cumin seeds
2 dry, hot red chiles, broken into pieces
Pinch of *hing*

Rinse the *toor dal* in very hot water a few times to remove the oily coating of the *dal*, and drain well. (Or soak the *dal* in hot water for half an hour, rinse well, and then drain.) Boil the water and add the *dal*. Simmer the mixture briskly for 15 minutes. Then add the powdered spices, gingerroot, minced green chiles, salt, and tamarind paste. Cover and cook the *dal* for the next half hour while preparing the vegetables.

Heat one tablespoon of oil in a frying pan or wok, and add the onion. When the onion is limp, add the cut-up vegetables, and fry for several minutes. Add the coconut and stir-fry for another minute. Add the vegetable mixture to the pot of cooking *dal*, and stir well. Add the halved tomatoes and simmer the *dal* at low heat.

To prepare the *vaghar*, heat the 2 teaspoons of oil in a small saucepan, and add the mustard seeds. When the seeds begin to pop, add the cumin seeds and wait for 30 seconds. Then add the broken pieces of dry chiles and a pinch of *hing*. Immediately add this hot oil mixture into the pot of *sambhar*, and quickly cover the pot, so that the vapor from the smoky, hot oil does not fill up the kitchen. Keep the pot covered for five minutes, then turn the heat off. Uncover and adjust the seasoning to taste. Remove the pieces of hot chile from the pot, or instruct your dinner guests to remove them from their individual portions. Garnish with the cilantro, and serve. As noted before, you will not need anything else except a bowl of rice to call this dish a complete meal.

DAL-DHOKALI (DAL WITH CHICK-PEA FLOUR DUMPLINGS)

8 cups water
1 cup *toor dal*
¼ teaspoon each turmeric, coriander, and cumin powder
1 teaspoon minced gingerroot
1 or 2 hot green chiles, minced after seeds and core are removed
1 teaspoon each *amchoor* powder and brown sugar,
or 1 tablespoon lemon juice combined with 1 teaspoon brown sugar
1 teaspoon salt
1 large tomato, cut into chunks

For the Dumplings
¼ cup *besan* (chick-pea or garbanzo flour)
¼ cup whole wheat flour
1 tablespoon garlic paste made with 3 cloves garlic, ¼ teaspoon cayenne, and 1 teaspoon minced cilantro (see page 39)
1 tablespoon oil
¼ teaspoon salt
up to 2 tablespoons water

For the Vaghar
1 tablespoon oil
¼ teaspoon black mustard seeds
3 or 4 whole cloves
1 dried hot red chile, cut into small pieces
Pinch of *hing*

Soak the oily *toor dal* in very hot water for half an hour and rinse thoroughly, or rinse it with very hot water several times, until all of the oil is removed from surface. Bring the eight cups of water to boil in a large pot, and add the rinsed *dal*. Continue to cook vigorously for the first 10 minutes; then cover and cook over moderate heat for the next 30 minutes. While the *dal* is cooking slowly, prepare the dumplings.

Combine the two flours in a small mixing bowl, and add the garlic paste and oil. Crumble all of these ingredients together using your fingers or a fork. Then add just enough water (a tablespoon or two is all you need) to gather the ingredients into a stiff, pie crust-like dough. Knead the dough into a small ball, and set it aside.

Stir the *dal* and add the powdered spices, gingerroot, minced chiles, *amchoor* and sugar (or lemon juice and sugar), and the salt. Continue to simmer the *dal* over low heat.

To roll out the dumplings, moisten the palms of your hands, the rolling surface, and a rolling pin with some cooking oil. Take the dough ball and flatten it out using your palms. Then roll out the dough into a flat, thin sheet about as thick as a tortilla or *chapati*. Then cut the dough into 1" squares or diamond-shaped pieces *(dhokalis)*. The *dhokalis* should be dry enough to lift up from the rolling surface. Take a few *dhokalis* at a time, and slide them into the cooking *dal*. Stir the *dal* while adding the dough pieces, making sure that they do not stick together. Then add the tomato chunks to the soup pot. Cover and cook over low heat for five to seven minutes so that the dumplings are poached. Turn off the heat.

To prepare the *vaghar*, heat the oil in a small pot, and add the mustard seeds. When they begin to pop, add the whole cloves and the dry chile pieces. When the oil begins to smoke, quickly add the pinch of *hing*, and add the hot mixture to the pot of *dal-dhokali*. Cover the lid right away, so that the vapor from the smoky, hot oil does not fill up the kitchen. Keep the lid shut for a full five minutes, then uncover and stir carefully. Separate the dumplings if they are stuck together, but be careful not to break too many of them. Adjust the seasoning to taste. The *dal* is now thick, spicy, and ready to be served.

MIXED BEAN SPROUTS

Sprouts with long shoots, such as mung bean or soybean sprouts used in Chinese cooking and alfalfa sprouts used in salad in Western countries, are hardly used in Indian cooking. However, beans and lentils such as mung, adjuki, brown lentil, and garbanzo, are sprouted in India. This can be done in your kitchen by soaking the beans in water overnight and then hanging them in a cheese cloth for several hours until short shoots appear. (Mixed bean sprouts are also sold in small bags in health food stores.) They are briefly cooked as follows.

2 tablespoons oil
2 tablespoons green onion, finely chopped
3 cloves garlic, minced
2 cups mixed bean sprouts with short shoots
1 teaspoon salt
¼ teaspoon cayenne
Juice of 1 lime or lemon

Heat the oil in a frying pan, and sauté the onion and garlic until they are wilted. Add the mixed bean sprouts, and cook them over moderately high heat for several minutes, until all the ingredients are well-blended. Add the salt, cayenne, and lime or lemon juice, and serve.

This hot bean sprout salad can also be served either at room temperature or cold and included in a picnic basket or bag lunch. It is sold as a popular street food in Gujarat. The sprouts can also be incorporated into a fried rice dish, as in the recipe on page 140.

KADHI OR YOGURT "CURRY"

I believe the origin of the word "curry" lies in a British mispronunciation of this dish, called *kadhi*. I don't know how all Indian dishes came to be known as curries, but this delicious soup is the only one that should be referred to as *kadhi*. Unlike most *dals*, this is a light soup where, instead of beans, a bit of *besan* (garbanzo flour) is used with yogurt to form a sauce-like soup. Like the chicken soup of Europe, *kadhi* is meant to clear up your sinuses, help you with the symptoms of a cold, and generally lift you up when you're feeling down and out.

Another misnomer associated with this soup is "curry" leaves. Since the sweet *neem* leaf is always used in flavoring *kadhi*, this leaf seems to have been mislabeled as the "curry" leaf.

Unfortunately, there is no dairy-free *kadhi* recipe. You need the yogurt, or at least the buttermilk, to make yogurt soup.

2 cups unsweetened yogurt or buttermilk
6 cups water
3 tablespoons *besan* (chick-pea or garbanzo bean flour)
1 teaspoon salt
½ teaspoon turmeric powder
1 teaspoon garlic/cayenne paste # 2 (see page 40)
A few sprigs of dry or fresh sweet *neem* (curry) leaves or chopped cilantro

For the Vaghar
1 teaspoon oil
¼ teaspoon black mustard seeds
⅛ teaspoon cumin seeds
1 dry, red hot chile, broken into three pieces
A pinch of *hing*
1 teaspoon brown sugar (optional)

Combine the yogurt (or buttermilk), water, *besan*, salt, and turmeric in a mixing bowl with a whisk, egg beater, or a fork, breaking any lumps formed by the flour. Heat this mixture in a soup pot over low heat, stirring frequently. During the first 10 minutes, you need to stir the soup almost constantly, as the soup may boil over or the *besan* may stick to the bottom. After the first few minutes of cooking, the soup quiets down.

The next 30 minutes of slow cooking will turn the yogurt, water, and flour into a nice, thick, sauce-like soup. When the soup is cooked down to half its original volume, add the garlic/cayenne paste and the *neem* (curry) leaves or cilantro. Keep the soup hot over *very low* heat, or turn the heat off while preparing the *vaghar*.

In a very small pot, start the *vaghar* by heating the teaspoon of oil. Add the mustard seeds; when they begin to pop, add the cumin seeds and the dried chile pieces. Quickly throw in the *hing*, and add this hot oil mixture to the pot of *kadhi*. Cover the pot immediately, so that the vapor from the smoky, hot oil does not fill up the kitchen. Turn off the heat and keep the lid on for the next five minutes. Uncover and adjust the seasoning to taste. Some people like to add a bit of sugar at this point to counter the tart flavor; others like it hot and sour. Remove the pieces of hot chile from the pot, or instruct your dinner guests to do so from their individual portions. Add the garnish and serve.

DAL CHOWDER WITH SALSA

This inter-ethnic recipe was inspired by a friend who was recovering from having her wisdom teeth pulled. She needed to eat something soft, nutritious, and tasty. At the moment, I was at work, so I had minimal time and not much to cook with (a hot plate). I had to be quick in inventing this recipe, using only the ingredients I had on hand.

3 cups water
1 cup red lentils (*masoor dal*), rinsed and drained
1 tablespoon oil
1 teaspoon finely grated or minced gingerroot

1 cup corn kernels scraped from a large corn cob (or frozen and thawed kernels)
1 cup fresh salsa,
or mix 1 cup tomato chunks, combined with 1 tablespoon each minced onion and cilantro, and 1 teaspoon minced hot green chile, after having removed seeds and core
Salt to taste
Juice of fresh lemon to taste

Bring the water to a boil. Add the lentils and cook them for fifteen minutes over moderate heat. Then turn the heat down, and simmer the lentils for the next few minutes. While the lentils are simmering, have the salsa ready.

Heat the oil in a frying pan, and add the gingerroot, salsa, and corn kernels. Stir-fry this mixture for five minutes, and add to the cooking *dal*. Raise the heat back to medium, and cook the *dal* for 10 more minutes or so until it is thick and creamy. Add the salt and lemon juice to your taste, and serve.

CHAPTER SEVEN
RICE AND RICE DISHES

Rice is certainly one of the oldest known cultivated foods known. There is evidence that rice was eaten in India some five thousand years ago. Supposedly, it was then brought to China and the rest of Asia before coming to Europe and the Americas. After the cultivation of rice was mastered, it became one of the single most important crops in Asia, and remains so to this day. It has been estimated that rice is part of the daily diet of more than half the earth's population.

In contrast, to many American cooks, rice is a merely a starchy pasta substitute and a rainy day side dish. Currently, however, more Americans are eating rice, in part due to increasing awareness of its health virtues and the promotion of its culinary versatility by a growing Asian-American population. This nutritious grain is quick to prepare and easy to digest, making it a good food for the very young, the elderly, sick people, and those who are allergic to other glutinous grains such as wheat. Therefore, knowing how to prepare rice more than one way is always useful for the health-conscious cook.

In India, rice is a staple food that is eaten by almost everyone at least once daily. Great respect is given to this grain in India, so much so, that offering rice has become a symbol of prosperity during religious holidays. The custom of throwing rice at a wedding has even survived the long journey to the West. There is a special holiday in India that marks a certain stage in the development of a young girl into a gradually maturing young lady. On this holiday, called *poshi punam* (literally "soft full moon"), all little girls aged 11 through 15 throughout India are supposed to be initiated into the art of cooking rice. That day, the young girl prepares *kheer* (see page 162), a kind of rice pudding for her brother(s). This may be the first time a young girl has prepared rice, but by the time she is a woman, she will be expected to have learned how to prepare rice in many different ways.

In India, there are many varieties of rice classified and priced according to their colors, textures, and where they were grown. Generally speaking, white rice is more popular in Indian cooking than whole grain brown rice, which contains the bran. Because of its cosmetic virtues—white and fluffy—when cooked, nutritionally inferior white rice is preferred by many cooks. However, many village folks use whole grain brown rice (and other whole grain rices) by default, because the milled variety is not available to them. The late Mahatma Gandhi tried to bring back the practice of eating hand-pounded rice, but, unfortunately, the great profits to be made by large, industrialized mills are slowly causing refined rice to win out.

Some white rice is better than others, depending on how it is processed. In most parts of the modern world, whole grain brown rice is sent to the mill to be scraped and polished. This milling removes most of the grain's vitamins and minerals. But rice that has been hand-pounded to make it light in color retains much of its nutrients. *Basmati* rice imported from India is usually made "white" using this method of hand-pounding. Another way of processing brown rice, which was popularized in this country some time ago, is parboiling and converting. With this method, brown rice is first parboiled to loosen its bran. The minerals and vitamins which dissolve in the parboiled liquid are later sealed back into the processed grain using a pressure cooking method. The liquid with the bran is then discarded. What remains is a creamy colored white rice which has much of the nutrients of the original grain, minus the bran. This rice is also quick and easy to cook and, in my opinion, is a good alternative to milled white rice, (which is often coated with talc).

In the recipes to follow, I have used long-grain brown rice, the hand-pounded imported white *basmati* rice, and converted, parboiled rice. Feel free to experiment with other varieties such as the Lundberg rice available in health food stores. Do not use instant rice or commercial white rice which is coated with talc. The talc is not good for you and is not easy to remove from the grain, even by rinsing it.

First, I will give you basic recipes for preparing regular, converted, and *basmati* white rice. Next, I will show you how to prepare whole grain brown rice. Many recipes using rice as a main ingredient will follow.

If you have a rice cooker and have success using it, keep it by all means. I prefer to cook rice on my back burner in any heavy-bottomed pot while chopping vegetables or preparing another dish. Brown rice cooks especially well if you use a heavy iron Dutch oven.

BASIC WHITE RICE
This recipe will work for any packaged or bulk white rice, except for imported basmati.

1 cup white rice
2 cups water
½ teaspoon salt optional

Rinse the rice, drain it, and set it aside. Boil the water in a pot, and add the rice, along with the optional salt. Stir the rice thoroughly. When the water comes to a second boil, lower the heat to medium so that it simmers gently. Cover and cook for 15 to 20 minutes. Rice does not like to be disturbed while it is being cooked, so don't open the lid for the first 15 minutes. Then, remove the lid to see if the rice is cooked. If the grains feel too hard when pressed between your fingers, add a few tablespoons of water, cover, and cook for five more minutes. By now the rice should be soft and fluffy when stirred with a fork. Keep covered for a few minutes before serving.

CONVERTED WHITE RICE: Converted white rice can be cooked in the same manner as above, except you need not rinse it. It takes a little less time to cook converted white rice than regular white rice. You can also follow the instructions given on the box.

BASMATI RICE

This delicious variety of rice is now available in many specialty stores, health food stores, and even in the gourmet section of supermarkets. The unique, nutty texture and fragrance of this cooked grain is attributed to the special soil in which it was grown. When the seed is brought elsewhere, such as to Indonesia, Thailand, or the United States, the resulting crop does not have the same flavor. Therefore, if you want authentic *basmati*, you need to get the imported Indian or Pakistani variety, both of which grow in the same type of soil. Brown *basmati*, grown in the U.S., has its own special flavor and texture. Prepare brown *basmati* using the recipe for Basic Brown Rice which follows.

This delicate white *basmati* rice cooks in 10 minutes, so being in a hurry to make an Indian dinner is a good excuse to use it.

1 cup imported Indian or Pakistani white
    basmati rice
2 cups water

Rinse the rice thoroughly using *cold* water. Drain it completely and set it aside. Boil the two cups of water, and add the drained rice. Again, bring the mixture to a boil, and then turn the heat to low or moderate to simmer the rice slowly. Stir the rice, cover it, and cook for 10 minutes. Gently fluff the rice with a fork, and see if it is fully cooked by pressing a grain with your fingers. Some aged grain may need further cooking. In that case, use an additional two tablespoons of water, and cook the rice a bit longer. Keep the cooked rice covered for a few minutes before serving.

Some people add a little salt and/or butter to their rice. But I do not like to alter the flavor of this special rice by adding anything to it.

BASIC BROWN RICE

Brown rice requires a longer cooking time and more water than white rice, but many people overcook it, creating a mushy porridge. If you have a Dutch oven or other iron cooking pot, use it for preparing brown rice. The heavy pot acts like a pressure cooker, cooking the rice faster and using less water. However, I find an actual pressure cooker is ill-suited for cooking brown rice.

1 cup long-grain or short-grain brown rice,
    or brown *basmati* rice
2½ to 2¾ cups water
½ teaspoon salt (optional)

Wash the rice, drain it, and set aside. Bring 2½ cups of water (and the optional salt) to boil in a heavy pot. Add the rice. Bring to a boil again, and cook the rice over moderate heat for five minutes. Then lower the heat, cover, and simmer it for 25 minutes. Then open the lid and check the rice to see if it is done. The finished rice must be soft enough to press easily between your fingers, but will not be as fluffy as white rice. If needed, add a few tablespoons of water, cover, and cook the rice for 10 more minutes, until soft. If you are cooking the rice in an iron pot, keep it covered for ten minutes after the initial cooking of half an hour. This will finish cooking the rice, leaving it soft and flavorful.

KESARI BHAT (SAFFRON RICE)

For special occasions, saffron rice is colorful and festive, although the high cost of saffron makes it something you'll only want to savor occasionally!

¼ teaspoon saffron threads
3 tablespoons hot milk or water
1 cup converted, regular, or *basmati* white rice
2 cups water
¼ teaspoon salt (optional)
1 teaspoon melted butter or oil

Soak the saffron in a bowl of hot milk or water to release its color and flavors. Set it aside. Boil the water with the optional salt. Unless you are using converted, parboiled rice, rinse it and drain it completely. Add the rice to the boiling water, and stir it thoroughly. Then allow the mixture to come to a second boil, and lower the heat. Cover and cook the rice for five minutes (or a bit longer for regular white or converted rice), then add the saffron liquid. Cover and cook until the liquid has been absorbed and the rice is done. Transfer the cooked rice to a serving platter, and serve.

SAFFRON RICE WITH NUTS AND RAISINS: Cook the saffron rice as instructed in the previous recipe. Transfer the cooked rice onto a serving platter. Sauté ¼ cup each of nuts and raisins (for 4 cups of cooked rice) with a bit of oil or butter until fragrant, and use them as topping for the saffron rice.

RICE WITH NUTS AND RAISINS

4 cups cooked white or brown rice (see pages 132-33)
1 tablespoon butter, *ghee*, or oil
¼ cup raisins, yellow raisins (sultana), or currants
¼ cup cashew, almond, or pistachio pieces

Heat the butter, *ghee*, or oil in a frying pan over low to medium heat. Add the raisins (or currants) and the nuts, and sauté them for five to seven minutes until fragrant. Layer them on top of the cooked rice, and cover the pot. Serve the rice mixture as it is, since the topping looks pretty. Or mix the nuts and raisins gently into the rice, and serve.

PEAS *PILLAU*

In this recipe, white *basmati* rice works the best, since it cooks for the same amount of time as the peas, but brown or converted rice can be used.

1 tablespoon butter or oil
¼ cup onion or scallion, finely chopped
1 hot green chile, minced after removing core and seeds
½ fresh gingerroot, minced
4 whole cardamom pods
3 whole cloves
1 stick whole cinnamon, broken into small pieces
1 cup white or brown *basmati* rice, washed and drained
1 cup fresh peas, or frozen peas, thawed and drained
¼ teaspoon turmeric
2 to 2½ cups water
1 teaspoon salt
Juice of ½ lime or lemon or 2 tablespoons fresh pomegranate seeds for garnish

If using white *basmati* rice, wash and drain the rice completely. Melt the butter or heat the oil in a pot over low heat. Add the onion, chile, and gingerroot. Sauté for five minutes until the ingredients become soft. Then add the whole spices and the rice, and stir-fry for a minute. If using white *basmati* rice, add the peas now and stir-fry for another minute. Then add the turmeric, water, and salt. Cover and cook for 10 minutes, or a bit longer until the rice is cooked and all the liquid is absorbed. If using converted or brown *basmati* rice, add the peas during the last 10 minutes, since they will take less time to cook than the rice. Sprinkle on the lemon or lime juice, and serve. When fresh pomegranate is in season, top the dish with these seeds instead of using the lemon or lime juice before serving.

PEAS *PILLAU* WITH BROWN RICE: If you want to use brown rice in this recipe, use a long-grain variety. Wash and drain the rice. Follow the above recipe until the addition of the rice. Then add 2½ cups water, cover, and cook the rice over moderate heat for 30 minutes. Then add the peas, cover, and cook for seven to ten more minutes. Keep the cooked rice covered for five minutes. Add the lime or lemon juice, and serve.

KHICHADI

Khichadi (pronounced as kitch-a-dee) is the daily fare for many a humble Indian. It is a good food for young children and is served daily in *ashrams* (religious communes) across India. *Khichadi* is considered a humble food because it is prepared with inexpensive, brown short-grain rice, and the finished product has a consistency like porridge.

As tradition goes in India, *khichadi* is never served to a guest, at least not on the first day! But it is a very nourishing dish, rich in protein (with the complimentary amino acids of rice and beans), minerals, and vitamins. The oldest man living in the village where I was born attributed his longevity to his daily diet of *khichadi*. While the name *khichadi* covers a variety of similar preparations, it generally means a combination of brown rice cooked with a *dal*—usually *mung dal*. The different variations of *khichadi* depend on the choice of beans that are used. So you can have *chana dal khichadi* or *masoor dal khichadi*. Here is the basic recipe for this unpretentious, but nutritious, dish.

1 cup short-grain brown rice
½ cup *mung dal* with the skins on
3½ cups water
1 teaspoon salt
1 tablespoon butter, *ghee*, or oil (optional)

Wash the rice and *mung dal*, and drain completely. Set them aside. Boil the water in a heavy-bottomed pot (a cast iron Dutch oven would be perfect). Add the rice, *mung dal*, and salt. Allow the mixture to come to a second boil, then reduce the heat so that the grains simmer gently. Cover and cook for about 40 minutes. At the end of this time, both the rice and mung should be cooked to a soft, somewhat mushy consistency. Turn off the heat, add the optional butter, *ghee*, or oil, and keep the pot covered for 5 to 10 minutes. Uncover and stir well with a wooden spoon. Serve the *khichadi* hot or at room temperature with a hot vegetable dish. In Gujarat, day-old, leftover *khichadi* is served for breakfast with yogurt.

MASOOR DAL KHICHADI: Substitute ½ cup of *masoor dal* for the *mung dal*. Since *masoor dal* cooks faster than brown rice, cook the rice first for 20 minutes, then add the *masoor dal* to the cooking rice.

YELLOW *KHICHADI*: Usually *khichadi* is considered more suitable for dinner or supper than for lunch in India. But when *khichadi* is made for lunch, you would add ¼ teaspoon turmeric to make it colorfully yellow.

BLACK-EYED *KHICHADI*

I came to the United States from India to attend a school near Albany, New York. At that time, there were no Indian import stores or special spice shops in Albany, so I had to make do with whatever local ingredients I could find for my Indian cooking. Instead of using traditional *mung dal* for *khichadi*, I cooked black-eyed peas with brown rice and came up with this delicious American *khichadi*.

⅓ cup dry black-eyed peas

3 cups water

1 teaspoon salt

⅔ cups short-grain (preferred) or long-grain brown rice

1 tablespoon butter or oil (optional)

Soak the black-eyed peas in enough water to cover for at least an hour. Then drain the peas and set aside. The soaked peas will take the same time to cook as the brown rice. (If you forget to soak your peas, you need to boil them for half an hour to soften them a bit. Then drain the boiled peas, and set them aside.)

Boil the water in a large pot, and add the rice and salt. Add the peas and cook them together for a few minutes over high heat until the water begins to boil. Then lower the heat and cover the pot. Cook for 40 to 45 minutes until both the rice and peas feel very soft when pressed between your fingers. Turn off the heat, add the optional butter, and keep the pot covered for a few minutes. The trapped heat will further soften the *khichadi*, as it should be nice and mushy. Serve hot or at room temperature with a piping hot entree.

RICE AND VEGETABLE *BIRIANI*

This substantial dish, in which many vegetables are cooked with rice, can be a meal-in-a-pot. Take it to a pot luck, serve it to guests, or prepare as a colorful, holiday centerpiece. Any way, you will be delighted!

1 cup eggplant, cut into ½" pieces

1 cup carrots, cut into ½" pieces

1 cup fresh peas, or frozen peas, thawed and drained

1 cup cauliflower buds, separated from the stem

2 tablespoons oil or butter

1 medium onion, finely chopped

1 bell pepper or medium-hot green chile (such as an Anaheim), chopped after removing seeds and core

1 large tomato, cut into chunks

4 whole cardamom pods

4 whole cloves

1 large stick cinnamon, cut into small pieces

2 cups uncooked white rice (converted or other variety, washed and drained)

1½ teaspoons salt

4 cups water

Juice of 1 lemon

Cut the vegetables as directed, and set them aside. Then heat the oil or butter in a saucepan, and add the onion and pepper. Stir-fry these vegetables over moderate heat until they are very soft, then add the whole spices. Continue to sauté until the onion is brown. Then add the chopped tomato, and stir-fry the mixture for a few minutes until the tomato turns into a paste with the rest of the ingredients. Now add the rice and sauté only for one minute until it is coated with the tomato mixture. Then add the rest of the vegetables, and stir all the ingredients together for two minutes. Add the water and salt, and mix all the ingredients thoroughly. Lower the heat so that the rice and vegetables simmer gently. Cover and cook for 30 minutes, then check to see if the *biriani* is finished. The rice should be fluffy and the vegetables soft, but not mushy. If the rice is not sufficiently cooked, add a few more tablespoons of water, cover, and cook for a few more minutes. When the *biriani* is done, stir it gently with a fork, and add the lemon juice. Season to taste and serve.

COCONUT RICE

Here is a rice dish that can be served on a special occasion or holiday. It is a bit time-consuming to make just for an ordinary dinner, but it comes out looking like a cake—quite suitable for any celebration.

2 cups of fresh coconut milk made from
    ½ coconut (see page 36),
or 2 cups canned coconut milk,
or 2½ cups coconut milk if using brown
    basmati rice
1 tablespoon butter, *ghee*, or oil
3 whole cloves
4 cardamom pods
1 stick cinnamon, broken into small pieces
1 cup white or brown *basmati* rice, washed
    and drained
1 teaspoon salt

Heat the butter, *ghee*, or oil in a saucepan over low heat. Add the cloves, cardamom, and cinnamon. Stir-fry for a few minutes until fragrant. Then add the rice and sauté for five minutes, until it is well-coated with the spices. Turn off the heat. Heat the coconut milk in a separate saucepan without boiling it. Pour the milk over the stir-fried rice. Cover the rice and continue to cook over moderate heat for five minutes. Then lower the heat and simmer the rice gently, still covered, for five minutes if using white *basmati* rice, 20 to 30 minutes if using brown *basmati* rice, or until the liquid has been absorbed. Keep covered for a few minutes, then transfer the rice onto a serving platter. Some people like to preserve the round, cake-like shape of this dish by placing the serving platter upside down over the pot of rice and turning both over quickly. You can also decorate this dish with edible gold leaf before serving.

LEFTOVER RICE

A whole cookbook can be (and probably has been) written on how to utilize leftover rice. You can store leftover rice in the refrigerator for up to a week and unrefrigerated for a day. However, the formerly soft and fluffy rice will turn into a soft mush or be very stuck together—not very appetizing, even after reheating. Leftover rice is best reheated by first gently stirring with a fork to separate the grains. Then add a couple tablespoons of water per cup of rice to the pot, cover, and heat it on low for five minutes. Better yet, rejuvenate leftover rice by transforming it into a brand new entree using the following recipe or its variations.

VAGHAREL THANDA BHAT (FRIED LEFTOVER RICE)

2 cups cooked rice
1 tablespoon oil
2 or 3 sprigs green onion, chopped finely
1 mild green chile, minced after removing
   seeds and core
¼ teaspoon black or green whole cumin
   seeds, or sesame seeds
¼ teaspoon turmeric
2 to 3 tablespoons water
1 tablespoon lemon juice
Salt to taste (optional)

Separate the cooked rice using a fork. Set it aside in a bowl. In a frying pan, heat the oil and add the onion and chiles, and stir-fry them for five minutes. Then add the seeds and cook for another minute. Next, add the rice and sauté for a few minutes while adding the turmeric and enough water to make the rice moist. Sprinkle with lemon juice. Adjust the seasoning to taste, add the optional salt, and serve.

SPICY FRIED LEFTOVER RICE: To make extra-spicy fried rice, add ¼ teaspoon cayenne and/or 1 tablespoon grated gingerroot along with the turmeric.

LEFTOVER RICE FRIED WITH YOGURT: To make a very moist fried rice, add ¼ cup of yogurt instead of the water, and omit the lemon juice.

LEFTOVER RICE FRIED WITH VEGETABLES: To make colorful fried rice, add ¼ cup shelled peas and/or shredded carrots along with the rice. (You may need extra water to cook the vegetables).

LEFTOVER RICE FRIED WITH MIXED BEAN SPROUTS: To make a whole meal out of leftover rice, first prepare Mixed Bean Sprouts, using the recipe on page 127. Add 1 cup of the spicy, cooked sprouts to the leftover rice while frying. Sprinkle with 2 tablespoons of lemon juice, and serve.

FRIED RICE USING FRESHLY COOKED RICE: All of the above variations of fried rice can, of course, be prepared using freshly cooked rice. In that case, first cook the rice and allow it to cool completely to room temperature. Then use any of the above recipes to fry the rice.

CHAPTER EIGHT
BREADS

The statement that bread is the staff of life takes on a full range of meanings in Asian cooking. First of all, bread is always homemade daily; the concept of a commercial bakery is still novel in most Asian countries, especially in India. Fresh bread is prepared from unrefined whole grain flour; thus it is very nutritious and delicious.

The northwest state of India, Gujarat, is well-known for its light flat breads called *rotlies* or *chapatis*. This bread is freshly made at least twice a day. One of the joys of eating in a Gujarati home is being served freshly cooked flat breads while you are eating. The women of the household, who traditionally eat after everyone else is finished, dutifully prepare the bread while you are eating, so the moment you have finished your last *chapati*, you will immediately be served a fresh, piping hot bread before you have a chance to refuse it. Nowadays, many modern couples who work out of the home often hire a cook just to prepare the *chapatis*, so that the entire family can enjoy their lunch together with fresh, hot *chapatis*.

There are many varieties of unleavened, homemade bread in various regions of India made from many different grains, such as wheat, millet, corn, rice, *juar* (a type of buckwheat), and even beans in combination with grains. In North India, there are breads baked in clay ovens called *naan*, which are a result of

the influence from Mogul or Persian cultures. *Naan* is a popular bread in the North where restaurants, and even fancy home kitchens, are equipped with a wood fire clay oven called a *tandoor*. *Naan* made in a conventional gas or electric oven is not the same, therefore, I am not including a "mock" *naan* recipe in this book. However, *pita* bread, which is similar to *naan* and easily found in many markets, can be substituted when your menu calls for *naan*.

Different crops produce grains suitable for different types of breads. For example, soft, light-colored Indian spring wheat berries are considered to be ideal for making *chapatis*. Although flat bread is made from many grains, wheat is the most commonly used grain for breads in many parts of India, so most of the recipes in this chapter call for wheat flour. However, there are regional recipes for breads made from other grains. I have included some of these wheat-free recipes for those who are allergic to wheat or who want to cook bread with other grains.

A young girl in India grows up watching her mother and other women of the family make different types of breads: the everyday variety and fancy, stuffed breads for special occasions. She acquires the techniques necessary to make perfect breads at a very early age, since this is a daily need. After making hundreds and thousands of *chapatis*, I think it's simple and easy to mix the flour, knead the dough, roll out the bread, and cook them to perfection. But this was not an easy process when I first began to learn. When I was a teenager, I produced *chapatis* with a variety of shapes and thicknesses until I finally learned to roll them perfectly round with a uniform texture. Then a few years later, I came to America to go to college. After not having made *chapatis* for few years in America, my *chapati*-making skills had deteriorated. When I went back to India after having spent several years traveling around the world, I was expected to help prepare *chapatis* for the family. I rolled out my *chapatis* as round as I could, being out of practice for some time. When I served them to my father, he looked at them and then casually asked me if those shapes were maps of some of the countries I had traveled!

Do not be put off by your first few *chapatis*. They may fail you. With a little patience and a lot of practice you, too, will be a good bread maker. Making bread is also easier when the technique is demonstrated to you. The step-by-step illustrations given in this chapter should help you.

SELECTING AND BLENDING FLOUR

The texture of the ground flour is very important to the final quality of the cooked bread. Indian wheat has a high gluten content which gives a perfect texture to Indian flat bread. Also, in India, flour is ground to a specific consistency for a particular bread. When you go the flour mill (which can be found on almost every corner of town), you can tell the miller that you want your berries to be ground into *chapati* flour or *parotha* flour.

Outside of India, I have experimented with many grades of wheat flour for making my *chapatis*. I have gotten the best results from combining equal portions of whole wheat flour, whole wheat pasty flour, and unbleached white flour. If you are a purist, you may combine equal parts of whole wheat and whole wheat pastry flours, which works out fine for *bhakharis* or *parothas*, but your *chapatis* may come out more like crackers.

MAKING DOUGH

Making the dough for Indian flat breads is simpler than kneading leavened bread. There is no yeast to mix, and there are no air bubbles to work out. You simply add water, a bit of oil, and the optional salt to the flour(s), and mix them to a uniform, play-dough-like consistency.

You will notice in the bread recipes that the amount of water called for is approximate. That is because the amount of moisture in the air would influence how much water you will need for the bread dough. Start with half the suggested amount of water, and keep adding more, a spoonful at a time, while mixing the dough, until a soft dough is achieved.

CHAPATIS

Chapatis (also known as *rotis*, *rotlies*, and *phulkas*) are soft, thin, unleavened bread rounds that look very much like Mexican corn tortillas. Many Gujarati women prepare *chapatis* twice a day, and, if any are leftover, they will be saved for next morning's tea.

1 cup each whole wheat flour, whole wheat
    pastry flour, and unbleached white flour,
or 1½ cup each whole wheat flour and
    unbleached white flour
3 tablespoons of vegetable oil
¾ cups or a bit more water
½ teaspoon salt (optional)
Butter, *ghee*, or margarine as needed to
    spread lightly on the cooked bread

First, read the introductory notes on flour and dough on pages 142-43. Start off by combining the flours, oil, ¾ cup of water, and the optional salt in a large mixing bowl. Then begin kneading the flour. If the mixture looks too crumbly, add more water, a tablespoon at a time. Stop as soon as you have a uniform, soft ball in your hand. If it is too sticky, add a little bit of oil to your palms and to the dough, and knead for two more minutes. The entire process of forming the dough takes only about ten minutes. Then cover the dough with a moist tea towel, and set it aside. Some cooks feel that letting the dough sit for about 20 minutes makes for better *chapatis*. I have made *chapatis* with the dough made ahead of time and with freshly made dough, but I haven't noticed any difference. Do not make the dough hours ahead of time and refrigerate. This will make the dough dry and tough.

To roll the *chapatis*, have a rolling pin ready (preferably the thin, tapered Indian *velan*), and prepare a clean, dry surface for rolling. Keep ½ cup flour and a bit of oil handy. Then divide the ball of dough into 12 to 16 equal, lemon-sized pieces, and flatten them out using the oily, hollow palms of your hands as illustrated. The flattened pieces should be about 1½" in diameter. Now, if you have a willing partner who will cook the *chapatis* while you roll, the task will be faster. If not, it is best to roll out and cook the *chapatis* in groups of three—one at a time.

Dust the rolling surface lightly with some flour. Oil the rolling pin and your palms. Then roll the dough pieces out, starting from the edges; the middle seems to get larger by itself. Try to make your *chapatis* as round and evenly flat as possible. The *chapati* should not be thin in one spot and thick in another. When the *chapati* is six to seven inches in diameter, set it on a dry surface, and roll out the next two *chapatis* in the same manner.

To cook the *chapatis*, heat a heavy cast iron griddle or Indian *tava* over medium heat, and wait until thoroughly hot. Keep a dry kitchen towel or cloth napkin handy. Have a dish of melted butter, *ghee*, or margarine nearby, ready to be spread over the cooked *chapatis*, as well as a plate to stack them on. Place one *chapati* on the hot griddle, and cook it very briefly (for about 30 seconds), and turn it over using a metal spatula. Cook on the second side for twice as long, and then turn it over again. Using a dry kitchen towel or napkin, press down lightly over the surface of the *chapati*. If the bread swells in some places and forms pockets or bubbles, this is a good sign. Sometimes the entire round inflates into a single pocket—a perfect *chapati*. Turn the *chapati* over a couple times until both sides are cooked and the surface is speckled with brown flecks. When done, transfer the *chapati* to the plate, and spread ¼ teaspoon butter, *ghee*, or margarine evenly over its surface. Cook the next two *chapatis*, and stack them on the plate. To keep them warm and moist, cover the *chapatis* with a cloth towel. Roll and cook the next batch. Serve them right away or keep them warm.

When planning the meal, make the *chapatis* just before serving, so they will stay warm and soft. If you need to reheat them, wrap them in aluminum foil in groups of three, and place them in a preheated 300°F oven for a few minutes.

BHAKHARIS (GUJARATI STYLE)

Bhakharis are thick, hearty *chapatis* which can be made for a simple, quick supper or even for breakfast.

1 cup each whole wheat flour and whole
  what pastry flour,
or 1½ cups whole wheat flour and ½ cup
  unbleached white flour
2 tablespoons vegetable oil
Up to ½ cup water
Melted butter, *ghee*, or margarine as needed

Combine the flours and oil, and gradually add up to a half cup water, making a dough that is somewhat stiff and dry. Knead the dough for about ten minutes, and gather it into a ball. Oil the surface of the ball, and set it aside, covering it with a damp cloth. Begin heating a heavy griddle or skillet over low heat, so that it will be uniformly hot by the time you have rolled out your first few *bhakharis*. Set aside some melted butter, *ghee*, or margarine in a small bowl. Set a plate nearby to stack the cooked *bhakharis* on.

Divide the dough into eight to ten pieces, and flatten them out using oiled hands. Roll out the first four *bhakharis* into six-inch rounds. They will be thicker than *chapatis* and may have uneven edges due to the dryness of the dough; that is O.K. Increase the heat under the griddle to medium high. Place one *bhakhari* on the hot griddle, and turn it over with a metal spatula after a minute. Cook the other side for a minute and a half, and turn it over again. Soon after having turned it for the second time, push the surface of the *bhakhari* lightly, using a cloth napkin. This will create some pockets or make the whole round into one big pocket. Turn it over a couple of times to finish cooking until the *bhakhari* develops a few brown and black specks on the surface. Remove it from the griddle and immediately rub ½ teaspoon of hot butter all over the surface of the *bhakhari*. The entire process of cooking one *bhakhari* should take two to three minutes, turning it often and quickly. Cook the rest of the *bhakharis* in the same manner, and stack them on a plate after having buttered the surface. Roll the rest of the *bhakharis,* and cook them as described above.

If you are not ready to serve the *bhakharis* immediately, store them on a plate covered with a cloth or a metal, dome-like cover to keep them moist. They can be reheated briefly before serving. These hearty breads are traditionally served with a thick *dal*, yogurt soup, or saucy vegetable dish.

ROTLA (MILLET BREAD)

In some parts of India, wheat is more expensive than other grains such as millet, which is easier to grow in arid areas. A *rotla* tastes doughier than a delicate wheat *chapati*, and is not as appealing to city dwellers. However, for many country folks, this hand-patted, thick, hearty and nutritious millet bread is their daily fare. The dark green, tear drop-shaped Indian millet grain is difficult to find in the West, but rye flour comes close to the taste and texture of Indian millet flour. Here is a recipe combining three grain flours which create a wheat-free dough that resembles the Indian *rotla*, but it is not as difficult to roll.

3 cups of imported Indian millet (*bajri*) flour, if available,

or 1 cup each rye flour, brown or white rice flour, and buckwheat flour (or finely ground cornmeal)

3 tablespoons oil

1 teaspoon salt (or less)

Approximately 1 cup or a bit more water, as needed

Melted butter, *ghee*, or margarine as needed to spread on the cooked bread

Combine the flours with the oil and salt. Then add ¾ cup of the water, and start mixing the dough, adding more water as needed to make a smooth, but not very sticky, dough. More flour or water can be added, a little bit at a time, to obtain a uniform consistency. Oil the surface of the dough to help form a dough ball, and set it aside.

Have a heavy griddle ready, and prepare to roll out the dough. In India, millet bread is often hand-patted instead of rolled, but rolling is easier for the novice, in my opinion. You will need to sprinkle some flour on the rolling board for this dough. Divide the dough ball into six to eight pieces, and flatten them using oiled hands. Dust the top of each piece with flour to prevent them from sticking to the rolling pin, then roll out into thick, four-inch wide rounds. These discs are meant to be thicker and smaller than *chapatis*. You can also use waxed paper on the rolling surface and on top of the dough to make the rolling process easier.

Roll out all the pieces, and set them aside. Then heat the griddle and place one round at a time on it to cook. The first side should be cooked for less than a minute; then turn it over to cook the other side. The second side can be cooked for a minute as well. Continue to flip and cook both sides at least once more, so that both sides are cooked thoroughly and brown specks appear on the surface. While cooking, push down the bread gently using a cloth napkin to encourage the formation of air pockets. When the *rotla* seems done, place it on a platter, and spread a little butter, *ghee*, or margarine on one side. Keep the cooked *rotlas* stacked on the platter until ready to serve.

PAROTHA

Parotha (pronounced pa-RO-tah) is a flat bread similar to *chapatis*. However, after rolling each bread, it is folded, oiled, and rerolled, and refolded, reoiled, and rerolled again, repeating the process as many time as the cook desires to create a multi-layered, flaky, puffed pastry-like bread. There are various folding and rolling techniques to make *parotha*, such as making two circles and rolling them together, making coils with the dough and then rolling them into a circle, or the one described below. In this method, a round is first folded into a half circle, then folded into a quarter circle, spreading the surface with *ghee* before each folding. After rolling, the *parothas* are pan-fried using *ghee* or oil (whereas *chapatis* are cooked on a dry griddle or skillet).

1 cup each whole wheat flour, whole wheat
    pastry flour, and unbleached white flour,
or 1½ cup each whole wheat flour and
    unbleached white flour
3 tablespoons oil or *ghee*
1 teaspoon salt
¾ cup or a bit less water

To make the dough, first combine the flours, salt, and oil. Then begin adding the water, starting with ½ cup, while kneading the dough. You need to make this dough somewhat stiff and drier than *chapati* dough, because it will get wetter as you apply the butter or oil while folding. While kneading the dough, add a little more oil to get a smooth texture, and gather it into a ball. Cover with a moist towel, and set it aside.

Next, divide the dough into six to nine pieces, and flatten them using oiled hands. Set the pieces aside under the moist towel. Have ¼ cup of melted butter, *ghee* or oil ready. Keep some flour handy to dust the rolling area. Take one piece of dough, and roll it into a four-inch round. Then oil the top of the round thoroughly but lightly. Fold the oiled round in half, and again lightly spread some oil or *ghee* on the surface. Fold the half again (making a quarter circle), and dust lightly with flour. Roll out this quarter circle until it has stretched out to twice its original size. If you have more patience or desire, oil it again, fold it again, and roll it out. Be careful not to use too much oil before folding, and do not dust too much flour while rolling. The repetitious folding and oiling is done to create more layers, but folding the *parotha* once into a half circle and then into a quarter circle is sufficient. Finish rolling all of

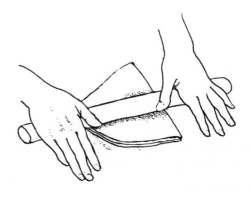

the *parothas*, and set them aside on waxed paper in a single layer so that they do not stick.

To cook the *parotha*, keep the remaining melted butter or oil near by. Lightly oil a heavy griddle or skillet, and heat it over medium heat. Place a *parotha* on the pan, cook on one side briefly, and flip it over using a metal spatula. Apply a teaspoon of oil or *ghee* on top, spreading it evenly. Turn over once again and spread oil on the second side. Gently press and rub the surface of the *parotha* with the back of a spoon to make the cooking process faster. When brown spots appear and the *parotha* looks cooked, transfer it onto a platter. Each *parotha* takes about two minutes to fry, so if you have two griddles, you can make the frying process twice as fast. Serve the *parotha* as soon as they are done, or reheat them in a 300°F oven in a covered casserole dish before serving.

STUFFED *PAROTHAS (ALU PAROTHAS)*

Potato-filled wheat pastries, such as *knishes*, *piroshkis*, and *gorditas de papa*, are popular food items all over the world. In this recipe, you will make two bread rounds, place potato filling in the center, seal the two rounds, and roll them together to create a pastry-like flat bread. Spreading them with *ghee* or oil and cooking them on a griddle or skillet completes this delight.

Filling

2 large potatoes (about ¾ lb.)

2 tablespoons oil

2 tablespoons of scallion or onion, finely chopped

⅛ teaspoon cumin seeds

¼ teaspoon salt

⅛ teaspoon turmeric

A few pinches of cayenne

Parotha Dough

1 cup each whole wheat flour and unbleached white flour,

or ⅔ cup each whole wheat flour, whole wheat pastry flour, and unbleached white flour

½ teaspoon salt

2 tablespoons of oil

½ to ¾ cup water

Ghee or oil for pan frying

Prepare the potato filling by boiling and peeling the potatoes, then mash them to a coarse consistency. Don't puree in a food processor or they will turn gummy. Heat the 2 tablespoons of oil in a frying pan, and sauté the scallion or onion for two minutes. Add the cumin and then the spices, salt, and potatoes. Stir-fry the mixture for five minutes, then transfer it onto a platter, spread it out, and let it cool.

First, make the *parotha* dough as described on page 148, making it a bit stiffer. Sprinkle a little flour on the rolling board. Take one of the dough pieces, and roll it into a circle about three inches in diameter. Roll out a second piece of dough the same way. Lightly oil the surface of both circles. Next, take a tablespoon of the cooled potato filling, and place in the center of one of the circles. Spread the filling evenly, leaving a half-inch space free around the edges, as illustrated below. Cover this round with the second round. Pinch the edges of the rounds together to seal. Then gently roll the parotha into a seven-inch round, turning it from one side to the other and dusting the board with some flour so that it does not stick while you are rolling. If a little bit of filling oozes out while rolling, it is all right. Seal and continue to roll carefully so that the two rounds do not separate. Prepare three more stuffed *parotha* in the same manner. Set the remaining dough pieces in a bowl, and cover them until ready to stuff and roll.

To cook the parotha, heat a heavy griddle, skillet, or *tava*, and set a small bowl of melted *ghee*, butter, or oil nearby. Place one *parotha* on the heated griddle, and cook for nearly a minute. Turn it with a metal spatula, spread a teaspoon of oil or *ghee* evenly over the surface, and cook for a minute on this side. Turn again, spread the oil or *ghee* on the other side, and cook for 30 seconds. Flip the *parotha* over a few more times, pressing lightly with a napkin to allow even cooking. When brown specks appear and the *parotha* looks cooked, remove from the griddle, and set aside on a plate. Cook the next *parothas* in the same manner. The entire process for frying the four *parothas* should take 10 minutes.

Roll the remaining *parothas* after stuffing each of them. Cook them in the manner described above. Keep the *parothas* warm by covering the plate with a cloth napkin. Serve them hot or at room temperature. They can be rewarmed in a very low oven (250°F) in a covered casserole dish.

ALU GHOBI PAROTHA: Boil, peel, and mash the potatoes for stuffing as described on the previous page. Mince 1 cup of cauliflower buds, and add to the mashed potatoes before you stir-fry them for stuffing. Cool the stuffing and proceed with the recipe as described.

ALU PALAK PAROTHA: Boil and peel the potatoes. Mash them to make the stuffing as described in the previous recipe. Add 1 cup of minced spinach or other leafy green, such as watercress, radish leaves, or even beet greens, to the two cups of potatoes. Stir-fry the potato/leaf mixture a bit longer than the previous recipes to allow the liquid from the cooking leaves to evaporate. Follow the main recipe to cook the *parothas*.

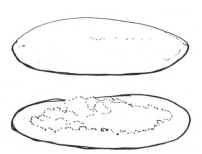

PURAN POLI (PAROTHA STUFFED WITH SWEET DAL)

This semi-sweet bread is prepared for special holidays or guests. Despite being sweet, it is a nutritious addition to your menu, since the bread is made with whole grain flour and is stuffed with cooked beans.

Filling

½ cup *toor dal* (other skinless *dals* can be substituted)
⅓ cup or less brown sugar or Indian *jaggery*
6 to 8 pinches of cardamom powder

Dough

1 cup each whole wheat flour, unbleached white flour, and whole wheat pastry flour
3 tablespoons oil
½ teaspoon salt
Approximately 1 cup water

Melted butter, *ghee*, or oil for pan-frying

Prepare the *dal* filling by boiling the *toor dal* vigorously in three cups of water for five minutes to remove the lentil's oily coating. Then strain the *dal* and discard the water. Boil two cups of water, then add the *dal* and allow it to cook over medium heat for 25 to 30 minutes, until the *dal* is very soft.

While waiting for the *dal* to cook, prepare the dough. Combine the flour, salt, and oil in a mixing bowl. Add water as needed to prepare the dough exactly like the *parotha* dough described on page 148. Set the dough aside after coating with oil to prevent it from drying.

Lower the heat under the *dal*, and add the sugar or *jaggery* and ground cardamom. Continue to cook, stirring the mixture until it looks like a thick pudding. Spread it on a platter to cool, and set aside. While the *dal* mixture cools, it will solidify enough to be used as the filling.

Divide the dough into 10 to 12 pieces, and form each piece into a ball. Flatten each piece using oiled hands, and set aside. Follow the directions for rolling out and filling the stuffed *parotha* on page 148, substituting a tablespoon of the cooked *dal* for the tablespoon of potato stuffing. After filling the *puran poli* with *dal*, roll it out in the same manner as the *alu parotha* (a thick, six-inch round), being careful not to squeeze out the filling.

When four of the rounds are done, heat a heavy iron griddle, skillet, or *tava* over medium heat. Place the *puran poli* carefully on the cooking surface, and cook the bread in the same fashion as for *alu parotha* (see pages 149-50). Cook on both sides for a minute, then spread a teaspoonful of *ghee* or oil lightly and evenly on each side. Turn it over a few times, allowing the *puran poli* to cook evenly until brown specks appear on the surface. Gujaratis love to drench the cooked *poli* with extra *ghee* as soon as it comes off the griddle.

Stack the cooked *polis* on a plate, and serve them with a saucy vegetable dish and a *chutney*.

THEPLAS (Flat Breads with Leafy Greens)
This interesting and nutritious bread is often made to use up leftover rice and bitter, spicy greens. What is more, this bread can be easily made without using wheat flour, as an alternative for people who cannot tolerate wheat. If you do not have leftover rice, the dough can be made using a combination of rye, buckwheat, and rice flour. Watercress or arugula leaves can used in place of traditional fenugreek or mustard greens.

The dough can be made in the same manner as the plain *chapati* dough described on pages 143-145, with the addition of minced leafy greens. Using a food processor to make the dough speeds up the process, but hand-mixing works well. After the dough is made, the *theplas* are rolled into somewhat thicker and smaller rounds than *chapatis*. Then, unlike *chapatis* which are dry-roasted, *theplas* are pan-fried on both sides with a small amount of oil.

1 cup cold cooked rice, or ¾ cup rice flour
1 cup each whole wheat and unbleached white flour,
or 1 cup each rye and buckwheat flour (for a wheat-free version)
1 cup finely chopped, leafy greens, such as fenugreek leaves, mustard greens, watercress, or arugula,
½ teaspoon salt
3 tablespoons oil
1 or 2 cloves of garlic, minced
¼ teaspoon turmeric and ⅛ teaspoon cayenne (both optional)
½ cup or a bit more water
Flour for dusting the rolling surface
Oil for spreading as needed

The dough will be a bit sticky due to the addition of leafy greens. If you use a food processor, place all the ingredients (except for the last three) in the processing bowl, and blend them briefly. Add the water last, as needed, until a sticky ball of dough starts to form. Add a bit of flour and/or oil to unstick and remove the dough from the food processor.

If you are making the dough by hand, chop the leaves very finely, and add the rest of the ingredients. Add the water last, as you need to make a dough that is not too crumbly or too sticky. Add a little more flour or oil if the dough is too sticky or dry.

Divide the dough into eight equal pieces, and work with one piece at a time, leaving the rest of the dough covered in a mixing bowl. Flatten the piece of dough by pressing between your palms. Dust the rolling surface and roll out the dough piece into a five-inch circle. You may need to flour the rolling surface and flip the circle while rolling it to prevent it from sticking. Roll out four of the *theplas*, and set aside to pan-fry.

Keep some oil in a bowl nearby the frying pan. Heat the pan over moderate heat, and add a rolled *thepla*. After it has cooked for a minute, turn it over and spread a teaspoon of oil evenly on its surface. Then gently turn it over again, and spread another teaspoonful of oil on that side. Flip the *theplas* a few more times, using a bit more oil on both sides, and cook them until brown specks appear and the bread looks done. Stack the *theplas* on a plate. Roll out the remaining pieces in the same manner, and fry them as described. The *theplas* remain moist even after they are cold. That is why they are a popular lunch box or picnic item in India. Serve *theplas* with a *suki bhaji* (see the recipes on pages 79-88) or with plain yogurt.

PURIS (Deep-Fried Puffed Bread)

Puris are delicate, light breads that are made for special occasions. Puris taste good whether they are hot or cold. This makes them perfect breads for a party where hot dishes are difficult to coordinate. The dough is made using the same ingredients and directions as *chapati* dough (pages 143-45)—only a bit stiffer. After rolling the *puris*, they are deep-fried in hot oil where they inflate like a balloon to form a puffed bread that is a delight to eat. I often make this bread when I give Indian cooking demonstrations to American school children, since they find puris visually fascinating to watch, as well as delicious to sample.

1 cup each whole wheat flour, whole wheat
    pastry flour, and unbleached white flour,
or 1½ cup each whole wheat flour and
    unbleached white flour
½ teaspoon salt
3 tablespoons oil
¾ cup water
vegetable oil for deep frying

Combine the flours, salt, and three tablespoons oil in a mixing bowl. Begin to add water starting with ½ cup, and add more as you need to bind the mixture together into a smooth, stiff dough. Oil the surface of a board and your hands, then transfer the dough onto the board. Knead the dough by pushing it back and forth with the palms of your hands while wrapping it around itself. After a few minutes the dough will be smooth. Gather the dough into a ball, and transfer it back to the mixing bowl. Cover it with a towel, and set aside.

Fill your wok or frying pan with about two cups of oil, and set it on the stove. Set a slotted serving spoon and a basket or a bowl lined with some towels near the stove for the cooked *puris*. Divide the dough into two portions. With one half of the dough ball, make 10 to 12 small pieces, and flatten them out using the oiled palms of your hands. *Puri* rounds are much smaller than *chapatis*, so start with small pieces of dough. Keep the other half of the *puri* dough covered.

Roll out four to six pieces at a time into small rounds, about three inches in diameter. Heat the oil until very hot, but not smoky. Slip a *puri* into the hot oil, and get ready for the action. The *puri* will first drop to the bottom, then rise to the surface. As soon as it reaches the surface, turn it over with a slotted metal spoon, and push it gently with the back of the spoon. The *puri* will now inflate. Turn the *puri* over again, and cook until both sides are golden but not browned. Remove the cooked *puri* from the oil using the slotted spoon and draining the excess oil. The first *puri* may not inflate—if the oil was not hot enough or the *puris* were not evenly rolled, they will have trouble puffing. (They will still be delicious.)

Store the cooked *puris* in the bowl or basket. Finish rolling and frying the rest of the *puris*. Rolling the *puris* in a group of six and then frying them works well. However, if you a have a cooking partner, one can roll while the other fries, making the task faster and more fun. Another trick for making five or six puris quickly is by first rolling a big oblong piece, then cutting small rounds using a round cookie cutter. Serve the *puris* hot, warm, or at room temperature.

MASALA PURIS (SPICY PURIS): Add ½ teaspoon turmeric powder, ¼ teaspoon cumin, and ⅛ teaspoon cayenne to the flour mixture, and proceed as for plain *puris*.

MITHI PURIS (SWEET PURIS): Add 3 tablespoons of sugar or honey and ½ teaspoon cinnamon powder to the flour mixture. (Use less water if using honey). Proceed as for plain *puris*.

MAKAI ROTI (Indian Corn Bread)

This Punjabi bread is often made using a mixture of wheat flour and cornmeal, plus corn kernels when fresh corn is available. It can also be made with *masa harina* (Mexican cornmeal) and wheat flour. I am also including a variation that combines cornmeal with other flours to create a wheat-free bread, since wheat-free bread recipes such as these are difficult to find.

½ cup cornmeal or *masa harina*

1½ cups whole wheat flour (finely ground, if possible)

1 cup corn kernels, scraped from a fresh corn cob, or frozen kernels, thawed (optional)

1 teaspoon salt

1 to 2 teaspoons minced hot chiles (such as jalapeño), with seeds and core removed

1 tablespoon oil

water as needed

If you are using corn kernels, it is easier to combine all the ingredients in a food processor. Place all the ingredients except the water in the blending bowl. Combine very briefly so as not to crush the corn kernels too much. Then add water as needed, a few tablespoons at a time, until the dough begins to form. As soon as the dough ball starts forming, turn the processor off and gather the sticky ball in a mixing bowl. Add more flour and cornmeal as needed to form a uniform dough. If you are making the dough by hand, you may need a little more water, since the liquid from the kernels is not secreted when mixing by hand. At any rate, this dough is somewhat sticky and tricky to roll out.

In order to roll the corn bread rounds, you will need to dust the rolling surface from time to time with flour or cornmeal. Using two layers of waxed paper is very helpful. Divide the dough into six to eight pieces, and flatten them out. Then roll each piece into a thick, *chapati*-like round.

Heat a heavy griddle or skillet over high heat, and place one *roti* on it. Flip it over after it has been cooked for 30 seconds, and spread ½ teaspoon oil evenly over the surface. Turn it over again and repeat the application of oil. Cook on both sides, flipping a few times until brown and black specks appear on the surface. Pan-fry the second *roti* in the same manner. Stack the breads on a platter. Finish rolling and cooking the rest of the *makai rotis*, and serve them hot or warm.

WHEAT-FREE *ROTIS*: Replace the wheat flour with ¾ cup rice flour and ¾ cup rye (or buckwheat) flour. The dough is a bit drier and harder to roll, because it lacks wheat gluten. Use waxed paper to help you roll out wheat-free *roti*.

PUDLA (or *PUDA*)

This spicy, pancake-like bread is sometimes referred to as a "vegetarian omelette" (since eggs are not considered vegetarian by Indian Hindus).

1 cup *besan* (chick-pea or garbanzo flour)
½ teaspoon salt
¼ teaspoon cumin seeds
⅛ teaspoon turmeric powder
A few pinches of cayenne powder,
or 1 hot chile, minced after removing seeds
    and core
¼ cup minced onion or scallion
Juice of ½ lime or lemon
½ cup diced tomato (optional)
½ cup water

In a mixing bowl, combine all the ingredients using a fork or whisk, breaking up any lumps. You should have a thick batter—a bit thicker than pancake batter. Adjust the batter by adding a bit more water or flour. Set the batter aside.

Heat a heavy griddle or crêpe pan over moderate to high heat. When the pan is hot, add a tablespoon oil, spreading it all over its inner surface. Then place two tablespoons of the batter in the center, spreading it quickly and evenly in a circular motion using the back of a ladle and leaving some free space at the edge of the pan. The pancake circle does not have to be round, but it should be uniformly thick. Cook the *pudla* for a minute on the first side, then flip it over using a spatula. Spread another tablespoon of oil on the second side of the *pudla*, and cook for another minute. Lower the heat and cook the *pudla* for two more minutes, turning it over a few more times and making sure it is well-cooked on both sides. The cooked *pudla* will look golden with some brown specks. Stack the cooked *pudlas* on a plate, and serve warm with plain yogurt or a *chutney*.

PUDLA WITH YOGURT: Use ½ cup yogurt and a few tablespoons of water in place of the ½ cup of water to make the batter. Omit the lemon or lime juice. Follow the remaining recipe directions.

RICE AND *BESAN* PUDLA: Use ½ cup cooked rice and ½ cup *besan* to make the *pudla*. Follow the remaining recipe directions.

PUDLA WITH CORNMEAL AND RICE FLOUR: Use equal portions of *besan*, cornmeal, and rice flour to make the batter.

CHAPTER NINE
SWEETS

A chapter on Indian sweets and desserts could fill up a whole book, since sweets play an important role in the multitude of holidays and feasts that are so much a part of India's rich culture. Sweets represent everything that is joyful; they symbolize prosperity and good fortune. However, this book's focus is the nutritional aspects of diet, so I prefer to discriminate among the many possible dessert recipes. I personally do not like the over-sweetened, cream-laden Indian sweets, so most of the recipes that follow are nutritious, as well as easy to prepare.

As a rule, sweets are not served at the end of the meal every day in India. They are reserved for holidays and for guests. However, there are so many holidays on the Indian calendar and so many relatives who drop by unannounced that sweets are not difficult to find in an Indian household. Most Indian sweets are time-consuming to prepare. Many of them require cooking milk for a long time until it condenses into an almost-solid mass. These sweets can be purchased from professional sweet makers, called *mithai walas*, who are an institution in their own right in India. In a special section of the market, they sit on a high altar of cushions in their shops, drinking many cups of *chai* all day long, stirring milk in great big woks and carefully reproducing age-old recipes. Even though I was never too fond of sweets, I have vivid memories of the aromas that would come from that colorful and popular section of the town, especially during religious holidays when the "sweets" bazaar becomes really hectic. During this time, many families purchase large quantities of sweets for feasts and celebrations.

In contrast to the big towns, the villages have no bazaars just for sweets. Many devoted cooks throughout India savor the challenge involved in producing traditional sweets and do not mind spending the long hours necessary to prepare them. Also, orthodox Hindus who adhere to strict dietary practices would not trust the preparation of any food they ate to someone who is not of their own family.

During the holiday season, women will stock up on the different costly items necessary for making sweets. Many days of preparation then begin. Houses fill up with delectable aromas, and children squeal with delight and anticipation. I remember how my mother used to hide the sweets (which were made days before the holiday) away from us—the kids—lest the temptation be too great.

In India, most homemakers devote the last several weeks of the Hindu calendar to preparing food for the holidays, much of that being sweets. These weeks in October and November are filled with many holidays, one right after another. In northwest India, the holidays begin with the days of the dead, called *Sraddha*, in which we commemorate the memory of those who have died. At this time, each family chooses a day on which the dinner is prepared as an offering for a deceased person. The menu must consist of that person's favorite foods, including a sweet. When the dinner is

ready, the youngest member of the family takes a helping of the prepared sweet, folds it within a *chapati*, and places it on the roof of the house. When the birds gather to eat this food, it is said that the soul of our ancestor being honored has flown down in the body of a bird and has taken the offering. When this is done and the ancestor is satisfied, everyone else can start the feast.

Following the holiday for the dead is the celebration called *Dashera*, literally meaning "ten days." On these festive days the victory of Lord Rama over the evil Ravana is celebrated. The story of the Hindu epic *Ramayana* goes like this: Prince Rama was chosen as heir to his father's throne when he reached adolescence. However, due to a family quarrel, he was exiled to the jungle for fourteen years. During his peaceful and simple life in the jungle, his beloved wife Sita was kidnapped by the wicked demon Ravana, who came dressed like a *sadhu* (holy man) and took her to his kingdom of Lanka. Rama sent his friend Hanuman, the Monkey King, to talk to Ravana about Sita's return. But the arrogant Ravana replied that Rama must come with his army to release his wife. In the jungle, where Rama had no army, he and Hanuman trained a strong army of monkeys and declared a war against Ravana. The battle was fought for ten days, and Rama became victorious on the tenth day. Thus, the ten days are celebrated with much festivity, and a different sweet is made for each day. During the evenings, people dress up in their fine clothes and gather in the streets for music and dancing, but the last day is the most important. On the tenth evening, huge paper and wood statues of the good lord Rama and the evil Ravana are erected in the town square. The hollow replica of Ravana is filled with fire works. At the end of the evening, after much music and dancing, a single flaming arrow is shot by the statue of Rama into the statue of Ravana. As soon as it strikes its adversary, a most wonderful display of fireworks is set off, filling up the sky with colors and accompanied by the shouts and applause of spectators. More music and dancing begin as if the real battle and victory had just taken place. The evening ends with a great feast and a variety of sweets.

After *Dashera* comes the most important holiday of the year, *Divali*—the festival of lights—which falls on the last four or five days of the Hindu calendar. Each day corresponds to a different event which took place during the golden age of Rama's reign. During these holidays, walls are painted and floors are decorated with sand paintings. During the evening, houses are illuminated with countless candles and oil lamps. The sky is made bright with many colorful fireworks.

This is the time to bring out all the important sweets which have been bought or prepared for days in advance. Families and friends will visit each other during *Divali*, exchanging and sharing sweets. The last evening of this holiday is *Laxmi Puja*—worshipping the Goddess of prosperity—with offerings of fruits and sweets in the hope that the following year will be fruitful for all. The next day is the Hindu New Year's Day, and breakfast is prepared with at least one sweet so that the new year will start with sweetness. On this day, Hindu people walk miles and miles to visit as many temples as they can. They gather at the temples to exchange good wishes for the new year, and many sweets are distributed during elaborate ceremonies. At the end of New Year's Day, people return to their homes tired and hungry. With their dinner that evening they eat the remaining sweets so that every dinner of the new year will be sweet.

In contrast to my enthusiasm for the season of sweets and celebrations is my opinion that many of these sweets are too sweet and contain too many calories, especially for adults who do not exercise regularly. I have avoided taking the trouble to learn how to make many of these sweets, as most of them are not that nutritious. They do take a long time to prepare. If I did learn how to make them, my younger

son Sanjay would want me in the kitchen for longer than I am already there! The sweets I have included in this chapter are those that are relatively easy to make and are more nutritious than other desserts. I have also cut down on the amount of sugar (or other sweetener) and butter or *ghee* in these traditional recipes. Feel free to alter them further to suit yourself, making them either less filling or richer.

In India, sweets are traditionally served with the meal in order to complement the entire range of flavors one encounters during the meal: sour, salty, hot (spicy), astringent, bitter, and sweet. The idea is to incorporate all the tastes in one *thali* (banquet), not to serve sweets at the end to override other flavors, as is the case with Western tradition. Whether you serve Indian sweets along with your meal or at the end, remember to serve them in small portions.

SHEERA (or SUJI HALVA)

Sheera is one of the quickest and easiest Indian sweets to prepare, yet it is no less important than more elaborate Indian desserts. In fact, *sheera* is prepared for various religious holidays, such as for *pujas* (temple services), where it is first offered to God, and then distributed among the participants of the ceremony as *prasad* (God's leftovers). Needless to say, children cannot wait for the service to end so that they can have this delicious, free *prasad*.

1 cup uncooked cream of wheat or rice cereal
3 to 4 tablespoons butter, *ghee*, or margarine
2 cups hot (not boiling) water
½ cup brown sugar or *jaggery*,
or ⅓ cup honey
2 tablespoons chopped cashews or almonds
¼ cup golden or black raisins
few pinches of ground cardamom

Melt the butter or margarine in a heavy skillet over low to medium heat, and add the cream of wheat or rice. With a wooden spoon, sauté the mixture for about 10 minutes until it turns golden. Do not burn. Either reduce the heat to low, and stir frequently while preparing for the next step, or turn the heat off. In a small saucepan, heat the water and add the sugar or honey. Cook gently until the sweetener melts and the liquid is very hot, but not boiling. Add the liquid to the stir-fried cream of wheat (or rice), and blend. Add the nuts, raisins, and cardamom, and stir-fry over low heat for about three minutes, until all the liquid has been evaporated and the thick mass starts drawing away from the sides of the pan. To serve it hot, spoon the *sheera* into individual bowls or dessert cups. To serve it cold, transfer the *sheera* to a platter; spread it out and pat it evenly with the back of a spoon. You can now cut the *sheera* into small squares or diamonds to serve at room temperature. You can also refrigerate the *sheera* platter, and cut the *sheera* right before serving.

KHEER

Kheer is a sweet rice dish that is prepared on festive occasions; both the sweetness and the rice are symbols of happiness and prosperity. This is a lighter rice pudding than European rice pudding made with eggs. It can be made without milk, as demonstrated in the following variation.

1 cup uncooked, long-grain white rice (parboiled is fine),

or 1 cup uncooked short-grain brown rice

2 cups water for cooking the rice (2½ cups for brown rice)

6 cups low-fat or whole milk, or coconut milk

1 cup or less sugar or honey

2 to 3 tablespoons butter, *ghee*, or oil

½ cup raisins (preferably yellow sultana)

⅛ teaspoon cardamom powder (freshly ground, preferred)

¼ teaspoon saffron threads (optional), soaked in 2 tablespoons of warm water or milk for 10 minutes

¼ to ½ cup shelled, chopped pistachios or blanched, chopped almonds

Cook the rice in a large pot according to your favorite rice recipe (or see the recipes on pages 132-33); keep it slightly undercooked or "al dente." Making *kheer* with brown rice would be frowned upon by traditional Indian cooks, but try the recipe with brown rice anyway. It takes a bit longer, but brown rice *kheer* is delightfully creamy and satisfying.

When the rice is nearly cooked (about 15 minutes for regular or converted white rice, 8 minutes for *basmati* white rice, and 25 to 30 minutes for brown rice), add the milk. Cook uncovered over medium heat, stirring frequently to prevent it from sticking to the bottom of the pan. When the liquid is almost completely evaporated (which will take about 30 to 40 minutes depending on what type of rice you are using), add the sweetener, butter, cardamom, saffron, and raisins. Continue to cook, stirring often to evaporate more of the liquid until it has thickened to a pudding-like consistency. Transfer the *kheer* to a serving bowl or individual cups, and top it with chopped nuts. *Kheer* can be served hot, at room temperature, or chilled. It thickens more if you refrigerate it.

VEGAN *KHEER*: To make the rice pudding without milk, substitute coconut milk and follow the above recipe. You can make the coconut milk using the directions on pages 36-37, or use canned coconut milk. You can also omit the butter. Coconut milk has enough oil in it to make this pudding nice and creamy.

FIRNI

Similar to rice pudding, this dessert is a bit quicker and simpler to make than *kheer*. *Firni* is traditionally made with whole milk which is reduced to half its volume by stirring and cooking it down for 40 minutes. An alternate recipe uses half-and-half to make it quicker. However, I prefer the traditional version which is creamier but less rich. You can also thicken the milk faster by adding non-fat powdered milk to the liquid milk, stirring the mixture very frequently so that the milk solids won't stick to the bottom.

2 quarts whole milk,
or 1 quart milk and 1 cup non-fat powdered
    milk
6 tablespoons uncooked cream of rice cereal
¾ cup or less sugar, honey, or maple syrup
½ teaspoon rose water
2 tablespoons butter, *ghee*, or margarine
½ cup blanched, chopped almonds, or shelled,
    chopped pistachio nuts

Pour the milk into a large, thick-bottomed saucepan or wok, and bring to a simmer over high heat. Reduce the heat to medium, stir often, and cook for about 40 minutes, until the milk has reduced quite a bit and has gotten thick. If you are using the combination of liquid milk and non-fat powdered milk, stir the mixture more frequently. Then reduce the heat and slowly add the cream of rice to the pot of cooking milk with one hand, while stirring with the other hand. Make sure to break apart any lumps which may form from the cream of rice. Add the sweetener and continue to cook while stirring for another 10 minutes, until the mixture approximates the consistency of thick pancake batter. Then add the butter and rose water. Transfer the mixture to individual serving cups or bowls. Decorate with the nuts as a topping. Chill in the refrigerator before serving.

VEGAN *FIRNI*: Omit the butter. Substitute coconut milk for the dairy milk (either freshly made from the recipe on pages 36-37 or canned). Follow the above recipe. This recipe can also be prepared with plain soymilk or an extra-thick soy beverage, such as Soyamalt. The cooking time should be quite short, with about 10 minutes of stirring if you are using the thick soy beverage. Do not use much sweetener if you use soymilk that has already been sweetened.

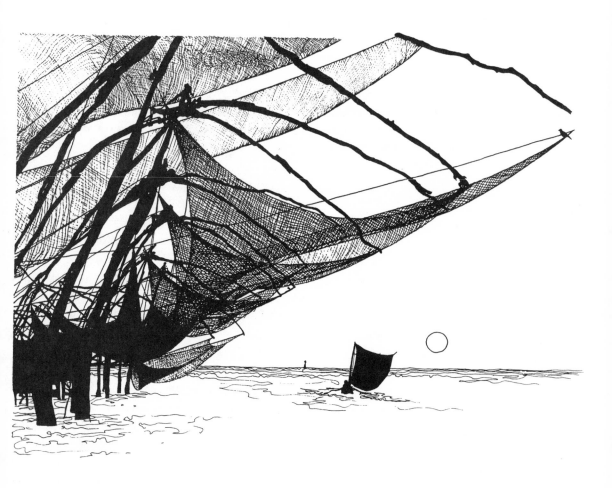

CHIKKIS OR SESAME HALVA

The word *halva* means "sweets" in Arabic, therefore several recipes given in this chapter are called *halva*: Carrot *Halva*, Suji *Halva*, Bedam *Halva*, etc. However, outside the Middle East or Asia, *halva* is thought of only as a sweet treat made from sesame seeds. Here is a recipe which is very similar to that familiar sesame *halva*. I learned this recipe while on the beautiful beaches of Goa, on the western coast of India. During the time when I stayed in Goa, a little girl would pass on the beach in front of my house, selling *chikkis* that her mother had made. I recall vividly how she ran quickly across the sand, carrying her jar of *chikkis* every afternoon, as I—her regular customer—waited eagerly for the treats which were perfect partners for my afternoon tea. We became friends and when I was leaving Goa, the girl came to my home and presented me with her mother's recipe. Years later, I started to make *chikkis* regularly for my six-year-old daughter Serena and her girl friend Sonia. Each day after school, they would wait for me to make the *chikkis* as eagerly as I had waited for them in Goa. I distinctly remember how they couldn't wait until the *chikkis* were cool enough to handle so they could eat them.

1 cup sesame seeds
4 tablespoons melted butter, *ghee*, or oil
¼ cup whole wheat flour
½ cup brown sugar or honey
2 tablespoons water (1 tablespoon if using honey)

Using a wide pan or wok, roast the sesame seeds over low heat, stirring them rapidly and being careful not to burn them. When the seeds begin to redden, immediately transfer them to a mixing bowl. Clean the wok or pan by wiping with a paper towel, and place one tablespoon of butter, *ghee*, or oil in the pan. Place over low heat, and stir in the flour. Sauté the mixture for three minutes, until the flour turns golden. Transfer the flour to the bowl of sesame seeds. Wipe the pan (wok) again, and add the remaining butter, *ghee*, or oil and the brown sugar or honey. Cook them together for a minute or so until they are combined, then add the water. Cook the mixture while stirring for about four minutes to create a thick syrup. Then add the sesame seed and flour mixture to the cooking syrup. With a continual, steady motion, stir the mixture for about five minutes until a solid mass is formed. Transfer the mixture to a wide platter or a mixing bowl. When the mixture has cooled down just enough so that it can be handled, divide it into six to eight small portions. Quickly start forming balls, about the size of a lemon, using the palms of your hands. This task is tricky; you have to make these balls while the mixture is still quite hot or else it will begin to fall apart. Arrange the balls on a plate, and serve. An alternate method is to spread the sesame meal mixture evenly on a platter, and allow to cool. Cut into squares to cool.

Chikkis can be eaten hot or cold. They will keep for days without refrigeration.

CARROT HALVA

This dessert is time-consuming, since you will be stirring the milk and carrots constantly until they become an almost solid mass. However, it is worth the experience making and eating this nutritious dessert. Some cooks shorten the time by adding powdered milk to the recipe, but the taste is not the same.

1 quart milk
2 cups grated carrots (approximately 3 medium carrots)
¼ cup almonds, blanched and chopped
2 tablespoons butter
¼ teaspoon ground cardamom
½ teaspoon saffron thread, soaked in 2 tablespoons of hot milk for 15 minutes
¼ cup honey or about ½ cup sugar (or adjust to taste)

Begin by heating the milk in a wide pan or a wok. Add the carrots and cook over medium heat, stirring frequently. After the first fifteen minutes of stirring, lower the heat and prepare the blanched almonds. (While preparing the nuts continue to watch and stir the mixture frequently.) To blanch the nuts, boil them in a cup of water for a few minutes, then dunk them in cold water. Remove the loosened skins from the nuts by peeling or by rubbing them with your hands. Chop the nuts with a knife, or crush them using a blender or food processor. Set them side.

Next, adjust the heat under the carrots to medium. Stir frequently, scrapping up any solids from the sides and at the bottom of the pan. After the milk and carrot mixture has been reduced to half its original volume (which takes about half an hour from the start), lower the heat again. Continue to stir occasionally while roasting the nuts. Melt the butter in a small pot, and stir-fry the nuts for a few minutes until they are golden. Add them to the cooking carrots. Then add the rest of the ingredients, and continue to stir and cook the mixture to an almost solid consistency. To facilitate the evaporation of the liquid, stir with a rapid circular motion. When almost solid, transfer the *halva* to an oiled platter, and spread it evenly, patting it with the back of the stirring spoon. Allow the *halva* to cool to room temperature, then chill it in the refrigerator. The cooling and chilling will further solidify the *halva* to the point where you should be able to slice the dessert into pie-like wedges or small squares or diamonds. Serve the *halva* in small portions as it is quite rich.

CARROT PUDDING: Cook the mixture only until it forms a pudding-like consistency. Divide the pudding into individual dessert bowls or cups. Serve carrot pudding chilled.

BESAN HALVA (or *MOHAN THAL*)

This is a fudge-like sweet made with high-protein chick-pea flour, nuts, butter, and sugar.

¼ cup sugar
3 tablespoons water
¼ cup melted butter, *ghee*, oil, or margarine
1 cup *besan* (chick-pea or garbanzo flour)
3 tablespoons shelled pistachios or almonds
⅛ teaspoon freshly ground cardamom

Combine the sugar and water in a small pot, and cook over low heat for six to eight minutes, until it forms a syrup and begins to simmer. Turn off the heat but keep the syrup warm.

Chop the pistachio nuts using a knife, blender, or food processor. Set the chopped nuts aside. In a heavy frying pan, warm the butter, *ghee*, or oil over low heat, then add the *besan* and sauté for five minutes. Add the chopped nuts and continue to stir-fry for 10 to 15 minutes, until the mixture turns a copper color. Next, heat the syrup for a minute, then add to the *besan* and nut mixture. Continue to cook for a few minutes until all the ingredients are well-blended into a thick, stiff mass. Add the cardamom. Lightly grease a platter and transfer the *halva* onto it, spreading it evenly using the back of a spoon. When the *halva* is cool enough to touch, make it more compact by rubbing the surface with your hands. When it is at room temperature or chilled in the refrigerator, it will be solid enough to cut. Cut the *halva* into diamond-shaped pieces to serve.

LADOOS (SWEET BALLS)

This is my favorite Indian sweet, because it is wholesome, and it also evokes fond memories of the celebration called *Ganesh Chaturthi*, the Elephant God's birthday. Ganesh, the elephant god, is admired by Indian ladies because he is a great lover of good food. On his birthday, women prepare a great feast which always includes *ladoos*, while the men and children build a mud statue of Ganesh and decorate him with colorful ornaments. When the feast is ready, the *ladoos* are offered to Ganesh as *bhog* (sacrifice). Then, the town's people gather together and take the mud statue of Ganesh down to a river in a gay, colorful procession with music and dancing. At the river's edge, the procession stops and Ganesh is taken down to the deepest part of the water for his *samadhi* (disappearance into eternity). The crowd excitedly bids Ganesh farewell with a lot of chanting and asks him to return early next year. The people then return home and begin their feast, which includes *ladoos* with the meal.

Ladoos literally means "sweet balls." They can be prepared from whole wheat flour, *besan*, or a variety of grain meal mixes. In my home town, this recipe using whole wheat flour and cream of wheat was the standard for *ladoos* made on *Ganesh Chaturthi*.

1 cup whole wheat flour
½ cup uncooked cream of wheat cereal
¼ cup melted butter, *ghee*, or oil
4 tablespoons water
½ to ¾ cup melted *ghee* or oil for deep-frying
⅛ teaspoon ground cardamom seeds
½ to ¾ cup brown sugar
⅓ to ½ cup melted butter, *ghee*, or margarine
1 teaspoon white poppy seeds (optional, sesame seeds can be substituted)

In a mixing bowl, combine the flour, cream of wheat, and the ¼ cup of melted butter, *ghee*, or oil, mixing them together with your fingers. Then add the water and knead the mixture into a very stiff dough. Knead the dough for about ten minutes to combine the ingredients; they are dry enough that they tend to crumble apart. That is O.K. Divide this stiff dough into as many handfuls of egg-shaped pieces as you can. Squeeze each of the pieces within your clenched fist to form an oblong-shaped ball. Set these pieces (called *muthia* or fistfuls) aside.

In a wok or a heavy pot, heat the *ghee* or oil for frying, and deep-fry the dough pieces (*muthias*) until they are golden brown, two or three at a time. Move them around in the hot oil to allow them to cook on all sides. Take them out using a slotted spoon, and drain as much oil as possible back into the wok. Set the fried *muthias* aside. Allow them to cool enough to handle. Then break each of the *muthias* into two or three pieces so that they can be cooled quickly. Set them aside to cool further.

Next, you will be breaking and crumbling those fried dough pieces into a cornmeal-like consistency. This is done by using a special wooden hammer in India, but having a food processor or blender is easier. Place the dough pieces into a blender or food processor and blend in a coarse consistency. Transfer the *ladoo* meal into a mixing bowl, and take out any big chunks that may be in this mixture. Next, add the cardamom, sugar and the ⅓ to ½ cup melted *ghee*, butter or margarine. Blend all the ingredients well. Now you are ready to make the balls. (This task is still done by hand in India, and I don't know of any mechanized way to do it.) Take ½ cup of this wet meal in your hand, and form a small compact ball, as though making a snow ball to throw. Make as many balls as you can from the meal. Set the balls onto a platter, and garnish by rolling them in white poppy seeds (traditional in India) or sesame seeds. Serve *ladoos* hot or cold.

BADAM PAK

Some Hindu holidays require "fruit fasting," where the observant are allowed to consume only nuts and fruits. This dessert is suitable for that sort of fasting.

1 cup blanched almonds (see directions on page 166 for blanching)
¾ cup water
A few pinches of cardamom,
or 1 teaspoon rose water (but not both)
3 to 4 tablespoons honey or sugar
2 tablespoons oil

Place the blanched nuts and water in a blender or food processor, and blend until the nuts are well ground and become thick like a milk shake. Transfer the nut mixture to a heavy-bottomed pot, and cook for 10 to 15 minutes to evaporate some of the liquid. Then add the sugar or honey and oil, and reduce the heat. Cook the mixture, stirring it continuously for 15 to 20 minutes until it gets to be sticky, thick, and lumpy. Add the ground cardamom or rose water to flavor the *badam pak*. Divide the dessert into individual bowls or plates, and chill before serving. Alternatively, you can form the dessert into small balls, then flatten them out to look like small cookies. Chill and serve.

PANEER PENDA (CHEESE FUDGE)

Traditionally this dessert is made with home-made cheese *paneer* (see pages 34-35), but ricotta cheese is an ideal substitution. Although I like to avoid refined sugar, in this recipe white sugar, or at least turbinado sugar, is necessary to get a satisfactory texture.

½ cup butter (preferably unsalted)
1½ cups paneer curds (without setting or shaping), or ricotta cheese
¾ to 1 cup white or raw turbinado sugar
1 cup milk powder (non-fat is fine)
¼ teaspoon ground cardamom

Choose a wide pot, such as a deep, cast iron skillet or Dutch oven. Melt the butter and add the ricotta or *paneer* to it, and blend them together well. Over medium to low heat, cook the mixture, stirring frequently for about 40 minutes until it becomes very thick. Then add the sugar, which will liquefy the mixture somewhat. Cook for an additional 20 minutes, stirring vigorously and making sure the mixture does not stick to the bottom or sides of the pan. Next, slowly add the powdered milk with one hand while continuing to stir with the other hand. Break apart any lumps which may develop, and turn the heat down to low. Blend in the cardamom and transfer the *halva* to a greased platter while it is still hot. Spread the *halva* out evenly, cool at room temperature, then chill the *halva* in the refrigerator. Cut into small squares or diamonds, and serve.

VEGAN VARIATION: Substitute dairy-free margarine for butter, and use firm tofu in place of cheese. Add soymilk powder or omit the powdered milk altogether. You will get a somewhat less solid *halva* with the tofu alone. This does not taste as rich as cheese fudge, but it tastes quite good.

DATE *HALVA*

Another simple, virtuous dessert for fruitarians.

2 cups dates, seeds removed and finely chopped
1 cup almonds, chopped or blended to a coarse meal using a blender or a food processor
4 tablespoons of melted butter, *ghee*, or margarine
2 tablespoons of honey
few pinches of cinnamon or nutmeg

Prepare the dates and nuts as described in the list of ingredients. Set them aside, separately. Heat 2 tablespoons of butter, *ghee*, or margarine in a wok or a frying pan, and add the nut meal. Sauté the mixture until the nuts turn a reddish color. Transfer the nuts to a platter. Wipe the pan or wok clean, and heat the remaining butter, *ghee*, or margarine. Add the honey and cook them together briefly. When the mixture starts to bubble, add the dates and stir-fry for about ten minutes. Then stir in the almonds, and cook all the ingredients together for few minutes, being careful not to burn them or allow them to stick them to the bottom of the pan. Transfer the *halva* to an oiled platter, and even out into a flat circle. Sprinkle with cinnamon or nutmeg, and chill. Cut into small pieces and serve.

GULAB JAMUN

I was going to omit this decadent dessert, but my cooking class students protested and begged me to include it. They were extremely curious as to how this mouth-watering dessert (which they always order at restaurants) is prepared. So, here you have it.

I must admit that *gulab jamun* is a romantic dessert; it literary means rose berries. So whoever coined this dessert must have thought that if rose bushes were to bear sweet fruits, they would be sweet, soft, spongy, and aromatic just like *gulab jamun*.

1 cup instant, non-fat, powdered milk or powdered soymilk
¼ cup unbleached white flour
3 pinches of baking powder
3 tablespoons melted butter, *ghee*, or margarine
3 tablespoons liquid (milk or water)
1 to 1½ cups melted *ghee* or oil for deep-frying
1 cup sugar
3 cups water
1 to 2 teaspoons rose water

In a mixing bowl, combine the milk powder, flour, baking powder, and the 3 tablespoons of melted butter, *ghee*, or margarine after it has been cooled. Add the liquid (milk or water), and knead the mixture into a stiff dough. Sprinkle more liquid if needed to form the dough. Break off small pieces of dough, and form small, compact balls the size of a walnut, using oiled hands. You should have approximately 18 to 20 balls. Set the balls aside on a platter. Heat the *ghee* (which is traditionally used in this recipe) or oil in a wok, and deep-fry the balls, three or four at a time, until they are golden brown on all sides. Remove them from the oil with a slotted spoon, draining the oil as you lift them out. Set the balls on a platter which has been lined with towels to absorb the excess oil.

To prepare the syrup, combine the sugar and water in a saucepan, and cook them uncovered over moderate heat for about 20 minutes. Then turn the heat down, and add the fried balls to the syrup. Cook the balls in the syrup over low heat for about 10 minutes. When the balls start to float and swell and the syrup turns dark, turn off the heat. Remove the *jamun* from the syrup using a slotted spoon, and arrange them in a serving bowl. Stir the rose water into the syrup, and pour the syrup over the balls. Allow the *gulab jamun* to cool, then chill before serving. Some cooks store the syrup and balls separately in the refrigerator, if they prepare them days ahead of time. When you are ready to serve them, reheat the syrup and pour it over the balls. This way the balls don't disintegrate in the syrup while being stored in the refrigerator.

CHAPTER TEN
BEVERAGES

TEAS

There is only one species of plant that truly qualifies as a tea plant: *Camellia sinensis*. It grows throughout Asia and in parts of Africa and South America; "tea" (as we commonly know it) is the beverage prepared from its leaves. (Herbal teas are, correctly speaking, herbal "drinks" or "infusions.") The tea plant most likely originated in China, and in many parts of the world such as Japan, India, Russia, and areas of Africa, the word *cha* or *chai* is used for tea, influenced perhaps by its birth place. According to one mythical Chinese story, a Buddhist monk was responsible for the origin of tea. This fellow could not keep from dozing off when he was trying to concentrate on his meditation. He was so grief stricken that he finally cut off his eye lashes to punish himself. At the very spot where the eyelashes landed on the ground, a tea plant began to grow. The monk brewed the leaves of the plant, and the resulting tea kept him refreshed while he meditated.

The distinct flavor of any tea is determined by where it is grown, how it is pollinated, and how the leaves are treated once they are picked. The plantations of Sri Lanka produce hearty Ceylon tea, those of India's highlands yield flavorful Darjeeling brew, and the mountains of China favor aromatic green tea. Unprocessed, harvested leaves are used for green tea, fermented leaves are used to make black tea, and partially fermented leaves are produced for oolong tea.

The leaves of common tea—*Camellia sinensis*—contain caffeine, which acts as a stimulant. This is why we feel a lift from afternoon tea. Cup for cup, however, tea generally contains less caffeine than coffee. An average cup of coffee may contain 90 mg of caffeine, while a cup of tea may contain only 45 mg. The amount of caffeine in a cup of tea will, of course, vary according to the strength and variety of the brew. Tea is also known to have some healing and soothing properties. Tea has been prescribed for relief from common colds and sore throats by grandmothers all over the world since the beginning of civilization. In addition, tea drinking plays a special social role in many societies. Tea stalls, tea houses, and tea rooms serve as public gathering places in many countries.

CHAI

Next to water, tea is the most widely consumed beverage in India. Any time is tea time, according to a popular Indian saying. The act of serving and offering tea is considered a demonstration of one's friendship and hospitality. Tea also plays an important role in the business world. It is quite common for a shopkeeper to ply a prospective customer with cups of *chai*.

Indian *chai* is generally brewed with water and milk which have been boiled together. This way of making tea may have been invented to preserve milk for the whole day. Later, the British segregated the water and milk to make "English tea," or what we call "tray tea," which requires separate utensils for the hot water, sugar, and milk.

Rich, sweet buffalo milk is favored over cow's milk in most parts of India. The ratio of water to milk in a particular cup of tea varies depending on the time of day, personal taste, or the occasion. Morning tea may be stronger and contain more milk than afternoon *chai*. Children's tea has lots of milk and no tea leaves (see the Yogi Tea recipe on page 176). In Gujarat where I grew up, there is an old maxim which states that if you are preparing some tea and a respected friend enters the house, you add extra milk to make up the needed cup. However, if a person of questionable importance drops by when you are making tea, you just add enough water to make the extra cup.

The type of tea leaves used for *chai* will, of course, affect the taste of the prepared tea. I like to drink a combination of aromatic Darjeeling or Assam with a strong Ceylon or India tea. Green tea leaves are not suitable for Indian *chai* with milk. Buy several varieties of loose tea in bulk, make your own blends, and store them in your kitchen pantry.

In India, tea is brewed with sugar, as it is assumed that everyone loves very sweet tea. If you are traveling there and don't like your tea so sweet, remember these few important Hindi words: *bahot kum sakkar* (very little sugar).

2 cups of water
1 cup milk (more if richer tea is desired)
1 to 2 heaping teaspoons loose tea leaves
Sugar or honey to taste

Heat the water and milk together in a saucepan until the mixture comes to a boil and the liquid begins to rise. Turn off the heat and add the tea leaves. Cover the pot with a tight fitting lid, and allow the tea to steep for five minutes. Strain the tea leaves out and serve, along with your choice of sweetener.

MASALA CHAI

Masala chai is tea made with milk and spices. If you are a frequent *masala chai* drinker, prepare a *chai masala* using the directions given on page 39, and store it in a jar. If you use *chai masala* infrequently, whole spices can be ground while the milk and water are heating. *Masala chai* is very soothing when you have a bad cold or a sore throat.

2 cups water
1 cup milk
A few pinches of *chai masala* (see page 39), or 2 cardamom pods, 1 whole clove, and a small stick of cinnamon, all ground coarsely
1 to 2 heaping teaspoons loose black tea

Prepare the *chai* in same manner as the basic *Chai* recipe, except add the spices to the brewing water and milk. Strain and serve with a sweetener.

VEGAN CHAI: *Chai* prepared in the above manner using soymilk instead of dairy milk is gaining popularity with the vegan crowd. Make vegan *chai* following either of the above *chai* recipes, substituting soymilk in place of dairy milk. It's quite good.

KASHMIRI CHAI

This is the only Indian tea recipe that I know which is made with green tea leaves and without milk. It is served in parts of North India as a beverage. Interestingly, in other parts of India, green tea is served as a remedy for colds (instead of the black tea made with milk).

3 cups boiling water
1 or 2 heaping teaspoons green tea leaves
¼ teaspoon finely minced or grated fresh gingerroot
Honey or sugar for sweetener as needed

Pour the boiled water over the tea leaves and ginger. Cover and steep for five minutes Strain the beverage and serve with honey or sugar.

VARIATION: When available, use 1 teaspoon of fresh or dried, minced lemon grass in addition to the tea leaves. This variation is customary in the northeast mountain areas of India.

ICED TEA

This beverage is now becoming popular in the larger cities in India, although I had never experienced iced tea when I grew up in a small village. On a hot day, iced tea is truly refreshening and quite simple to make. You won't have to use poor-quality, expensive, powdered ice tea mixes after learning this method.

6 cups water
3 teaspoons of your favorite loose black or green tea
A few fresh mint leaves, chopped (optional)
2 or 3 lemons or limes
Sugar to taste

Boil half of the water, and chill the other half. Add the tea and mint leaves to the boiling water. Remove from the heat, cover, and steep the tea for seven minutes. Strain the tea into a pitcher. Add the chilled water, the lemon or lime juice, and sugar to taste. Serve in tall glasses with ice cubes.

HOT MILK DRINKS

GARAM DOOTH (HOT FLAVORED MILK)

This beverage is a favorite among Indian vegetarian mothers who want good quality protein for their finicky children who refuse to drink plain milk. It is also a soothing drink for the elderly and others who use it as a sleep aid.

3 cups milk
2 or 3 whole cardamom pods, crushed lightly
2 tablespoons chopped almonds
2 tablespoons raisins or currants
Optional sweetener to taste

Combine all the ingredients in a saucepan, and heat thoroughly. Allow to stand for a few minutes. Then divide the beverage into two glasses, and add the optional sweetener (although the nuts and raisins sweeten the drink sufficiently). Serve it with a spoon.

YOGI CHAI

This is a misnomer, because the beverage does not contain tea leaves, and, therefore, will not give you a lift. However, it is a soothing and tasty drink. The recipe is suitable for yogis, children, and others who need to avoid an artificial caffeine boost.

2 cups water
2 cups milk (or soymilk for the vegan variation)

⅛ to ¼ teaspoon *garam masala* or *chai masala*, or 2 cardamom pods, 1 whole clove, 1 stick of cinnamon, and 1 teaspoon grated gingerroot, coarsely ground
Honey or sugar for sweetener

Combine all the ingredients except for the sweetener, and bring them to a boil. Strain out any whole spice pieces, if you prefer. Serve with your choice of sweetener.

KESARI DOOTH

The eleventh day of each month is called *Ekadeshi*. On this day, devout Hindus will eat only fruits, nuts, milk, and honey. This hot milk drink made with saffron threads is favored among those who can afford it.

3 cups milk
12 to 14 whole saffron threads, or ⅛ teaspoon chopped threads
A few pinches of freshly ground cardamom powder and cinnamon powder
¼ cup shelled, crushed pistachio nuts
honey to taste

Heat the milk in a saucepan. Take out ¼ cup of hot milk, and soak the saffron in it. Add the powdered spices and pistachios to the milk, along with just enough honey to sweeten it lightly. Add the saffron and the soaking milk, and mix well. Scald the liquid until it starts to froth, stirring frequently to prevent it from sticking to the bottom of the pan. Transfer to a pitcher and whisk before serving.

COOL DRINKS

SUGARCANE JUICE

Many popular cool drinks are sold in Indian bazaars during the long, hot summer months. The one I miss the most is sugarcane juice. Fresh sugarcane looks like a bamboo reed and is filled with cool, sweet liquid. Unlike refined sugar, sugarcane contains many micronutrients, in addition to providing quick energy.

Fresh sugarcane itself is difficult enough to find outside of the tropics, not to mention the presses used by the *raswalas* who sell cane juice in the streets all over India. The vendor pushes long stalks of sugarcane through one end of a hand-operated juice extractor that looks like an old-fashioned laundry wringer. At the other end of the machine, there is a pot which collects the juice. The vendor adds some lemon or lime juice and a bit of fresh ginger to complement this sweet drink, which is served over a large cube of ice. So if you happen to come across a sugarcane vendor on a hot summer day in India, ask him for *ek ganna ka ras* (one sugarcane juice).

Here are some other cold drinks which you can serve on a hot tropical day.

MANGO JUICE

This is another popular Indian drink which is now bottled and sold everywhere. But if you have the ambition, nothing compares to freshly made mango juice.

In India, most bottled or canned fruit juices, like apple or orange juice, are very expensive. The one fruit abundant enough during its peak season to make juice from is the mango. Juicing mangoes are small, round, and soft to the touch. For instant gratification, you can buy one of these small mangoes, squeeze it gently by rolling it between your hands to loosen the juice inside, pluck the dark top end off, and suck the juice out. People buy them by the basket in India to make juice to have with their meals. Outside of the tropics, mangoes are expensive, so if you are lucky enough to come across some very ripe mangoes at a reduced price, this drink is well worth a try.

10 medium or 6 large, very soft, ripe mangoes
(black spots on skin O.K.)
Juice of 1 lemon or lime
Juice of 3 oranges
Sugar, if needed

Wash the mangoes and squeeze each fruit by rolling it gently but thoroughly between your hands, as illustrated. Set them aside. Take one mango at a time, and cut off the tip where it comes to a point. With firm, steady pressure from your hands, squeeze the juice into a mixing bowl. Set the empty peels and pits aside. More juice can be extracted from the pits and peels after all the mangoes have been juiced by squeezing each piece individually. If there are too many fibers, strain the mango juice using a colander with fairly large holes. Add the lemon juice and orange juice, and mix well. If the juice is too thick, add some water, but the beverage can be as thick as a milk shake. Taste for sweetness and add sugar only if needed. Serve chilled.

GINGER DRINK

Ginger drinks are made using similar recipes in India, Ceylon, and parts of Indonesia. It is considered a healthful stimulant in that it energizes you through your digestive system and not through your nervous system, as is the case with caffeine.

2" piece fresh gingerroot, grated or minced
6 cups water
Juice of 1 lemon
Honey to taste

Boil the water and gingerroot together for five minutes, then simmer for five more minutes. Strain the liquid and add lemon juice and honey to your taste. Chill the drink and serve cold with ice. Or serve it as a hot drink, diluting it with more hot water.

ANISE DRINK

Anise seeds look a lot like caraway seeds and smell like licorice. The taste of this drink is something like root beer without the carbonation. It is served chilled during the summer and also given to children to relieve upset stomachs.

2 tablespoon anise seeds
3 cups water
Juice of ½ to 1 lemon
Sugar to taste

Boil the seeds in two cups of water for five to seven minutes. Pour the liquid with the seeds into a blender or food processor, and blend until the seeds are crushed. Strain the liquid using a fine mesh strainer. Add 1 cup cold water, and ice to chill the drink. Sweeten to taste and serve.

TAMARIND DRINK

Various delicacies are made from this tropical sweet and sour pod, which is full of vitamin C. This drink is now canned and sold in Latin neighborhood grocery stores in the United States. Most of these cans contain preservatives, and the drinks are over-sweetened. Here is how you can make fresh tamarind drink at home.

12 to 16 fresh tamarind pods,
  or a few tablespoons of dehydrated, compressed
  tamarind
1 quart chilled water
Sugar as needed

Follow the instructions which detail the process of making tamarind paste on page 40. You will get 1 to 1½ cups of thick liquid. Strain the liquid to remove the fibers. Stir in the chilled water and sugar to taste.

LASSI (pronounced la-cchi)

Lassi is another popular cool drink, made with yogurt or buttermilk, water, and ice. This drink, a type of Indian milk shake, is sold in tea stalls and restaurants throughout the cities, but it can also be made easily at home.

SWEET *LASSI*

2 cups buttermilk
2 cups unflavored yogurt
2 cups water
2 tablespoons sugar (or more for a sweeter *lassi*)
Crushed ice
A few ice cubes

Place all the ingredients, except the ice, in a blender or food processor, and blend well. You can also use a whisk for this purpose. Add some crushed ice, making sure not to thin the drink out too much. Serve in tall glasses with ice cubes. This drink is a blessing when a meal is too spicy for you.

KHARI LASSI (SALTY *LASSI*): Omit the sugar and add ¼ teaspoon each salt and cumin powder. Follow the rest of the recipe as above.

MANGO *LASSI*: Using the method described in the recipe for Mango Juice on page 177, extract juice from four well-ripen mangoes. Blend the mango juice with the yogurt and buttermilk mixture from the sweet lassi recipe above.

CHAPTER ELEVEN
SIMPLE MEALS, PICNICS & FEASTS

A well-planned, balanced menu can help nurture a healthy body and an alert mind. Careful menu planning can go a long way towards reducing the cost of your food, as well as assuring that your diet contains a sufficient variety of foods and nutrients. Planning ahead is also helpful to those of you who want to change your food habits, such as making the transition to a vegetarian diet after having eaten meat for most of your life. In that case, plan your menus with the idea of changing your food habits gradually. Begin by cooking one or two simple dishes at a time from this book, incorporating them into your own basic meal plans. Later, you can prepare a compete Indian meal, which may take a little time to prepare if you are new to Indian foods and/or vegetarian cooking. Western explorers risked their lives and fortunes searching for the fabled spices of the East. Now you can, with much less effort, rediscover some of the culinary joys of India.

All meals should be nutritionally balanced, visually appealing, and tasty. I think, however, that an Indian vegetarian menu contains unique flavors and a presentation that is distinct among other styles of food preparation. The simplest meal usually consists of a variety of colors and textures. The menu generally contains most of these basic items: a vegetable dish, a bean dish, a bread, and a chutney and/or yogurt. This is not to say all Indian meals always adhere to a strict formula.

The addition of fresh fruit or a sweet, or the absence of one of the entrees is most common. A menu can vary depending on regional tradition, seasonal availability of produce, and the occasion. For example, a simple Gujarati meal consists of one vegetable dish, a *dal*, a rice dish, and a flat bread. In fact, the phrase *dal-bhat-shak-rotli* is used as one word to describe a basic Gujarati meal. Examples of other regional menus are given here.

EVERYDAY INDIAN MEALS

You can serve Indian food in any manner that you find comfortable. It may be overwhelming or impractical for some of you make a whole Indian meal as shown in the examples that follow. You can abbreviate a menu by omitting the more time-consuming dishes. Or you can make a few Indian entrees to be incorporated in your non-Indian meal. At any rate, let me first take you on a visual journey of how everyday family meals are traditionally served and eaten in India.

Even in the most modern Indian households, the ritual of eating together with your family members is a tradition kept as sacred as the holy cow. All meals, or at least one meal, is shared with the entire family. This family meal used to be lunch, but with more and more people working all day, the family meal is shifting towards early evening in the cities. In the rural areas, where crops and harvest directly affect people's lifestyles, the timing of family meals varies seasonally. In either case, the family meal is an important everyday event to be respected by all.

Breakfast is the simplest meal in North India, usually consisting of *chai* (tea) or hot milk or yogurt with *thundi rotis* (cold bread) leftover from the evening meal. In the South, an elaborate, late breakfast of freshly made *dosa* (crêpe-like, spicy pancakes made from rice and beans) and *rasam* (clear, hot-and-sour soup) with coffee is more common.

Most Indian homes do not have a dining table, so people gather around a dining area, either in two rows or a circle, and eat on the floor. Traditionally, men folk and children eat together (or the children are fed first), and women eat together after everyone else is finished. Nowadays, you may find more and more families eating together at the same time.

An Indian meal is served to each individual on a large, high-lipped metal plate known as a *thali*. The *thalis* are made from brass, copper, or stainless steel (currently the most popular metal). When not in use, the *thalis* are polished clean until they sparkle and then placed on display on the kitchen shelf.

Most dry entrees, such as rice and bread, are served on the *thali*, while the *dal*, vegetables, and yogurt (or *raita*) are usually served in small metal bowls that are placed around or in the *thali*.

A small heap of chutney is usually placed next to the rice in the *thali*. The food items are mixed and eaten by hand, without the use of forks or knives. The dinner ends with a drink of water which is always served with a meal. The empty *thali* is used as a sort of portable sink in which the diners can rinse their hands. *Chai* or other drinks (if in the menu) are served later.

A SIMPLE GUJARATI SUPPER

Khichadi (brown rice with mung): page 136
Kadhi (yogurt soup): page 128
Spinach *Bhaji* (stir-fried spinach): pages 82-83
Bhakharis (thick flat bread): page 146
Coriander *Chutney*: page 67
Garam Dooth (warm sweet milk): page 176

A COMPLETE GUJARATI DINNER OR LUNCH

Masoor Dal (soup): page 112
Plain *basmati* rice: page 133
Cauliflower With Parboiled Potatoes: page 91
Kachumber (cucumber salad): page 109
Chapatis (thin flat bread): pags 143-45
Raisin *Chutney*: page 66
Sweet *Lassi* (yogurt shake): page 180

A HEARTY PUNJABI MEAL

Matar Paneer (peas with cheese): page 100
or *Matar Tofu* (peas with tofu): page 100
Rice and Vegetable *Biriani* (pilaf): page 138
Punjabi Chana (garbanzo beans): page 121
Puris (deep fried puffed bread): pags 154-55
Mint *Chutney*: page 69
Masala Chai (spiced tea): page 174

NORTH INDIAN FANCY DINNER

Navaratan Shak ("nine jewels" vegetables):
    page 94
Rice with Nuts and Raisins: page 134
Toor Dal (soup): page 116
Parotha (multi-layered bread): pages 148-51
Carrot *Raita* (carrot & yogurt salad): page 108
Peanut *Chutney*: page 66
Mango *Lassi* (mango yogurt shake): page 180

A MADRASI LUNCH

Sambhar (soup with vegetables): page 125
Brown or white rice: pages 132-33
Date *Chuntey*: page 68
Tamarind Drink: page 179

SOUTH INDIAN BRUNCH

Patra (spicy, rolled leaf pastry): pages 62-63
Tamarind *Chutney* (sweet & sour dip):
            page 67
Banana *Raita* (banana-yogurt salad): page 108
Lassi (yogurt shake): page 180

PICNICS AND COOKOUTS

In India, village folks who live in the countryside do not have the need to go out and have a picnic. During the busy sowing and harvesting seasons, farmers bring their meals to the fields out of necessity. Food fresh from the farm, such as the first corn of the season, is included in their lunch before it even gets to the town. Among my fondest memories of the monsoon season in my village is the sight of an open fire in the green corn fields, around which a group of farmers would be gathered, roasting the freshly picked corn. The smoke of the fire and misty air blended perfectly with the smell of the cooking corn. After the corn was cooked, the lightly charred ears would be rubbed with lemon juice, a little bit of salt, and cayenne pepper. Apart from these impromptu food samplings, country folk do not have much time to organize picnics.

In contrast, city people grab every chance they get to go on a picnic. It can be a company event, a sunny Sunday, or a national holiday. Indian city people love to get away from the crowded streets and go to the many parks and reservoirs to party, get together, and eat outdoors. Often, the cooking is done early in the morning and packed by noon. Some preparation may be done the day before to ensure variety in the menu. Here is a picnic menu I recall having with my friends.

GUJARATI PICNIC MENU

Green *Theplas* (flat bread make with leafy greens, rice, and other grains): pages 152-53

Rice and Vegetable *Biriani* (rice cooked with vegetables): page 138

Fried Cabbage: pages 86-87

Alu Matar (potatoes with peas): page 84

Kachumber (cucumber salad): page 109

Peanut *Chutney*: page 66

Banana *Raita* (yogurt salad with bananas): page 108

Kheer (rice pudding): page 162

Fresh fruits

Lots of *Masala Chai* (spiced tea): page 174

COOKOUTS

Residents of big cities like Bombay and Delhi have adopted Western-style barbecues where working folk get together on a hot Sunday afternoon and cook together in someone's yard or patio. The non-vegetarians might roast chickens or kebabs, but there are always vegetarians who bring their own contributions, such as fresh corn to be roasted as described on page 184 or *ola*-roasted eggplant (see page 96)

Outdoor cooking can be a satisfying change from a small, overheated or overcrowded kitchen where the cook is often isolated from his or her guests. And the pleasure of outdoor cooking should not be experienced only by meat-eaters. So, if you are invited to a typical, meat-centered barbecue, I hope preparing some of the items from this book will be helpful to share with other vegetarians.

FEASTS

Food preparation for feasts, weddings, and important holidays may take a few days or even weeks in India. Typically, the sweets are made first because they keep for a long time. Sometimes the chutneys, appetizers, and breads (like puris) are made a day ahead of time. For holidays, friends, relatives, or neighbors will cook the time-consuming items together, taking turns going from one house to other. This way, the labor feels more joyful, and the boring tasks turn into a work party.

Following is a suggested menu for a special feast. The list seems quite extensive, but it is within the range of any cook. Try to plan the feast some days in advance. It is extremely helpful if you can get someone to help you, especially if the feast is for more than eight people. But too many cooks can spoil the "*dal*," so try to limit the number of persons in your cooking party. Read through the recipes to make sure you have the dry goods, fresh ingredients, and utensils necessary. Plan out the timing for each dish. Some recipes take twice as much time when you double the amount; others do not. Plan which dishes will be cooked first, second, and so on. For example, all Indian sweets can be cooked a week in advance. If you are making *matar paneer*, the cheese and tomato sauce can be made several days in advance, kept refrigerated, and assembled on the day of the party. The *chutney* or *raita* can be made many hours or a day in advance. The rice, *dal*, and vegetables can be the first things to be prepared on the day of the party. The *dal* and vegetables can be reheated easily

just prior to being served. The rice can be kept at room temperature. The last items to be cooked should be the appetizers and the breads, since it is very important that they be as freshly made as possible when served. For these last two stages, a helping hand is most beneficial. You can prepare the dough and assemble the ingredients for the appetizer and bread ahead of time, so when the help comes, you are ready to roll, cook, or fry.

Depending on the size of the party and the occasion, the feast can either be served in a buffet/banquet style or in a succession of courses, starting with an appetizer, a few chutneys, and then the *thali* with other items, except for the bread. The bread will come last, piping hot, one or two at a time, so that it does not cool off while you are eating your meal. The second serving of *dal* and vegetables is also traditionally reheated. Most Indian dishes are served hot except for the chutneys, salads, *papadam*, and sweets. Rice is served at room temperature, since it is usually eaten with hot *dal* or vegetables.

Just before eating, a short *sloka* (prayer) is said to honor the occasion. Then, a piece of the food is thrown into the fire as an offering to the God of Fire, *Agni*, in the hope that His Greatness, who is responsible for such feasts, will bring about many more celebrations.

A SUGGESTED MENU FOR A SPECIAL FEAST

Carrot *Halva*, page 166
Besna Halva (*Mohan Thal*) page 167
Pakora or *Samosa*, pages 50-51 or 56-57
Mint *Chutney*, page 69
Tropical or Raisin *Chutney*, pages 68 or 66
Cucumber *Raita*, page 107
Rice With Nuts and Raisins, page 134
Toor Dal or *Masoor Dal*, pages 116 or 112-13
Matar Ghobi (Peas and cauliflower) page 85

Eggplants With Boiled Potatoes, page 90
 or *Matar Paneer* or *Matar Tofu*, page 100
Punjabi Chana, page 121
Puris, pages 154-55
Papadam, page 49
Sweet *Lassi*, page 180
 or *Masala Chai*, page 174
Fresh tropical fruits such as mangoes,
     pineapples, and papaya

MAIL ORDER SOURCES FOR INDIAN SPICES AND OTHER INGREDIENTS

To find a source of Indian ingredients in your area, check your local yellow pages under Indian grocers, speciality shops, farmers' markets, or health food stores. If you have an Indian restaurant in your area, they may be able to help you locate hard-to-find ingredients.

The following grocers can supply Indian ingredients through the mail if you are unable to locate a source near you:

ARIZONA
Bombay Bazaar
334 E. Camelback Road
Phoenix, AZ 85012-1614
602-265-8781

CALIFORNIA
Bazaar of India
1810 University Avenue
Berkeley, CA 94703-1516
510-548-4110

New Bombay Bazaar
548 Valencia Street
San Francisco, CA 94110
415-621-1717

Haig's Delicacies
642 Clement Street
San Francisco, CA 94118
415-752-6283

India Food Mill
650 E. San Bruno Avenue
San Bruno, CA 94066
415-583-6559

Other Avenues Food Store
3930 Judah Street
San Francisco, CA 94122
415-661-7475

India Spices and Broceries
5994 West Pico Blvd.
Los Angeles, CA 90035
213-931-4871

CONNECTICUT
India Spice and Gift Shop
3295 Fairfield Avenue
Bridgeport, CT 06605
203-384-0666

FLORIDA
India Grocery Store
2342 Douglas Road
Coral Gables, FL 33134
305-448-5869

GEORGIA
Taj Mahal Imports
1612 Woodcliff Drive
Atlanta, GA 30329
404-321-5940

ILLINOIS
Apna Bazaar
2314 West Devon Avenue
Chicago, IL 60659
312-262-4200

KANSAS
India Emporium
10458 Metcalf
Overland Park, KS 66212
913-642-1161

MASSACHUSETTS
India Foods & Spices
80 River Street
Cambridge, MA 02139
617-497-6144

MICHIGAN
India Bazaar
23626 Vanborn Road
Dearborn Heights, MI 48125
313-295-2121

MINNESOTA
Patel Groceries & Video
1848 Central Avenue NE
Minneapolis, MN 55418
612-789-8800

MISSOURI
Seema Enterprises
10635 Page Avenue
St. Louis, MO 63132
314-423-9990

MONTANA
Good Food Store
920 Kensington
Missoula, MT 59801
406-728-5823

NEW JERSEY
Dana Bazaar
291 Central Avenue
Jersey City, NJ 07307
201-656-7396

NEW MEXICO
Ganesh Indian Groceries
6320-D Linn Northeast
Albuquerque, NM 87108
505-268-3342

NEW YORK
Patel Groceries
3145 Coney Island Avenue
Brooklyn, NY 11235
718-743-4318

House of Spices
8280 Broadway
Jackson Heights, NY 11373
718-476-1577

Kalustyan's Groceries
123 Lexington Avenue
New York, NY 10016
212-685-3451

NORTH CAROLINA
Payal Indian Grocery
6400 Pineville Road
Charlotte, NC 28217
704-521-9680

OHIO
India Groceries and Gifts
4412 Cleveland Avenue
Columbus, OH 43231
614-476-8555

OREGON
International Food Bazaar
915 SW 9th Avenue
Portland, OR 97205
503-228-1960

PENNSYLVANIA
Spice Corner
904 S 9th Street
Philadelphia, PA 19147
215-925-1660

TEXAS
India Grocers
5604 Hillcroft
Houston, TX 77036
713-782-8500

Taj Mahal Imports
26-C Richardson Hghts Village
Richardson, TX 75080
214-644-1329

WASHINGTON
Ayengar Association
2516 NE 95th Street
Seattle, WA 98155-2428
206-524-4040

Glossary

ADU Fresh gingerroot 22
ALU or BATATA Potato
AJOWAN Oregano seeds 21
AMCHOOR Mango powder 27
ANAR DANA Pomegranate
  seeds 26
ASAFETIDA Hing 25
BASMATI RICE An aromatic rice
  grown in North India 16,
  133
BESAN Chick-pea or garbanzo
  flour 18
BHAJIA (or PAKORA) Deep-fried
  vegetables in batter 50
CHAI Tea 173-74
CHANA DAL Split chick-
  peas 110
CHAPATIS Unleavened Indian
  bread 143-45
CHHASH Milk by-product or
  thin buttermilk 32
CHUTNEY Spicy condiment 64
CORIANDER LEAVES Cilantro,
  or Chinese or Mexican
  parsley 21
CURRY LEAVES Leaves of the
  sweet neem tree (kadhi patti
  or mitha neem patti) 23
DAL Split beans or dish made of
  beans 19, 110-112
DHANIA Coriander or
  cilantro 21
DOODHI Large, gourd-shaped
  squash (opo) 79
DOSA Spicy pancake 59-60
FARASAN Snacks 45
GALKA Squash similar to
  zucchini 79

GARAM MASALA Sweet spice
  mix made from cinnamon,
  cloves, cardamom pods, and
  other spices 24
GHEE Indian clarified but-
  ter 19, 33-34
GHISODA Squash which looks
  similar to cucumber 79
GULAB JAL Rose water 25
HALDI Turmeric 21
HING Asafetida 25
ILAICHI Cardamom pods 24
IMLI Tamarind 26
JAIFAL Nutmeg 26
JAIFAL PATTI Mace 26
JARA Slotted spoon for drain-
  ing 28
JEERA Cumin 21
KADHAI Indian frying pan, taller
  and rounder than a Chinese
  wok 27
KADHI Yogurt "curry" 128
KADHI PATTI Curry leaves 23
KALA MIRCH Black pepper 21
KANDA Onions 22
KARELA Bitter squash 79
KESAR Saffron 25
KEVRA JAL Screwpine water 25
KHAS KHAS White poppy seeds
  used to decorate sweets 26
LASAN Garlic 22
LILU LASAN Green garlic 23
LIMNU Lime 23
LOVING Cloves 24
MASOOR DAL Red lentils
  19, 110
METHI Fenugreek seeds 25

MIRCHI Chile or hot pep-
  pers 21, 23
MITHA NEEM PATTI Curry
  leaves 23
MUNG DAL Split mung
  beans 19, 110
NIMU Lemon 23
PAKORA or BHAJIA Deep-fried
  vegetables in batter 50
PANEER Indian homemade
  cheese 31, 34-35
PAPAD or PAPADAM Crispy,
  potato chip-like crackers 49
PHODINO Mint leaves 23
PURIS Puffed breads 154-55
RAI Black mustard seeds 21
RAITA Yogurt-based salad 107
RASADAR SHAK Vegetables
  with a sauce 89
SAUNF Anise 26
SAMOSA Deep-fried vegetable
  rolls 56
SUKI BHAJI Stir-fried vegetables
  without a sauce 79
TAJ Cinnamon 24
TAVA Concave griddle for
  cooking flat breads 28
THALI Individual, high-lipped
  metal serving plates 77, 182
TOOR DAL Yellow split
  peas 110
URAD DAL Split urad len-
  tils 110
VAGHAR Sautéing spices in hot
  oil 112
VARIALI Fennel 26
VELAN Indian rolling pin 28,
  144

Index

Alu Matar 84
Alu Parothas (Stuffed) 149-50
Anise Drink 179
Asparagus With Mixed
Vegetables 86
Aviyal 95

Badam Pak 169
Baked Eggplant With Yogurt
Sauce (Ola) 96
Banana Raita 108
Basic Garam Masala 38
Basic Tomato Sauce 41-42
Basmati Rice 16, 133
Batada Vada 55
Bean Sprouts, Mixed 127
Besan Halva (or Mohan
Thal) 167
Beverages 173-80
Bhajia (Pakora) 50-51
Bhakharis (Gujarati Style) 146
Biriani, Rice and Vegetable 138
Bombay Garam Masala 38-39
Breads 141-56
Bhakharis (Gujarati Style) 146
Chapatis 143-45
Makai Roti (Indian Corn
Bread) 155
Masala Puris (Spicy Puris) 155
Mithi Puris (Sweet Puris) 155
Parotha 148-49
Parothas, Stuffed (Alu) 149-50
Pudla (or Puda) 156
Puran Poli 151
Puris (Puffed Bread) 154-55
Rotla (Millet Bread) 147
Theplas 152
Broccoli with Carrots 85
Brown Rice, Basic 133
buttermilk 32-33

Cabbage 78
Cabbage, Fried 86-87
Cabbage Raita, Carrot and 108
carbohydrates 9
Carrot
and Cabbage Raita 108
Halva 166
Kofta 98
Pickles 75
Cauliflower 78
Eggplant With Thin Sauce 92
With Cream Sauce,
Steamed 97
with Parboiled Potatoes
(Broccoli) 91
Chai, see Tea
Chai Masala 39
Chana Dal 117
Chapatis 143-45
Chikkis (or Sesame Halva) 165
Chivra 46
Chutneys 64-72
Coconut 70
Coriander 67
Cranberry 71-72
Date 68
Garlic 69
Green Garlic 68
Green Tomato 72
Mint 69
Peanut 66
Raisin 66
Shanta's Tropical 68
Tamarind 67
Tomato 71
coconut milk 36-37
Coconut Rice 139
Cream Sauce, Indian 43
Cucumber Pickles 75
Cucumber Raita 107

Dahi Vada 54
Dal and Dal-Based Dishes 110-29
Bean Sprouts, Mixed 127
Chana 117
Dal Chowder With Salsa 129
Dal-Dhokali (Dal With Chick-
Pea Flour Dumplings
126-27

Doodhi-Chana-Nu-Shak 124
Kadhi or Yogurt "Curry" 128
Khata Mung (Sour Mung) 113
Kofta 98
Masoor 112-13
Moth (Adjuki Beans) 123
Mung (Dry) 114
Mung With Spring Herbs 115
Pancha (Five Bean) 119
Punjabi Chana 121
Rasam 122
Sabat Maahan (Whole Black
Lentils) 120
Sambhar 125
Toor 116
Urad 117
Black-Eyed Khichadi 137
Date Chutney 68
Date Halva 170
Dhokla 58-59
Doodhi-Chana-Nu-Shak 124
Dosa 59-60

Eggplant 78
Baked With Yogurt Sauce 96
With Boiled Potatoes 90
With Snow Peas or String
Beans 92
South India-Style Stuffed 105
Stuffed 103-104
Extra Creamy Raita 107

Farali Chivra 46
Farasan, see Snacks
fats 9–10
Firni 163
flours 17–18, 141-43
Fried Cabbage 86-87
Fried Zucchini, Ghisoda, Galka, or
Other Summer Squash 81

Garam Dooth (Hot Flavored
Milk) 176
Garam Masala 24, 38-39
Garlic Chutney 69
Garlic Paste (#1 and #2) 39-40
Ghee 33-34

Ghisoda or Doodhi With
  Tomato 93
Ginger Drink 179
Ginger Pickles 75
Green Garlic Chutney 68
Green Tomato Chutney 72
Gujarati-Style Stuffed
  Eggplants 103-104
Gulab Jamun 171

Hot Chile Pickles 73

Iced Tea 175
Idli 61
Indian Cream Sauce 43
Indian Potato Salad 82

Juice
  Mango 177
  Sugarcane 177
  Tamarind 179

Kachumber 109
Kadhi or Yogurt "Curry" 128
Karela, Dry 87
Karelas, Stuffed 106
Kashmiri Chai 175
Kesari Dooth 176
Khari Lassi (Salty Lassi) 180
Khata Mung (Sour Mung) 113
Kheer 162
Khichadi 136
kitchen equipment 27-28
Kofta 98
  Carrot 98
  Curry, Paneer and 99
  Dal 98
  Squash With Tomato Sauce 98
  Sweet & Sour 98

Ladoos (Sweet Balls) 168-69
Lassi
  Khari (Salty Lassi) 180
  Mango 180
  Sweet 180

Makai Roti (Indian Corn
  Bread) 155

Mango
  Juice 177
  Lassi 180
  Pickles 74
  Powder 27
Margarine ghee 34
Masala
  Chai 174
  Dosa 60
  Puris 155
Masoor Dal 112
Matar
  Ghobi 85
  Paneer 100
  Tofu 100
menus 183–184
micronutrients (vitamins and
  minerals) 10-11
Milk drinks 176
  Garam Dooth (Hot Flavored
    Milk) 176
  Kesari Dooth 176
  Yogi Chai 176
Mint Chutney 69
Mithi Puris 155
Moth (Adjuki Beans) Cooked With
  Coconut and Tamari 123
Mung Dal (Dry) 114
Mung Dal With Spring
  Herbs 115
Mushroom, Stuffed 101

Navaratan Shak 94

Okra 78, 83
  Hot & Spicy 83
  Stuffed 102
  With Green Tomato 83

Pakora or Bhajia 50-51
  Cheese 51
  With Besan and Cornmeal 51
  With Shredded Vegetable
    Batter 51
Pancha Dal (Five Bean Dal) 119
Paneer, making 34-35
  and Kofta Curry 99
  Balls 35

Paneer (cont.)
  Cubes 35
  Matar 100
  Penda (Cheese Fudge) 170
Papad (Papadam) 49
Parotha 148–151
  Alu Ghobi 150
  Alu Palak 150
  Puran Poli (Parotha Stuffed
    With Sweet Dal) 151
  Stuffed (Alu) 149-50
Patra 62-63
Peanut Chutney 66
Peas Pillau 135
Pickles 73-75
  Carrot 75
  Cucumber 75
  Ginger 75
  Hot Chile 73
  Mango 74
Potato Bhaji 82
Potato Raita, Cooked 109
Potato Salad, Indian 82
protein 8-9
Pudla (or Puda) 156
Punjabi Chana 121
Puran Poli (Parotha Stuffed With
  Sweet Dal) 151
Puris (Puffed Breads) 154-55
  Masal Puris (Spicy Puris) 155
  Mithi Puris (Sweet Puris) 155

Raisin Chutney 66
Raitas 107
  Banana 108
  Carrot and Cabbage 108
  Cooked Potato 109
  Cucumber 107
  Extra Creamy 107
  Radish 108
  Vegan 107
Rasadar Shak 89-96
  Aviyal 95
  Baked Eggplant With Yogurt
    Sauce (Ola) 96
  Cauliflower and Eggplant With
    Thin Sauce 92
  Cauliflower with Parboiled
    Potatoes (Broccoli) 91

Rasadar Shak (cont.)
Eggplant with Boiled
Potatoes 90
Eggplant With Snow Peas or
String Beans 92
Ghisoda or Doodhi With
Tomato 93
Navaratan Shak 94
Rasam 122
Rice and Rice Dishes 16-17, 131-
40
Basic Brown Rice 16, 133
Basic White Rice 17, 132
Basmati Rice 16, 133
Biriani 138
Black-Eyed Khichadi 137
Coconut 139
Kesari Bhat (Saffron Rice) 134
Khichadi 136
Leftover Fried (Vagharel
Thanda Bhat) 140
Peas Pillau 135
With Nuts and Raisins 134
Rotla (Millet Bread) 147

Sabat Maahan (Whole Black
Lentils) 120
Sakkarpara 48
Spicy 48
Sweet 48
Wheat-Free 48
Salad, Indian Potato 82
Sambhar 125
Samosa 56-57
Samosa Pie 57
Sauteed Mixed Squashes for the
Holidays 88
Sev 47
Shanta's Tropical Chutney 68
Sheera (or Suji Halva) 161
Snacks (Farasan) 45-75
Chivra 46
Dhokla 58
Dosa 59
Farali Chivra 46
Idli 61
Masala Dosa 60
Pakora or Bhajia 50-51

Snacks (Farasan) (cont.)
Papad or Papadam 49
Patra 62
Sakkarpara 48
Samosa 56
Samosa Pie 57
Sev 47
Upma 52
Vada 52
Spinach Bhaji 82-83
Squash Kofta With Tomato
Sauce 98
Stuffed Vegetables 101-06
Eggplants, South India-
Style 105
Gujarati-Style Eggplants 103-
104
Karelas 106
Mushrooms 101
Okra 102
Sugarcane Juice 177
Suki Bhaji 79-88
Alu Matar 84
Asparagus With Mixed
Vegetables 86
Broccoli with Carrots 85
Dry Karela 87
Fried Cabbage 86-87
Fried Summer Squash 81
Matar Ghobi 85
Okra 83
Potato 82
Sauteed Mixed Squashes 88
Spinach 82-83
Sweet & Sour Kofta 98
Sweet Lassi 180
Sweet Tomato Sauce 42-43
Sweets 157-71
Badam Pak 169
Besan Halva (or Mohan
Thal) 167
Carrot Halva 166
Chikkis (or Sesame Halva) 165
Date Halva 170
Firni 163
Gulab Jamun 171
Kheer 162
Ladoos (Sweet Balls) 168-69

Sweets (cont.)
Paneer Penda (Cheese
Fudge) 170
Sheera (or Suji Halva) 161

Tamarind Chutney 67
Tamarind Drink 179
Tamarind paste 40-41
Teas 173-75
Chai 173-74
Iced Tea 175
Kashmiri Chai 175
Masala Chai 174
Vegan Chai 174
Theplas (Flat Breads With Leafy
Greens) 152-53
Thick Tomato Sauce 42
Tofu, Matar 100
Tofu "Paneer" Cubes 36
Tomato Chutney 71
Tomato Sauce
Basic 41-42
Sweet 42-43
Thick 42
Toor Dal 116

Upma 52
Urad Dal 117

Vada 52-55
Batada 55
Dahi 54
Leafy 53
Mixed Dal 53
Vegan Dahi 54
Vegan Chai 174
Vegan Raita 107
vegetable ghee 34

water, importance in the diet 11
White Poppy Seeds 26
White Rice, Basic 132

Yogi Chai 176
yogurt 31-32
Yogurt "Curry" 128
Yogurt, Very Low-Fat 32

Ethnic Favorites from Book Publishing Company

A Taste of Mexico $13.95
Delicious Jamaica! 11.95
Flavors of India 12.95
From a Traditional Greek Kitchen 12.95
From the Global Kitchen 11.95
Good Time Eatin' in Cajun Country 9.95
Indian Vegetarian Cooking at Your House 11.95
Now and Zen Epicure 17.95
Olive Oil Cookery: The Mediterranean Diet 10.95

More Classic Cookbooks from Book Publishing Company

Almost No-Fat Cookbook 12.95
Almost No-Fat Holiday Cookbook 12.95
Becoming Vegetarian 15.95
Cookin' Healthy with One Foot Out the Door 8.95
Cooking with Gluten and Seitan 7.95
Fabulous Beans 9.95
Lighten Up! with Louise Hagler 11.95
Natural Lunchbox 12.95
New Farm Vegetarian Cookbook 8.95
Peaceful Palate 15.00
Shiitake Way 9.95
Soyfoods Cookery 9.95
Table for Two 12.95
Tempeh Cookbook 10.95
Tofu Cookery 15.95
Tofu Quick & Easy 7.95
TVP® Cookbook 6.95
Uncheese Cookbook 11.95
Vegan Vittles 11.95

Ask your local book or health food store to carry these titles or you may order directly from: Book Publishing Company
P.O. Box 99
Summertown, TN 38483
1-800-695-2241
Please add $2.50 per book for shipping and handling.